Rick Turner's Politics as the Art of the Impossible

Edited by Michael Onyebuchi Eze,
Lawrence Hamilton, Laurence Piper
and Gideon van Riet

WITS UNIVERSITY PRESS

Published in South Africa by:
Wits University Press
1 Jan Smuts Avenue
Johannesburg 2001

www.witspress.co.za

Compilation © Michael Onyebuchi Eze, Lawrence Hamilton, Laurence Piper, Gideon van Riet 2024
Chapters © Individual contributors 2024
Published edition © Wits University Press 2024
Cover photograph by Foszia Turner, Rick Turner at their home in Dalton Avenue, Bellair, Durban 1972

First published 2024

http://dx.doi.org.10.18772/22024078936

978-1-77614-893-6 (Paperback)
978-1-77614-894-3 (Hardback)
978-1-77614-895-0 (Web PDF)
978-1-77614-896-7 (EPUB)

This publication is peer reviewed following international best practice standards for academic and scholarly books.

Project manager: Elaine Williams
Copyeditor: Inga Norenius
Proofreader: Lee Smith
Indexer: Margaret Ramsay
Cover design: Hybrid Creative
Typeset in 11 point Minion Pro

CONTENTS

ACKNOWLEDGEMENTS   v

ACRONYMS   vii

INTRODUCTION   Michael Onyebuchi Eze, Lawrence Hamilton,
               Laurence Piper and Gideon van Riet   ix

PART I   RICK TURNER AND CONTEMPORARY BLACK THINKERS

CHAPTER 1   Decolonising Resistance: Political Freedom in Rick Turner
               and Steve Biko
               Michael Onyebuchi Eze   3

CHAPTER 2   Race, Political Change and Liberal Critiques: Rick Turner
               and Sam Nolutshungu
               Ayesha Omar   26

CHAPTER 3   On Biko's Turn on Turner
               Tendayi Sithole   45

PART II   TURNER'S THEORETICAL LACUNAE

CHAPTER 4   Women in the Frame: Reading Turner's *The Eye of the
               Needle* through Simone de Beauvoir's *The Second Sex*
               Paula Ensor   71

CHAPTER 5   Poverty and Misplaced Prioritisation: Evaluating 'Human
               Models' and 'Value Systems'
               John S Sanni   91

CHAPTER 6   Should We Take Turner's Democratic Model Seriously?
               Daryl Glaser   113

PART III   TURNER AND TEACHING PHILOSOPHY

CHAPTER 7   Rick Turner and Teaching Critical Theory
               Laurence Piper   137

CHAPTER 8   The Relevance of Rick Turner's 'Utopian Thinking' for
               a Critical Pedagogy
               Crain Soudien   157

PART IV   **RICK TURNER AND THE LEFT**

CHAPTER 9 Rick Turner, an Aboveground Radical
Billy Keniston   181

CHAPTER 10 Radical Contingency and Turner's Enduring Message
to Relative Privilege
Gideon van Riet   199

PART V   **ON THE NATURE OF POLITICAL THEORY**

CHAPTER 11 Rick Turner and the Vision of Engaged Political Philosophy
Christine Hobden   223

CHAPTER 12 What is the Point of Political Theory?
Lawrence Hamilton   241

CONTRIBUTORS   261

INDEX   263

ACKNOWLEDGEMENTS

I would like to thank my fellow co-editors for stimulating conversation at the conceptual stages of this volume. Working together with the editors and many other excellent contributors brings to light the famous African proverb that 'knowledge is the only thing that grows when it is shared'. A special thanks to Adam Branch, Jorn Rusen and Chiamaka Igboayaka from whom I have learnt the habit of creative disruption and epistemic empathy in knowledge production.

Michael Eze

I would like to thank the co-editors and contributors to this volume for their convivial excellence and forbearance. It has been too long in the making, but we got there in the end and learnt so much 'together'. Scare quotes are used here because all workshops were online, thanks to Covid and the fact that we all live and work in different parts of the world. I am also very grateful for the discussions with participants during two conferences at which versions of my chapter in this volume were presented, in Buenos Aires and Johannesburg, as well as formidable research assistance from Dr Candice Bailey. Finally, I would like to warmly thank the South African National Research Foundation for financial support during the research, writing and compilation of this book (Bilateral SARChI Chair Grant No. 103137).

Lawrence Hamilton

I would like to thank all the scholars involved in this project for the lively and constructive discussion and engagement on Turner. Your comments and criticism improved the quality of the work. To my fellow editors, who all took a turn at the wheel, thank you for your hard work. I really enjoyed this project. A special thanks to Raph de Kadt, who worked with Turner for a time, and introduced me to him. Thank you also for regaling me with tales of his exploits. Finally, thanks to Rick Turner, whom I never met, but who challenges me to be better than I am. Hopefully, one day, justice will be served.

Laurence Piper

I would like to thank Pia Bombardella, Andre Goodrich, Pieter Heydenrych, Andreas Langenohl and Amina Nolte for the frequent stimulating discussions we have had in recent years. I would also like to thank my fellow editors, Michael, Laurence and Lawrence, and all the contributors for their hard work and, at times, patience, through the long process of producing this volume. The Social Sciences Research Council/ African Peacebuilding Network is hereby acknowledged and thanked for funding part of the research on which my contribution is based, as part of the project 'Transitional injustice: The spatial politics of crime in contemporary South Africa', 2019.

Gideon van Riet

A Note on Rick Turner's Writings

Rick Turner published a number of works though not always under his name. There are also many unpublished works of his, which are difficult to trace. South African History Online has compiled a list of works by and on Turner. Readers interested in researching further works can find the information at http://www.sahistory.org.za/r-turner/his-writings.

ACRONYMS

ANC	African National Congress
ARC	Alliance for Radical Change
ARM	African Resistance Movement
BCM	Black Consciousness Movement
Cosatu	Congress of South African Trade Unions
IIE	Institute for Industrial Education
NBC	New Black Consciousness
NLRC	Natal Labour Research Committee
Nusas	National Union of South African Students
PAC	Pan Africanist Congress
SACP	South African Communist Party
SASO	South African Students' Organisation
UCT	University of Cape Town
WIL	Work-integrated learning

Michael Onyebuchi Eze, Lawrence Hamilton,
Laurence Piper and Gideon van Riet

THE MAKING OF TURNER

Richard Turner, known as Rick Turner, was a South African academic and activist. He was born to a farming family in Stellenbosch in the Cape in 1941, and lived only until 1978, when he was assassinated in his home in Durban, aged 37. Turner was married twice, first to Barbara Follett (née Hubbard) and then to Foszia Turner (née Fisher). Turner's eldest daughter, Jann Turner, is a Hollywood director, novelist, television director and screenwriter. Barbara Follett later became a British Labour Party member of parliament.

Rick Turner's life was a testimony to making the impossible possible. As a white South African from a privileged background, he rejected the racial supremacy, sexism and authoritarianism of apartheid rule, engaged in various forms of activism – such as supporting the dockworkers' strikes in Durban (today eThekwini) in 1973, and became an ally of the Black Consciousness leader, Steve Biko. It was almost certainly Turner's significant role in the 'Durban Moment' during the 1970s, when the city of Durban became the centre of the most vibrant resistance to apartheid, that led to his death. To this day the crime of his death remains unsolved and his assassin is yet to be brought to justice, although the case has recently been reopened, 45 years after his murder.

But Turner also made the impossible possible intellectually. In his search for a just alternative to the oppressive apartheid order, he was deeply influenced by both the Marxism of the New Left and French existentialism. While Marxism was common among many in anti-apartheid movements, Turner's blending of it with existentialism was singular. This came about from his time of studying towards his PhD under Henri Lefebvre at the Sorbonne in Paris, and gave his ideas a unique flavour that can be summed up in the italicised phrase: the point of philosophy is not just to interpret the world, but to change it, *not least by changing oneself.* This qualification of Marx's famous dictum is central to Turner's intellectual distinctiveness. A key example of his personal transformation was his choice to marry and live openly with a black Muslim person at a time when sex and marriage across race lines were illegal in South Africa.

Turner's affirmation of radical freedom as personal political practice, his emphasis on transforming consciousness as a condition of freedom and on the connection between personal and collective action, as well as his commitment to transforming the world into a just order based on human love, are ideas that he conveyed in his teaching at the University of Natal from 1970 until his death in 1978. Here, he quickly attracted attention for not only the radical nature of his ideas, but also for his teaching method, which was rooted in personal dialogue among equals rather than the dictates of an authority figure, as well as his calm engagement through reasoning and facts rather than emotion and invective. All these seemingly impossible things to believe in and act on at the height of apartheid, Turner did.

THE DURBAN MOMENT

The social and political context of Turner's adult life was the rebirth of overt political ferment in South Africa during the 1970s following the banning of black political organisations such as the African National Congress (ANC) and the Pan African Congress (PAC) in the early 1960s, and the relative lack of organised internal resistance during that decade. Central to this rebirth were the re-emergence of both the trade union movement and left-wing political movements, principally the Africanist student movement, that affirmed the significance of political consciousness and direct action for liberation. Notably, these events conjoined initially around the port city of Durban on the east coast of the country, and became known as the 'Durban Moment'.

The key event of the Durban Moment was the dockworkers' strike of 1973. This industrial action – illegal at the time – spread to other industries, leading to mass marches through the city. In the wake of these events, Turner and other University of Natal staff and students set up the Institute for Industrial Education, which engaged workers in Marxist ideas, and also set up the *South African Labour Bulletin*, a journal that operates to this day. By the mid-1970s, the union movement had gathered notable ground in South Africa. By 1976, there were 174 registered trade unions, although most of them were segregated by race and were for white, coloured and Indian workers rather than black workers. Confronted by growing resistance, the government established an independent commission called the Wiehahn commission in 1976. The commission recommended reforms that included the unbanning of black trade unions, which eventually took place in the 1980s.

Central to the ideology of the Durban Moment were New Left ideas that criticised structural Marxism for failing to create space for human agency. Turner was a central figure here, connecting political to personal liberation through an ethics of what he perceived as universal values articulated by the great religions. This emphasis on personal liberation as transforming a 'common-sense' consciousness shaped by oppressive regimes resonated deeply with the Africanisms emerging in the student movement and associated with Steve Biko in particular. In addition to these union and working-class consciousness aspects, the Durban Moment was associated with the non-violent philosophy of Mahatma Gandhi, who had also spent time in Durban in his youth.

A key feature of Turner's contribution was the linking of political thought to action through both his activism *and* his teaching and 'research'. Turner was part of a group of university academics who saw their role as transgressing university–society divides and supporting the education of the black working class as much as white middle-class students. In addition, though, Turner's blend of existentialism with New Left Marxism prioritised the role of consciousness-building for liberation in ways that necessarily implied both changing oneself individually and participating in collective organisation and action to change society. As critical theorists and what was later to become known as the Cambridge School have argued, words are forms of action ('speech acts', roughly conceived) and they are best understood as having been performed with the intention to communicate a particular meaning or set of meanings to an audience or set of audiences. A full understanding of texts and arguments can therefore be provided only by means of grasping what was intended by their propagation: grasping what they were intended to mean and how that meaning was intended to affect the ideological, social or political context in question.

As Wittgenstein convincingly insisted, this interpretive understanding could achieve nothing without an unambiguous focus on the fact that this was always a public not a private matter. In other words, at a similar time, but at great geographical and political distance from critical theorists and the Cambridge School, in Turner we have a particularly fascinating and radical practitioner of this form of doing politics (the idea that words are political deeds involved in at least a battle of ideas). Thus, his only substantial published work, *The Eye of the Needle* (2015 [1972]), is both a very theoretical work and, at the same time, a direct practical intervention into the politics of his time.

This volume is not primarily interested in recreating the ideological and other battles that marked Turner's times. It is more ambitious. Many of the contributors use Turner to interrogate our political context today, reflecting on how his ideas do (or do not) engage with contemporary priorities and problems. Again, like Turner, the wide variety of authors in this volume attempt a broad range of goals, not just intellectual history à la the Cambridge School, but direct intervention into our times, using Turner as an inspiration, a moment of discord, a fellow traveller or a blinkered idealist. *The Eye of the Needle*, seemingly a highly theoretical work, was also a direct practical intervention into the politics of Turner's time, which in an important sense, it could only have been. This volume raises the question of whether it could be more. Could it – or a revision of it – be a direct political intervention in our own troubled times?

THE MEANING OF *THE EYE OF THE NEEDLE*

Turner's philosophical and political arguments are overtly set in, and against, the context of racist apartheid oppression of the 1960s and 1970s. This was the heyday of white supremacy in South Africa, arguably at its most extensive and institutionalised form ever in human history, running through the body politic from the arteries in the heart to the capillaries of the fingertips. Turner's intellectual, political and personal rebellion against white oppression, economic exploitation and (to a lesser extent) patriarchal domination is most meaningful and impressive in this context. It is also a valediction of identities and values less affirmed today: a common humanity with a social order based on the principle of mutual love. Indeed, *The Eye of the Needle* is a direct challenge to white South Africans, in the name of their ostensible Christianity, to reflect on their core values using reason, and to reject domination based on race and exploitation based on class, and to imagine a utopian alternative.

Much has changed since Turner's time. South Africa, and the world, have moved on from formal apartheid; state socialism has crumbled in the face of global capitalism; the ideology of a common

humanity has yielded somewhat before a politics of particular identities; and the climate crisis looms large and menacingly over humanity's
future. In this new context, *The Eye of the Needle* appears out of time.
However, this is only true if one reads Turner narrowly. A deeper reading reveals multiple ways in which Turner's work can serve as a bridge
from the past to political theory debates in the present. For example,
despite the lacuna in his writings around any systematic gender critique, Turner's affirmation of radical individual freedom in respect of
political and economic relations can logically be carried through to relations around sexuality and gender – especially given his emphasis on
the importance of personal responsibility in relations of domination,
and on pursuing new forms of everyday practice that prefigure a free
and just society. Through this lens, the issues at the centre of contemporary Western 'culture wars' could be framed as another iteration of
working through the notion of individual freedom into cultural and
identity aspects of social relations.

Another, and perhaps the most important, way in which Turner serves
to bridge the past and the present is to connect to current debates on
postcolonial and decolonial thought, much of which was prefigured
in Biko's relation with Turner, and in the productive tension that existed
in the engagement between the two. In many ways, returning to Turner
cannot be done without reflecting on Black Consciousness thought,
and the demand for reflecting deeply on the origins and implications of
the forms of knowledge that enable colonial and apartheid domination.
In this regard, Turner offers a powerful lens through which to critique
the elisions, omissions, silences and repressions of Western thought, both
mainstream and radical.

Engaging Turner helps illustrate how Western thought has upheld
forms of domination and the façade that legitimates Western epistemology as the absolute source of value by ignoring consciousness
to the benefit of social structures or group identities. Thus, as much
as the formal rules of politics might change, the values, identities and
symbolic meanings in and around white supremacy, of which we may

be only partly conscious, might well endure. Turner helps to unmask the misrecognition of these cultural constructions that project Western epistemology as the universal source of value. Instead, he offers a social utopia which negotiates between contradictions and ambivalences, politics and power, rights and common good – with the goal of an emancipatory political philosophy based in a shared humanity. What we then have is a productive foil for engaging with contemporary global debates, including the changing role of universities, the relationship between knowledge and activism, the question of resistance and violence and the nature of critical reflection. Thus, returning to Turner helps not only to disrupt established histories and deprovincialise Southern perspectives on global issues, but also to bridge divides between politics and philosophy, teaching and learning, and the personal and the political. Turner helps rethink contemporary global challenges outside of their hegemonic historical framings.

While we come to honour Turner in this text, we also come to bury him. Our objective is less to canonise another forgotten white male who strayed too far South, than it is to call into question the canon in the present – including the South–North divide – by bringing Turner into collision with the critics of his time, and, especially, with the debates of the present. Engaging Turner and Black Consciousness helps to understand the eternal return to the question of race, the relentless reinvention of capitalist domination and the growing failure to deal with colonialism. Engaging Turner also offers new ways of thinking about new questions – questions of learning, knowledge and judgement; of being, resisting and leading; of our contemporary experiences of the stark exclusions and inequalities of today; and of how better to live and engage as human beings living in a variety of collective structures and forms of engagement, or lack thereof.

Turner insists that all the major challenges that confront humanity can be addressed, as they are the result of social relationships, and these in turn emerge from our collective human choice. Unlike many who see no alternative to the current order and its malcontents, Turner insists that all this is a misreading of human creativity. A misreading that, for example, makes it easier to imagine the end of the planet than the end of capitalism. But it is precisely this imagination that must change – by recognising the reality of contingency, and the value of transcending 'common-sense' thinking and dominant technocratic wisdom in favour of a better future. More specifically, Turner advocates for individual freedom, political (and thus material) equality and collective empowerment. He is insistent on the need for utopian thinking to achieve this goal. The objective of utopian thinking is to make us see that the seemingly impossible may, in fact, be quite possible. All we need to do is choose, behave and live differently to realise our values. In short, a second key contribution Turner provides for the present is the building blocks for an alternative theoretical structure that bridges the deep chasm between idealism and realism.

THE METHOD OF THE FUTURE

In the third decade of the twenty-first century we are again reminded of the need for academics, activists and ordinary people to think the impossible. The world is facing numerous crises that neither realism nor idealism, materialism nor ideational theory have been able to contend with by themselves. In South Africa, democracy has not brought with it the social, economic and political inclusivity many would have expected. Racial divisions have largely remained, while economic inequality has grown significantly. This inequality – as in other territories, especially in Africa and Latin America – is linked to increased levels of crime, a matter often politicised in quite unproductive ways. Ongoing police violence against black citizens, combined with high levels of incarceration, the increasing rate of school shootings and the influence of big capital in government in the USA, the supposed epitome of liberal democracy, are merely some of many examples.

As South Africa and the world face an increasing set of divisions between left and right, but also within left and right, Turner's attitude to praxes is extraordinarily instructive and inspiring. South Africa remains deeply divided along established and emerging fault lines. Many new issues are important, and 'hot takes' often misdirect towards the peripheral. This local and global set of complexities calls for responsible and considered praxes, and appropriate education and prose to precede it. In the era of social media, podcasts, and the quick and gratuitous production and consumption of opinion – not always reasoned positions – and in the context of increased opportunities for the spewing of hate as opposed to constructive dialogue, we must perhaps look to Turner as someone who would have acted more responsibly than many contemporary figures. This does not mean he would have been passive. What would Turner have said about practical politics today?

Turner used universal values as a loose anchor, a preliminary point from which to achieve loftier ideals. These ideals were for personal, political and economic liberation throughout society when these were seemingly unthinkable. The situation today is analogous, though the specifics are different. Once again, we must have the courage to think the unthinkable, but we must also have the courage to act politically, both personally and collectively. In today's context, would it be prudent to reflect on Turner's belief in linking thought to political action? This is an important question following the rise of forms of ethno-nationalism, populism and political polarisation globally, all forms of politics that not only threaten democratic institutions but also the very notions of truth and reasoned argument – fundamental principles of Turner's approach.

The answer in contributions to this volume is a qualified yes. Whether in respect of political-economic relations, the defence of democracy and human rights, the quality of education or health care and social protection, there is growing discord in South Africa and globally. Around the world, but especially in the global South, ordinary people still bear the brunt of what Elizabeth Povinelli would call (biopolitical) abandonment. The lessons to be taken from Turner for contemporary challenges are inspired by, rather than modelled on, his thought and his actions. Various contributions in this volume take up this challenge, more related to education than to research. None of them go as far as Turner did, argu-ably, because the context has changed. Education is now far more widely accessible. Engagement and activism through teaching and research, as is common for scholars informed by critical theory globally, is far more likely to have an impact now than was the case during the 1970s. Teaching remains a viable tool for effecting change, if the purpose is to develop critical thinkers and if teachers and lecturers, still largely a prod-uct of Western-centric curricula, remain humble and open-minded facil-itators, respectful of ideas proposed by students.

The challenge for advocates of freedom, equality and human solidar-ity is to affirm inclusive and democratic responsiveness, as against par-ticularism, populism and polarising narrow-mindedness. We require a reasoned and nuanced position that has been tested through rigorous dialogue before being executed in good faith. Through education on campus and activism in society, and vice versa, Turner inspires us not to be afraid but to be courageous; to start with imagining a better world from where we are with what we have, and then to act to get there, bear-ing in mind we might need to alter ourselves along the way.

THE MATERIAL AT HAND

Some contributions in this volume engage with Turner's theory and politics directly, while others use him as a base from which to speak to his context as well as to contemporary South Africa. Still others engage with Turner to consider the nature and purpose of political theory and philosophy in our contemporary global milieu.

The book is divided into five thematic foci speaking to his signifi-cance, his context, his continuity with history and the ways in which his work can continue to inspire and shape contemporary political theory. In chapter 1, 'Decolonising Resistance', Michael Onyebuchi Eze shows how Turner's political philosophy mirrors Steve Biko's Black Consciousness Movement. Although Turner's dream of a free South Africa was cut short, Eze examines ways in which his work continues to impact the political unconscious of contemporary South Africa in relation to emancipatory decolonisation. He historicises the ideological crossroads at which both Turner's and Biko's philosophies mirror and critique each other. For Biko and Turner, decolonising resistance goes beyond the material asymmetries of culture or simply the overcoming of negative freedom. As Turner (and later Biko) anticipated, the failure of the current decolonisation programme is that its only achievement has been to induct a few blacks into the privileged class while leaving intact the real mechanism of oppression, exploitative capitalism. The chapter draws lessons from both Turner and Biko for a new way of thinking about decolonisation that is neither racialised nor encumbered by asymmetries of material culture.

In chapter 2, 'Race, Political Change and Liberal Critiques: Rick Turner and Sam Nolutshungu', Ayesha Omar juxtaposes Rick Turner's political ideas with those of another South African social and political change theorist, Sam C Nolutshungu. This helps to broaden the scope of political theory in South Africa by re-centring previously marginalised voices and engaging comparatively with their ideas. The chapter reveals that Turner and Nolutshungu developed radical theoretical imaginaries in their accounts of race, liberalism and the philosophy of Black Consciousness. Unlike Turner, however, Nolutshungu's approach to social and political change hinged less on utopian thinking, and more on understanding the alignments of domination and submission conditioned by political rather than economic relations. The chapter further explores Nolutshungu's and Turner's critiques of liberalism and the liberating power of capitalism through their treatment of the ideas of John Locke. It concludes that both Turner and Nolutshungu were conservative optimists about the emancipatory potential of a liberal state in a future democratic dispensation. Finally, the chapter outlines Turner's and Nolutshungu's approaches to the Black Consciousness Movement as a vehicle for radical change.

Tendayi Sithole brings Turner and Biko into an interlocutory encounter, in the form of the protocols of the black critical rejoinder, in chapter 3. Writing 'On Biko's Turn on Turner', Sithole offers an entry into the politics of the otherwise that informs Biko's philosophy of Black Consciousness which, for Turner, is a point of contention. Black Consciousness is the centre of this intervention and Turner's conception of it is examined and criticised. It is from this stance that Biko's turn is formulated as a concept that is rooted in the decolonial turn. Turner's conception of Black Consciousness is exposed as doing what Biko criticised in the inaugural take of what Black Consciousness is and, by extension, its criticism of white liberals.

Paula Ensor draws on the work of Simone de Beauvoir, amongst other theorists, to illuminate important themes around freedom, work and the body. In chapter 4, 'Women in the Frame', she examines the so-called Durban Moment of the early 1970s, characterised by large-scale strikes and increased class consciousness, a moment and subject matter to which Turner is often linked. Ensor finds that there was little place for marginalised female workers in Turner's utopia. She concludes her contribution with a postscript on the Durban Moment, as a landmark moment in South African history that needs to be reinterpreted to reflect the oppression of women more appropriately and to acknowledge their agency more fully.

John Sanni, in chapter 5, 'Poverty and Misplaced Prioritisation', argues that a misplaced prioritisation is implied in Turner's critique of human beings' desire to own, accumulate and consume goods. Turner understands the human model as the ethical system that determines the internal morality of a society. By value systems, he means goals, mostly material, that people seek to achieve. South Africa offers a complex, though not unique, case of historical marginalisation, which escalates poverty. Turner's position makes an important contribution to addressing this problem. Focusing on South Africa, this chapter engages how sociopolitical conceptions engender misplaced prioritisation in the various ways of approaching the issue of poverty. Like Turner, he argues that the fixed nature of human models and value systems must be re-examined.

'Should We Take Turner's Democratic Model Seriously?' Daryl Glaser asks in his contribution, chapter 6. Taken 'literally', as a model for a new and better society, Turner's prescription, Glaser suggests, is implausible. To this end, Glaser offers overlapping historical moments: first, to see *The Eye of the Needle* as the product of a South African moment. For him, this moment is the most respectful treatment we can give the book, alongside an acknowledgement of its role in, notably, the intellectual evolution of 'workerism' in the 1970s. Another moment is to register the attractiveness of Turner's idealism. The book's ongoing relevance is its model of radical intellectual engagement and insistent critique, including critique of materialistic capitalism, Stalinism and narrow race politics.

In his engagement with Turner and critical theory, Laurence Piper contextualises Turner's ideas about education in relation to contemporary critical theory in chapter 7. For Turner, education should empower students to live democratically, not just educate them to get a job. Piper engages with the notion of 'critical thinking', which lies at the heart of Turner's account of education. For Turner, liberation was a process of personal and organisational transformation through reflection and conscious choice (critical thinking) to practise egalitarian democracy pre-figuratively. It was also, Piper argues implicitly, a process that requires a teacher, as revealed in Turner's practice as a public intellectual if not in his words in *The Eye of the Needle*.

In chapter 8, Crain Soudien examines Turner's emphasis on 'utopian thinking' with penetrating questions about its contemporary relevance for education and transformation. Would such an ideology, produced under circumstances of repression and dominance, have significance beyond South African epistemic space to encompass wider discussions on decolonisation, and the place of education in the struggle for human freedom and equality? Crucial attention is devoted to Turner's general comments on education and its role in the struggle for freedom, and his thinking on human becoming. Soudien further examines Turner's framing of consciousness, specifically as a social phenomenon and especially in its concern with the ethics of human behaviour.

Billy Keniston's chapter 9 analyses the extensive contestations regarding the question of non-violent versus armed struggle in the context of 1970s South Africa. Contrary to the standard heroic narratives produced by the ANC, Keniston argues that war was in the best interests of the apartheid state. Non-violent modes of resistance continued to play an important role in the opposition to apartheid, long after they were declared futile. Furthermore, throughout this period, the apartheid state remained consistently concerned about the threats posed by the 'homespun Marxism' of the New Left, and Rick Turner was one of their largest concerns. Understanding Turner's contribution to the political vision of this group of leftists, Keniston argues, is crucial to understanding the possibility of alternative paths towards liberation in South Africa.

Inspired by Peter Hudson's (2017) assertion that Turner anticipated the 'new Sartre', in chapter 10 Gideon van Riet engages with Rick Turner's thought amid particularly contemporary South African problematics of enduring, though reiterated, versions of insecurity. He brings Turner, as an existentialist, into conversation with poststructural works published after Turner's death, specifically Ernesto Laclau and Chantal Mouffe (2013). The chapter's main argument is that Turner's work, based on a sense of open-mindedness, or radical contingency in Laclauian vernacular, should not be viewed as hostile to – or impotent in light of – contemporary struggles. Instead, his general method of critically engaging with relative privilege in aid of radical and social democracy remains valid, while there remains room for strategically privileging specific causes. The key to addressing potential contradictions between Marxist reification and radical contingency lies in recognising that praxes are dynamic, that they result in collaboration across previous lines of division and that they aim to relieve contemporary South Africa's most pressing concerns, also as they morph.

Christine Hobden brings Turner's political philosophy into dialogue with contemporary feminist, anti-racist and decolonial thought on philosophical method in chapter 11. She explores how philosophical endeavour can and should be a tool to resist injustice. For Hobden, Turner offers an intellectual resource and practical inspiration to become engaged political philosophers. Engaged political philosophy holds, following Turner, that to truly come to philosophical grips with concepts such as freedom, democracy or equality, one must engage with how these concepts are lived in the world. An engaged philosopher seeks, therefore, first to understand society, and does so self-reflectively, aware that even our readings of the facts are shaped by our own position and worldview.

In the final chapter of the book, Lawrence Hamilton seeks to re-centre the thematic focus of the book by a pointed engagement with Turner vis-à-vis a key ontological question: 'What is the point of political theory?' Drawing on Turner's ideas about history, ethics, utopianism, judgement and change, Hamilton argues – sometimes in tension with Turner – that utopian thinking depends on a certain form of realism in political theory. For Hamilton, politics involves judgements within a particular concrete context regarding our agency, needs and interests. 'What is the point of political theory?' is therefore a practical question. It is about working out how best to proceed at a particular moment in local, national and global contexts. This requires capacities that constitute the art of good political judgement: an interlinked conception of individual and collective well-being and freedom; deliberation and critique; timing and courage; and, even, persuasive force. The epistemic utility, as Hamilton suggests, is thus a need for a set of radical representative institutions to enhance political judgement in democracies as well as a set of concomitant individual responsibilities to uphold realist, democratic and utopian possibilities.

We are all political agents that possess capacity for change and power to transform. In Turner we encounter the discursivity of politics as an art, a performance and as a revolutionary synthesis that is often contingent on utopia. In the history of South Africa, what Turner offers is to synchronise utopian ideals with the context of impossible circumstances. Politics offers a space of hope for future transformation; in other words, *not only*, as Otto von Bismarck (1815–1898) famously put it, 'the art of the possible, the attainable … the art of the next best'. For Turner, politics is also the art of the impossible made possible.

REFERENCES

Hudson, Peter. 2017. 'Let's Talk about Rick Turner'. *Theoria* 64 (151): 1–9.

Laclau, Ernesto and Chantal Mouffe. 2013. *Hegemony and Socialist Strategy*. London: Verso.

Turner, Richard. 2015 [1972]. *The Eye of the Needle: Towards Participatory Democracy in South Africa*. Kolkata: Seagull Books.

PART I

RICK TURNER AND CONTEMPORARY BLACK THINKERS

1

Decolonising Resistance: Political Freedom in Rick Turner and Steve Biko

Michael Onyebuchi Eze

Rick Turner's political philosophy and subjective location as an agent of transformation mirror Steve Biko's Black Consciousness Movement (BCM) in certain ways. Although Turner's dream of a free South Africa was cut short, one wonders – and for very good reasons – what impact his work might have had on the political unconscious of contemporary South Africa, particularly concerning emancipatory decolonisation. This chapter historicises the ideological crossroads at which Turner's and Biko's philosophies mirror and simultaneously critique each other. Like a man who saw the future, Turner anticipates Biko's prophetic critique of 'white' liberalism concerning the fractured decolonisation status in post-apartheid South Africa. For both Biko and Turner, decolonising resistance goes beyond the material asymmetries of culture or simply overcoming *negative* freedom. The residual legitimation of this claim has become more relevant in the context of emancipatory politics in contemporary South Africa. The new black bourgeoisie's entrenchment is central to this critical thesis on the weakness of the 'liberal programme' (see Biko 1972). As Turner (and later Biko) anticipated, the failure of the current decolonisation programme is only because the liberal programme managed to 'induct a few blacks into the privileged class while leaving intact the real mechanism of oppression, exploitative capitalism' (Turner 1978). The chapter draws lessons from both Turner and Biko for a new way of thinking about resistance that is neither racialised nor encumbered by asymmetries of material culture.

Drawing on Biko and Turner, I argue that the politics of resistance goes beyond the binary narration of Manichean aesthetics. In examining the structure of power and the mode of resistance in colonial South Africa, I show that resistance is not just a one-sided phenomenon within history but occurs simultaneously and is not dependent on the political positionality of the victim or the villain. In Biko's Black Consciousness philosophy, resistance is not categorised only in terms of domination, oppression or exclusion; he subverts these structures and mechanisms. Black Consciousness delegitimates the very ontology of systems of oppression. Thus, one is said to be dominated, excluded or oppressed if one possesses what Jürgen Habermas terms 'Anerkennungswürdigkeit' (recognition worthiness) within the system (Habermas 1979, 5).

In denunciation and subversion, Biko and Turner are taking the power of subjective legitimation away from the oppressor in a way that may be framed thus: 'I do not need you to recognise my humanity! Your recognition of my being is not a condition for my subjective legitimation; my worth is not dependent on your vision of history and its ontological reference.' Thus, Biko and Turner reject negotiation, for that is already a form of recognising that the oppressor defines the terms of my subjective engagement. Negotiation is not neutral, since the oppressor defines the very meaning of justice. Hence, a rejection, refusal and denunciation of the very structures of oppression and its notion of justice are requisite. The coloniser assumes an ontological moral authority, but so, too, does the colonised if they subscribe to negotiation in the context of coloniality. What must be rejected is not just the practice of coloniality, but also the language and metaphysical acceptance of coloniality as a regularised truth. It is this acceptance that Biko and Turner are at war with. As I show later, if the liberals are concerned about the residual consequences of apartheid, for Biko and Turner, it is the epistemic foundation – normalising colonial moral truth – that justifies the institutionalisation of oppression that is the problem. To fight the residual consequences is already an acceptance, as given, of the ontological truth of white superiority.

DECOLONIALITY AND THE EPISTEMOLOGY OF RESISTANCE: SOUTH AFRICA

In political theory, resistance is suggestive of sociocultural, political and sometimes violent opposition or a refusal to accept the status quo or unwillingness to yield to institutionalised powers. I choose the term 'power' instead of authority because resistance often emerges to challenge pre-existing authority, or when existing authority is in contestation as a legitimate political order. Power is understood here as the ability to coerce or control the actions of others, whereas authority arises when power gains legitimation or acceptance. Political resistance emerges to challenge institutionalised political power that lacks moral authority and legitimation. As is often the case, the notion of resistance is localised within contextual experiences reproduced within spatial boundaries. As Howard Caygill argues, resistance is 'rooted in practice and articulated in tactical statements and justifications addressing specific historical contexts' (Caygill 2013, 6). Resistance, therefore, ought to be understood within the context where it is provoked and generates emotive responses. Critical questions I address in this chapter include: Is resistance a historically contingent narrative with universal signification or imperative? If resistance is rooted in a specific historical context, can we articulate a normative framing for its legitimation as a moral practice? Relatedly, is resistance necessarily moral? What is the relationship between moral resistance and political power?

My hypothesis is that politics is rarely about morality. In fact, morality is an agenda of politics. Politics, for its part, is concerned with power. Resistance is a *performative negotiation* between politics, morality and power. Since politics is the bulwark for what constitutes our notion of morality or terms of justice, resistance emerges to renegotiate the ontological legitimations of the moral conditions and terms of justice. When politics becomes moralised, it automatically gives epistemic space for the emergence of resistance. Resistance is, therefore, a discursive displacement of political ontology and its legitimating powers and institutional hierarchies. The degree to which resistant ideologies lay claim to moral justification is dependent on the level of political positionality within a given historical context. As Adam Burgos (2017, 2) notes, resistance is *broadly* defined as 'group opposition, either formal or informal, against some element of the status quo that is dominating, oppressive or exclusionary'. Political resistance then becomes an act sanctioning a pre-existing 'institutional mechanism' that violates common interests (Burgos 2017, 2). From this perspective, the experience of domination, oppression or exclusion constitutes a substantive reference of resistance as the politics of the oppressed. Since these are violations of moral behaviour, resistance becomes a necessary evil, an imperative 'to resist exclusion, oppression, and domination as they exist within the societal status quo in societies claiming to be guided by the common interest' (Burgos 2017, 3). On this trajectory of analysis, the following implications emerge: (i) resistance occurs within a structural power relation; (ii) resistance erupts within the structural binaries, for example, victims versus villains or oppressors versus oppressed; (iii) motivations for resistance are often amorphous and multilayered, such as a desire for constructive progress, for improved principles, to maintain a fragile alliance of convenience or to disrupt the state; and (iv) resistance can also be non-political and subjective in its criterion of inducement. As Burgos notes, 'a democratic legitimate social formation would then be one that understands and fosters the necessity of continually being open to having its blind spots be pointed out by resistance movements, as well as how to productively respond to them' (Burgos 2017, 4).

In contemporary African political philosophy, Turner and Biko remain relevant in an attempt to configure a decolonised understanding of resistance. Their work offers a creative synthesis that fuses history and ideology to contest the legitimacy of the apartheid state on the one hand but also, on the other hand, a sociological and moral aspiration for an emancipatory politics that fosters an inclusive sense of justice. Like slavery and colonialism, apartheid needed an ideology of morality for its ontological legitimation. Racism infused meaning into culturally legitimating experiences of oppression. Racism became necessary for multiple reasons: (i) as a critical source of subjective legitimation; (ii) to enthrone 'whiteness' as moral grounds for colonial power; and (iii) as a cultural plebiscite for oppression, which, as Terrence Ranger observes, provides 'a model of subservience' through which Africans were drawn into the colonial culture (Ranger 1983, 212). As a model of coercion and of 'modern' behaviour, race becomes a cultural tradition to justify an evolving sociopolitical and economic mandate of oppression.

In South Africa, resistance and liberation movements emerged in the context of racialist capitalism – where race determines one's access to the sociopolitical, economic and cultural lifeworlds. To be black was to be excluded from the sociopolitical, economic and material world of apartheid South Africa. Blackness was not just an imposed category to facilitate domination and exploitation of black bodies – the concept freezes black subjectivity. Black oppression was thus normalised as public truth and a legitimate political reality. To be black is to be scorned, derided with contempt and self-hate, as Bloke Modisane (1960, 26) expounded: 'White is right, and to be black is to be despised, dehumanized, classed among the beasts, hounded and persecuted, discriminated against, segregated and oppressed by government and by man's greed. White is the positive standard, black the negative. Symbols of wealth… are allotted to the whites…inferiority, humiliation and servitude are the lot of the black people.' In the absence of teleological mobility, that is, frozen without sociopolitical and economic prospects, black subjectivity is anathemised, valued only insofar as it serves the whims of the white community. What this means, too, is that since political power is tied to race, to dethrone political control is to uproot and subvert the ontological roots of its legitimation, which are (i) white superiority (Turner) and (ii) subjective reclamation (Biko). The political resolution of apartheid is only possible when racial conflict is resolved through resistance to institutional hierarchies of oppression, as Njabulo Ndebele (1972, 8) acutely observes: 'There is a hierarchy of conflict in South Africa. The greatest conflict is that between the races. The race which is in power is the white race; that which seeks the power it does not have is the black race. The white race is able to control the black race, by force if necessary, in order to maintain its position of power.'

As Biko and Turner would have argued, the colonial social space that legitimated apartheid depended on the successful dehumanisation of black subjectivity. Upon this dehumanisation thrive the material asymmetries of apartheid in terms of racialist capitalism and access to sociopolitical and cultural worlds. The material oppression of blacks is only a symptom of the cultural processes of domination. Resistance is only viable in understanding that oppression is first and foremost linked to racialised ontology. This ontology gave epistemic currency to apartheid and its associated political economy of oppression. According to this view, a black person is a being that exists only as (i) an antithesis to white subjectivity, and (ii) a material burden for the colonial economy. A Manichean subject evolves: the colonised subject symbolically exists only so that the imperial subject recognises himself as a moral superior. As Philip Rief notes from Freudian psychology, 'the very reason that Hegel thought Africa not a proper subject for the historian, Freud would consider it most proper' because Africa gave Europe its identity by being the binary opposite of the undesired *other* upon which Europe anchored its moral gaze (cited in Ankersmit 2010, ix). Yet, this is a moral hierarchy that is violently enforced, as Doris Lessing (1950, 144) notes: 'When a white man in Africa by accident looks into the eyes of a native and sees the human being (which is his chief preoccupation to avoid), his sense of guilt which he denies, fumes up in resentment and he brings down the whip.'

A new understanding of colonised humanity emerges that is ambivalent and contradictory. The more savage the native becomes, the more human the coloniser becomes. The moment the colonised subject begins to become 'civilised' or look more like the coloniser, in that moment, he loses his right to legitimate presence, the right to be, and becomes a rabble-rouser, a bad subject and is disqualified. To be is to remain a constructed other, a subjective inferior and mirror for the self-affirmation of the coloniser. Aimé Césaire (1972, 41) elucidates: 'Colonization ... dehumanizes even the most civilized man; that colonial activity, colonial enterprise, colonial conquest, which is based on contempt for the native and justified by that contempt, inevitably tends to change him who undertakes it ... the colonizer, who ... gets into the habit of seeing the other man as an animal accustoms himself to treating him like an animal, and tends objectively to transform himself into an animal.'

Frantz Fanon (1963, 169) seems to concur: 'Colonialism is not satisfied merely with holding a people in its grip and emptying the native's brain of all form and content. By a kind of perverted logic, it turns to the past of the oppressed people, and distorts, disfigures and destroys it.' Chinua Achebe (1977, 792) shares this view: 'The West seems to suffer deep anxieties about the precariousness of its civilization and to have a need for constant reassurance by comparing it with Africa. If Europe, advancing in civilization, could cast a backward glance periodically at Africa trapped in primordial barbarity, it could say with faith and feeling: There go I but for the grace of God.'

In the context of South Africa, racial hierarchy constitutes the very ontology of apartheid ideology and its instrumental humanity. At the root of apartheid ideology is the denigration of Africans as inferiors and the imposition of Europeans as superiors. This assumption has political and ethical implications for the coloniser and the colonised. Thus, in resisting apartheid, priority is given to subjective restoration, for if the racial hierarchy collapses, political change becomes inevitable. Subjective restoration is the form of resistance that simultaneously emancipates the victims and ruptures the logic of oppression. With subjective reclamation comes moral restoration and the legitimation of black subjectivity. Accordingly, political freedom first starts with the decolonisation of the mind and subjective liberation. Resistance is, first and foremost, a resignification of blackness from a negative imposition of values to a positive meaning. Second, for political freedom, black people would have to take charge of their destiny and history. As Mikhail Heller and Moiseevich Nekrich (1986, 9) observe, 'Conquerors write the history of the wars: the victors take possession of the past, establish their control over the collective memory.' It is in contestation of this politics of memory that Biko noted in his introduction to *Black Viewpoint*, 'We have felt and observed in the past, the existence of a great vacuum in our literary and newspaper world. So many things are said often to us, about us and for us but very seldom by us' (Biko 1972, 1).

RESISTANCE AND THE LEGITIMATION OF POLITICAL CHANGE

Why was the government threatened by Turner and Biko? First, their subjective location was weaponised. Both their writings were banned (books banned, prohibited, indicted) and conceived by the government as a cancer on the tissues of their oppressive structures. Second, liberal agitations were tolerated, but the utopian vision of resistance that looks beyond the cosmetics of oppression became more dangerous than the oppressive structure itself. Their idea was a threat to the ideology of oppression.

The Bantu Education Act proscribed a reflexive education of blacks, any education that was beyond that of instrumental value in the service of the white community. Educational skills such as maths or science lead to vain expectations, as Dr HF Verwoerd noted: 'When I have control over native education, I will reform it so that natives will be taught from childhood that equality with Europeans is not for them...There is no place for Bantu in the European community above the level of certain forms of labour' (cited in Christie 1985, 12).

In this context, political domination is facilitated by inaccessibility to knowledge and knowledge production, that is, what to know, how it is known, where it is known and who has a right to know. According to Wilhelm Jordaan and Jackie Jordaan, Bantu Education authorities 'will determine what you know, how you know it and what you do with your knowledge' (Jordaan and Jordaan 1998, 599). Education is thus a thoroughly ideological project, in order to dominate through control and manipulation of the worldview accessible to the oppressed. It also imposes subjective alienation through the internalisation of these racist discourses. The implication is that 'when you control knowledge or information, you depict the world in a particular way, but at the same time distort it...through your verbal control of reality...you do not reflect it but create it according to your view, and persuade others to see it as you see it. This amounts to subtle domination to make others look at things your way' (G. Rossouw cited in Jordaan and Jordaan 1998, 599).

'Look[ing] at things your way' means accepting oppression as natural, or normalising whiteness as superior. Hence, education becomes a locus of absurdity that redeems and oppresses. As Dr AB Xuma, who led the African National Congress (ANC) between 1940 and 1949, bitterly complained: 'It has been felt that an educated African is a threat to the security of Europeans. And so, politicians have found that it has become more and more necessary to limit opportunity of Africans or at least to make it impossible for them to acquire the same qualification and the same skills' (cited in Dworkin 1993). This view was equally shared by Govan Mbeki, who said: 'Verwoerd believed that if we get the child into the classroom to accept domination, to accept a subservient position in society, they [the schoolchildren] will, in turn, spread it amongst the community and in the final analysis, the whole African population will accept subservience' (cited in Dworkin 1993).

Writing on his Black Consciousness agenda, Biko perceived education as a sociocultural project in the service of ideology. For Turner, apartheid is simply racialist capitalism, where race configures patterns of access to the sociopolitical and economic imaginary. Turner understands political decisions or policies in apartheid South Africa as a metonymical displacement for capitalist accumulation. Race becomes necessary as a justificatory ontology to legitimate the culture of oppression. What Biko and Turner have in common is their recognition that apartheid offered a myth of inferiority, but even if this is a false myth, it has an actual impact on the lives of the people. Both victims and villains are affected by it. Therefore, resistance does not start with dealing with the residues of oppression but with uprooting the ontological roots of racism, which are culture, knowledge production and, mostly importantly, capitalist accumulation.

Biko and Turner criticise white liberals for accommodating oppression. As Turner (1978) asks: 'Can we perhaps persuade them at least to eat old goats instead of our prize lambs?' Thus asking the right question instead of making moral compromises would be an initiative for a just political order. Structures of oppression are 'naturalised' as public truths. Consequently, ethics and morals become conceptualised as traditions rigidly codified and impossible to change. We conceive them as natural entities imposing certain rigidities on our behaviours (Turner 1978). Instead of asking the right questions, we are settled with cosmetic and redundant solutions; instead of upending the root causes of racism – for Turner, capitalist accumulation (racialist capitalism); for Biko, knowledge production (who, where and what is learnt) – we subscribe to piecemeal compromises. The liberal modernity offers liberatory compromises in which we throw charitable bones of humanity to the exploited, and despite this, Turner warns, 'the great core institutions remain, essentially unaltered and unalterable'. We ought to have, therefore, a critical attitude towards history; we have to 'grasp the present as history' (Turner 1978). For Biko (2005, 78), white liberals are complicit, and since they enjoy the benefits of oppression, they share in the metaphysical guilt for the sin of oppression; 'the very fact that those disgruntled whites remain to enjoy the fruits of the system would alone be enough to condemn them'. Drawing a parallel with the Nuremberg era, Biko cites Karl Jaspers at length:

> There exists amongst men, because they are men, a solidarity through which each shares responsibility for every injustice and every wrong committed in the world and especially for crimes that are committed in his presence…If I do not do whatever I can to prevent them, I am an accomplice in them. [I]f I have stood silent, I feel guilty in a sense that cannot in any adequate fashion be understood juristically or politically or morally…That I am still alive after such things have been done weighs on me as a guilt that cannot be expiated. (Karl Jaspers cited in Biko 2005, 78–79)

Biko rejects white liberals because even if they seek to identify with black people's struggle, they nevertheless lack subjective experience of what it means to be black, given that they are past and present beneficiaries of the colonial project. Besides, their theory of resistance offered as a metaphysical source of redemption is the product of the same Western intellectual history and culture that produced and nourished apartheid. This idea of liberation effectively preserves the metaphysical status of white superiority without creating space for the subjective mobility of blacks. The idea of liberation offers a sense of inclusion yet thrives by homogenising the revolutionary impulse into one historical experience of enlightenment humanism. How, then, would it be possible to articulate a theory of resistance thoroughly grounded in black people's experience as a racialised other? Black Consciousness rejects the default definition of blackness as a residual subjective of non-whiteness (see Adam 1973, 155). As Kogila Moodley (1991, 242) notes, the purpose of the BCM was to change this 'negative attitude about subordinate "non-whites" into an inverted, positive discourse of resistance. It offered psychological support to an oppressed group by providing a model for positive identification and sought to alter the contempt that the victims often felt for their own group'. Biko (2005, 53) notes:

> Black Consciousness is in essence the realization by the black man of the need to rally together with his brothers around the cause of their oppression – the blackness of their skin – and to operate as a group in order to rid themselves of the shackles that bind them to perpetual servitude. It seeks to demonstrate the lie that black is an aberration... Black Consciousness... seeks to infuse the black community with a new-found pride in themselves, their efforts, their value systems, their culture, their religion and their outlook to life.

White liberals are rejected because their empathy lacks subjective iden-tification and thrives only on the level of abstract experience without any access to the inner psychological trauma afflicting black identity. Biko infuses morality into context. He is aware that abstract moral-ity not only de-historicises but imposes misrecognition on reality and experiences. Biko understands, too, the signification of resistance from within the orbit of racialised oppression. White liberals benefit from white privilege, and their empathy springs from a need to assuage their metaphysical guilt. Besides, since political power is tied to race, admission of whites into the movement is to transfer the same political unconscious and mediate continued domination of black people, as Biko explicates:

> [Their] presence amongst us is irksome and of nuisance value. It removes the focus of attention from essentials and shifts it to ill-defined philosophical concepts that are both irrelevant to the black man and merely a red herring across the track. White liberals must leave blacks to take care of their own business while they concern themselves with the real evil in our society – white racism... the kind of twisted logic that the Black Consciousness approach seeks to eradicate. (Biko 2005, 24, 51)

If Biko rejects white liberals because their subjective location in history makes them metaphysical accomplices (or beneficiaries) of oppression, Turner, on the other hand, rejects them for more practical reasons. As Turner notes, the rejection of 'white liberals' is not motivated by the Sartrean thesis of anti-racist racism, but rather by ideological pragmatism: 'White opponents of apartheid are not a significant political force and are certainly not going to be the chief agent in the overthrow of apartheid. It would therefore be wrong for blacks to orient their political activity towards an appeal to whites to help them' (Turner 1972, 20). Turner's view was shared by Biko, who argued that even as the existing theory of resistance might offer a priori economic empowerment and forms of political justice, it still lacks the ontological mandate and vision necessary for an enduring political change. The vision is alienated, invented for a white audience. Bennie Khoapa (1972, 24) agrees: 'It is a mystification to preach universal brotherhood in a situation of oppression... it is too soon to love everybody... There is nothing ominous or subversive about this principle. It is simply an exigency of the situation. History has charged us with the cruel responsibility of going to the very gate of racism in order to destroy racism – to the gate, no further.'

The discursive power of invention comes with material authority to possess or dominate. As Chamcha noted in Salman Rushdie's *The Satanic Verses*, 'They describe us. That's all. They have the power of description, and we succumb to the pictures they construct' (Rushdie 2008, 172). 'Succumb[ing] to the pictures they construct' informs Turner's defence of Black Consciousness as an epistemic rebellion to this imposed convergence between politics and anthropology. The black person is a framed political subject, and claims on integration are only a metaphor for continued subordination and subjugation, as indicated in the South African Students' Organisation (SASO) policy manifesto #6: 'Integration in South Africa... in particular the Progressive Party and other liberal institutions – are not working for the kind of integration that would be acceptable to the Black man. Their attempts are directed merely at relaxing certain oppressive legislations and to allow blacks into a white-type society' (SASO 1971). Integration in this context is merely a political concession, not an ontological necessity, and hence suspect and distrustful, as noted in the SASO policy manifesto #5: 'Integration does not mean an assimilation of Blacks into an already established set of norms drawn up and motivated by white society' (SASO 1971). The upshot is that while integration is a political necessity, it ought simultaneously to possess an ontic commitment to what may be termed the 'teleological mobility' of agents within the system, free to choose and participate in the making of a new South Africa. Integration is not a predetermined metaphysical script or binary creation but suggestive of what I have termed elsewhere as a confluence of narratives. In the SASO manifesto, it means 'free participation by individuals in a given society and proportionate contribution to the joint culture of the society by all constituent groups' (SASO 1971, #5).

As shown earlier, decolonising resistance therefore unveils a tripartite process that includes not only the decolonisation of socioeconomic and political structures, but also a decolonisation of the mind and cultural 'imaginary' as reflected in processes of knowledge production and its legitimation of the realities of experience (Mignolo 2007, 450). Fanon (1963, 31) observes:

> The originality of the colonial context is that economic reality, inequality and the immense difference of ways of life never come to mask the human realities. When you examine at close quarters the colonial context, it is evident that what parcels out the world is to begin with the fact of belonging to or not belonging to a given race, a given species. In the colonies the economic substructure is also a superstructure. The cause is the consequence; you are rich because you are white, you are white because you are rich.

Decolonising resistance also attempts to transcend the binary construction of humanity and seeks instead to restore collective agency as central to decolonisation. Thus, subjective reclamation precedes material decolonisation, and decolonisation (of resistance) is simultaneously a critique of liberal modernity. The subject is neither just an abstract individual alienated from tradition or culture, nor merely an imperial subject – one that thrives through what has been clichéd as a differentiating order of otherness.

The liberal principle of resistance is imported from the dominating nation. In practice, resistance remains an instrument of domination and warfare imposed upon the people to suit the colonial mindset. It is a mechanical attempt to liberate through modification of behaviour based on white paternalism. It ignores the inequality of race without any historical infusion of the reality of the colonised experience. As Fanon (1963, 118) notes, liberation is necessarily contingent on one's 'knowledge of the practice of action', that is, the subjective location that fuses context with experience. The practice of action and its implication motivates Turner's (1972, 20) criticism of white liberals and their paternalistic white saviour consciousness: 'The point here is that this attitude remains arrogant, paternalistic and basically insulting. It involves the acceptance of the idea that to behave like whites is the ideal, it is to accept the concept of civilizing mission of the whites, the idea that, although blacks are not biologically inferior, they are culturally inferior. They may be educable, but they need whites to educate them.'

Turner was thus negotiating subjective revival not only in the political sphere but also within the socioeconomic and cultural spheres of apartheid South Africa. For him, oppression is fundamentally tied to the racialised ontology of black people within history. Subjective reclamation occurs by way of subversion of the epistemic eccentricities of coloniality as well as subversion of history and the fundamental logic of apartheid coloniality. In liberal modernity, whiteness is still a paradigm of rightness or humanity, while black inferiority is normalised and regularised as public truth both by villains and victims of oppression. Hence, effective resistance is not merely in physical encounters but also in refusal, denunciation and subversion of the ontological eccentricities of coloniality. Acceptance of the status quo is an endorsement of the epistemic currency for subjective (de)legitimation. Negotiating with the system is recognising the validity of the system. Integrating white activists into the struggle compromises resistance because they, too, are beneficiaries of the system, and blacks, Biko writes, should not 'seek to reform the system because doing so implies acceptance of major points around which the system revolves' (Biko 2005, 50). Subjective freedom is to be achieved only by a Black Consciousness attitude and not through collaboration with white interventionists:

> Whites are deriving pleasure and security in entrenching white racism and further exploiting the minds and bodies of the unsuspecting black masses. Their agents are ever present amongst us, telling us that it is immoral to withdraw into a cocoon, that dialogue is the answer to our problem... These in fact are the greatest racists for they refuse to credit us with any intelligence to know what we want. [T]hey want to be barometers by which the rest of the white society can measure feelings in the black world. This then is what makes us believe that white power presents its self as a totality not only provoking us but also controlling our response to the provocation. (Biko 2005, 51–52)

As a theory of resistance, decolonisation as both liberatory and emancipatory discourse succeeds not by negotiation but by epistemic subversion. The problem with negotiation is that equality, where it is invoked, is not synonymous with subjective equality in terms of the cultural procedures of power relations but masks its racism in terms of tolerance. Yet, what this shows is racism as denialism, liberation as exploitation, and resistance as contempt. Hence, as Fanon suggests, in decolonisation, the individual is not only a political subject but a being that is ontologically transformed:

> [Decolonization] influences individuals and modifies them fundamentally. It transforms spectators crushed with their inessentiality

into privileged actors, with the grandiose glare of history's flood-lights upon them. It brings a natural rhythm into existence, introduced by new men, and with it a new language and a new humanity. Decolonization is the veritable creation of new men. But this creation owes nothing of its legitimacy to any supernatural power; the 'thing' which has been colonized becomes man during the same process by which it frees itself. (Fanon 1963, 37)

In Black Consciousness, resistance means a recognition that liberation and dignity are synonymous. A free person is one with dignity. Freedom without dignity is no freedom; it is subjective imprisonment:

Liberation therefore is of paramount importance for we cannot be conscious of ourselves and yet remain in bondage. We want to attain the envisioned self which is a free self... the realization by the blacks that the most potent weapon in the hands of the oppressor is the mind of the oppressed... the realisation by the black man of the need to rally together with his brothers around the cause of their oppression – the blackness of their skin – and to operate as a group to rid themselves of the shackles that bind them to perpetual servitude. (Biko 2005, 50, 69, 92f)

RESISTANCE AS POLITICAL THEOLOGY

Although Turner and Biko agree on the extent to which direct engagement with or response to apartheid policies (as liberals do) constitutes a legitimation of apartheid ontology, they disagree as to what constitutes the epistemic grounding on which resistance ought to take off. For Turner, ground zero is in understanding apartheid as a simulation of capital accumulation. Disrupting the means of production or changing it will ultimately shape subjective relocation and rupture structural dehumanisation. Capital is what gives humanity. I am what I have or have access to. To deny people access to labour or capital is to deny them access to humanity. Disenfranchisement of property is a denial of humanity. Ownership of property gave subjective rights under the apartheid scheme. Race enabled the dispossession of property rights. Property rights legitimated oppression since the absence of economic capital not only disenfranchised but ultimately desubjectified. Thus, Turner asks, would emancipation be racial or capital reclamation? Indeed, Turner was prophetic, and liberal ideology would not usher in any metaphysical euphoria. Like Biko, he was suspicious of liberals and their ideology because they treat the symptoms and not the root causes of oppression. Liberal ontology does not yield to any metaphysical euphoria. In fact, Turner scoffed at the idea of white 'cultural superiority', which he finds 'laughable' since the 'main "contribution" of Western civilization to human history was the development of a new and higher level of exploitation of person by person, and of a new and higher level of materialism' (Turner 1972, 20).

On what ideological platform, then, could true political emancipation emerge? In *The Eye of the Needle*, Turner suggests that real subjective conversion comes by teaching Christian love to white people: 'If the Christian Churches can rediscover their transcendence and show the meaning of love to white South Africans then a peaceful resolution of the struggle will be possible' (Turner 1978). Yet, Turner is not naïve about the processes of power relations and their functional practices. Five years before the publication of *The Eye of the Needle*, he was very sceptical that Christianity could be a doctrine of liberation or emancipatory politics. Drawing an example from Europe, he showed how Christianity is implicated in the ideology of oppression: 'The theoretical Christian principles of Europe were contradicted by the factual concentration on the acquisition of material goods through the efficient exploitation of one's neighbours. Christian Europe was based on servile labour and, as it expanded internally with the development of industrial capitalism, and externally through imperial conquest, it refined the mechanisms of exploitation' (Turner 1972, 20).

Turner specifically refers to white Christianity, which he sees as a subterfuge for oppression. He advocates for a new interpretation of Christianity that is simultaneously a liberation theology. He finds within Christianity a space for subjective reclamation of all races. Colonial Christianity became implicated in racist discourses and the legitimation of oppression. In South Africa specifically, the Dutch Reformed Church became a state religion to give substantive moral legitimacy to apartheid policies. Segregation, for example, was justified by the 1974 communiqué by the General Synod of the Dutch Reformed Churches: 'Under certain circumstances and conditions, the New Testament does leave room for organizing the co-existence of different nations in one country through the policies of separate development' (Boesak 1976, 36). But this is not only an endorsement of segregation, it is also a divine mandate for whites to be overlords over blacks, as the Reverend EP Groenewald observed: 'It is [not only] God's will that separate people should maintain their separateness… it may be expected that the immature people shall subject itself willingly to the authority placed over it… [therefore]… it can be stated with gratitude that the race policy of the Afrikaner testifies to the reverence [the Afrikaner] has for God and his word' (cited in Boesak 1976, 35, 158). A peculiar interpretation of Christianity was hence used to justify active collaboration between the churches and the apartheid regime.

In appealing to Christian liberation principles, Turner was at pains to find ways in which Christian egalitarian principles could offer an ontological space to mobilise resistance to oppressive ideology. This concern was shared by many in the black liberation movements. The ANC Cape president in the 1920s, Pastor Zacheus Mahabane, for example, envisaged Christianity as an ideological platform for total liberation: 'The universal acknowledgment of Christ as common Lord and king [would] break down the social, spiritual and intellectual barriers between the races' (Walshe 1991, 31). Pastor Mahabane's vision is supported by Dr Alfred Bitini Xuma, the ANC president between 1940 and 1949, who suggested that the liberation movement be modelled on Christian ideals: 'The liberation movement is not anti-white in seeking full scope for African progress [on the contrary, it is] working for the good of all South Africans, working to promote the ideal of Christianity, human decency and democracy' (Walshe 1991, 31). And in 1960, Albert Luthuli denounced the churches for having abandoned their teleological mandate, which is the liberation of all peoples irrespective of race:

> [The] churches have simply submitted to the secular state for too long; some have even supported apartheid. While it is not too late for white Christians to look at the Gospels and redefine their allegiance, I warn those who care for Christianity, who care to go to *all* the world and preach the Gospel, that in South Africa the opportunity is 300 years old. It will not last for ever. This time is running out. (Luthuli 1962, 119)

This is the context in which Turner was seeking a reinterpretation of Christianity as a theology not just of redemption, but of political liberation – of all peoples. Drawing on egalitarian principles, Turner, it seems, is undercutting the material basis of capitalist Christianity: 'How practical is it to want a second car when the world is running out of petrol? How practical is it to try to pass a camel through the eye of the needle?' (Turner 1978). He suggests a change of attitude through teaching Christian love. In Christianity, Turner found a revolutionary synthesis for resistance, a triple manoeuvre of (i) rehabilitating black subjectivity from the truncated image of apartheid historicity; (ii) undercutting the very basis of racialist capitalism; and (iii) dethroning white privilege as a normative sociopolitical value. Given its nature as a religion, for Turner, Christianity bore the truth that could offer a space to challenge the dogma of oppression. Christian values, even as a dogma, could offer a higher value that remains transcendental and non-contestable by the oppressor – the oppressor is also a believer. Thus, Turner fuses theology with emancipatory politics: 'Christianity does not just condemn racism. It constitutes a challenge to all accepted values, an invitation to continuous self-examination, to a continuous attempt at transcendence... Christianity is incompatible not only with racism but also with many of the other norms regulating our behaviour, and in order to live in a Christian way we will need to radically restructure our society' (Turner 1978).

Radical restructuring was to preoccupy Biko, whose view is similar to Turner's:

> The only path open for us now is to redefine the message in the Bible and to make it relevant to the struggling masses. The Bible must not be seen to preach that all authority is divinely instituted. It must rather preach that it is a sin to allow oneself to be oppressed... This is the message implicit in 'black theology'. Black theology seeks to do away with spiritual poverty of the black people... Black theology seeks to depict Jesus as a fighting God. (Biko 2005, 32)

CONCLUSION

Resistance emerges when the legitimation of the state and its distribution of power, rights and privileges is in question. Resistance seeks to disrupt this structure of power relations and its associated privileges. What we gain from Turner and Biko is a new understanding of resistance that reconciles human freedom with evolving political ontologies. What both revolutionaries demand is a new ideology of resistance that is sensitive to the context of history and experience. They both reject white liberalism for its paternalist hierarchy. They seek to decentre resistance as a scripted mandate of abstract morality. They reject whiteness as a subjective location of rights and privileges. More specifically, since white Christianity is implicated in fostering and legitimating the ideology of oppression, in rejecting white Christianity, whiteness is dethroned along with its embedded power relations and social productions. Resistance is not merely a response to oppressive structures where the subject is embroiled with *familiar* terms of engagement dictated by conflict; resistance becomes a performative narrative that challenges and displaces illegitimate power with new social relations of engagement. In this way, agency is restored since the ideal of resistance embodies not simply a counter-oppressive impulse of oppression but a creative response to hierarchies of power.

In decolonising resistance, our revolutionary impulse assumes a new teleological aspiration that is not subordinated to pre-existing sociopolitical and epistemic structures or hierarchies of power but instead offers a theoretical utility that (i) illuminates institutional and sociopolitical conditions that mediate oppressive structures; (ii) fuses political freedom with subjective reclamation; (iii) mediates a new consciousness that recognises the ambivalence of conflict, its internal tension and series of contradictions; and (iv) ultimately prioritises the context of struggle that drives resistance. Resistance is thus both performative and pedagogic in terms that delineate rupture versus transformation or revolution versus emancipation. As noted earlier, 'the most potent weapon of the oppressor', Biko famously quipped, 'is the mind of the oppressed'. Resistance is subjective liberation from ideological blinders that perpetuate domination, or that legitimate the ideology of oppression; it is defiance in freedom and freedom as defiance. For Turner, resistance is not naïve optimism. In fact, resistance is necessarily a mode of contested violence that chokes both victims and villains through the *eye of the needle*, a metonymical expression of South Africa's impossible circumstances.

That is all!

REFERENCES

Achebe, Chinua. 1977. 'An Image of Africa: Racism in Conrad's "Heart of Darkness"'. *The Massachusetts Review* 18 (4): 782–794.

Adam, Heribert. 1973. 'The Rise of Black Consciousness in South Africa'. *Race and Class* 15 (2): 149–165.

Ankersmit, Frank. 2010. 'Foreword'. In *The Politics of History in Contemporary Africa*, by Michael Onyebuchi Eze, ix–xii. New York: Palgrave Macmillan.

Biko, Steve. 1972. 'Introduction'. In *Black Viewpoint*, 1. Johannesburg: Spro-Cas Black Community Programmes.

Biko, Steve. 2005. *I Write What I Like*. Cambridge: ProQuest.

Boesak, Allan. 1976. *Farewell to Innocence: A Socio-Ethical Study on Black Theology and Black Power.* New York: Orbis Books.

Burgos, Adam. 2017. *Political Philosophy and Political Action: Imperatives of Resistance.* London: Rowman & Littlefield International.

Caygill, Howard. 2013. *On Resistance: A Philosophy of Defiance.* London: Bloomsbury.

Césaire, Aimé. 1972. *Discourse on Colonialism.* New York: Monthly Review Press.

Christie, Pam. 1985. *The Right to Learn: The Struggle for Education in South Africa.* Johannesburg: Ravan Press.

Dworkin, Laurence (dir.). 1993. *Ulibambe Lingashoni – Hold up the Sun*, a five part video documentary series on the ANC and popular power in the making. Toron International and Thebe Investment Corporation production, produced by Afravision. Johannesburg: Impact Video.

Fanon, Frantz. 1963. *The Wretched of the Earth.* Translated by Constance Farrington. New York: Grove Press.

Habermas, Jürgen. 1979. *Communication and the Evolution of Society.* Translated by Thomas McCarthy. Boston: Beacon Press.

Heller, Mikhail and Aleksandr Moiseevich Nekrich. 1986. *Utopia in Power: The History of the Soviet Union from 1917 to the Present.* New York: Summit Books.

Jordaan, Wilhelm and Jackie Jordaan. 1998. *People in Context.* Johannesburg: Heinemann.

Khoapa, Bennie. 1972. 'The New Black'. In *Black Viewpoint*, edited by Steve Biko, 22–26. Johannesburg: Spro-Cas Black Community Programmes.

Lessing, Doris. 1950. *The Grass is Singing.* London: Michael Joseph.

Luthuli, Albert. 1962. *Let My People Go.* London: Collins.

Mignolo, Walter D. 2007. 'Delinking: The Rhetoric of Modernity, the Logic of Coloniality and the Grammar of De-Coloniality'. *Cultural Studies* 21 (2): 449–514.

Modisane, Bloke. 1960. 'Why I Ran Away'. In *An African Treasury*, edited by Langston Hughes, 26–29. Johannesburg: Crown Publications.

Moodley, Kogila. 1991. 'The Continued Impact of Black Consciousness in South Africa'. *The Journal of Modern African Studies* 29 (2): 237–251.

Ndebele, Njabulo. 1972. 'Black Development'. In *Black Viewpoint*, edited by Steve Biko, 2–10. Johannesburg: Spro-Cas Black Community Programmes.

Ranger, Terence. 1983. 'The Invention of Tradition in Colonial Africa'. In *The Invention of Tradition*, edited by Eric J Hobsbawm and Terence Ranger, 211–262. Cambridge: Cambridge University Press.

Rushdie, Salman. 2008. *The Satanic Verses.* New York: Random House.

SASO (South African Students Organisation). 1971. 'SASO Policy Manifesto'. Durban: SASO.

Turner, Richard. 1972. 'Black Consciousness and White Liberals'. *Reality* 4 (3): 20–22.

Turner, Richard. 1978. *The Eye of the Needle: Towards Participatory Democracy in South Africa.* Maryknoll (NY): Orbis Books. https://www.sahistory.org.za/archive/eye-needle-preface-richard-turner. Accessed 18 December 2023.

Walshe, Peter. 1991. 'South Africa: Prophetic Christianity and the Liberation Movement'. *The Journal of Modern African Studies* 29 (1): 27–60.

2

Race, Political Change and Liberal Critiques: Rick Turner and Sam Nolutshungu

Ayesha Omar

The fifty-year anniversary of the publication of Rick Turner's book, *The Eye of the Needle: An Essay on Participatory Democracy* (1972a), has prompted scholars to reflect on the meaning and value of this text in South African political theory and philosophy. Turner's life and writings exemplify an important political project that instantiates the struggle against apartheid. Perhaps more significantly, his book undergirds a particular moment in South African anti-apartheid intellectual history, and is generative of further contestation and debate. This is in reference to both normative questions, ideational possibilities and Turner's utopian vision for political reform and social change through the notion of participatory democracy. Many scholars have been generously attentive to Turner's scholarship, commenting variously on the substantive nature of his ideas and providing detailed analysis on its theoretical architecture. There is also a resurgence of citing Turner's continuing relevance for the social and political challenges facing contemporary democratic South Africa (see Fluxman and Vale 2004; Piper 2010; Keniston 2013; Friedman 2017; Macqueen 2018). After all, *The Eye of the Needle* represents Turner's attempt to produce a theory of political and social change for an ideal South African society. But in it is encoded a complex and sometimes bewildering set of ideas that signifies Turner's existentialist training, his mode of radical theoretical engagement, and the context of oppositional thinking that informs his scholarship.

Turner concedes that *The Eye of the Needle* was composed with the intent to influence political action rather than offer a ground-breaking academic argument. This text also speaks to a particular audience: 'Until white South Africans come to understand that present society and their present position is a result not of their own virtues but of their vices... they will not be able to communicate with black people, nor, ultimately, with one another' (Turner 1972a, 92). In this sense, political reform, for Turner, may be construed as a bold challenge to white society and to 'whiteness and its failings' (Friedman 2017, 14).

But like Turner, other South African intellectuals operating in a context of opposition and defiance to the apartheid system, and imbued with a similar spirit of radicalism, critiqued dominant theoretical and ideological constructs to develop visions for social and political change. In a somewhat alternative path of inquiry, this chapter seeks to locate how Turner's ideas can be brought into conversation with another South African theorist of social and political change. In particular, my task here is to illuminate the work of an arguably lesser-known black intellectual and political theorist, Sam C Nolutshungu, who articulates a theoretical vision for social change and political reform in his book *Changing South Africa: Political Considerations* (1982). This text was published some ten years after Turner's *The Eye of the Needle*. It remains striking that even in contemporary South Africa, no special issues, edited volumes or academic conferences have committed themselves to understanding Nolutshungu's ideas. As I have argued elsewhere, Nolutshungu's extraordinary ideas deserve singular attention yet remain overlooked and neglected (Omar 2021, 83).

The purpose of this kind of inquiry is twofold. First, to engage reflexively with intellectual history in South Africa by broadening its limited purview and approach. One way this may be achieved is by re-centring previously marginalised voices, for example, the writings of black theorists, and engaging comparatively with their ideas to garner more depth and nuance in South African intellectual historiography. Second is for these projects to enable a greater plurality of thinking in South African and African intellectual history by tending to the methodological urgencies and attendant concerns raised by the discipline of comparative political theory. Comparative political theory takes seriously the task of broadening the scope of how we practise political theory through the inclusion of historically marginalised ideas. It seeks to redefine the 'parameters of political theory' in a transformative manner, often guided by the imperatives of democratic or postcolonial concerns, 'to press for the inclusion of historically suppressed voices in a global conversation about a shared political future' (Williams 2020, 1). What I am suggesting here is that while Turner's ideas on political reform in the late apartheid period are routinely thought to offer bold and radical visions for a post-apartheid future, these ideas, when juxtaposed with other, equally daring and independent theoretical perspectives for change, enable us to see how the context was read and interpreted in deeply complex and alternating ways by black and by white South African intellectuals.

Moreover, these alternative perspectives offer us a way of reading the present in more subtle and enriching ways. As such, three main areas of comparative emphasis are explored in this chapter: race, liberalism and the role of the Black Consciousness Movement (BCM). These three areas provide important overlapping points of convergence. They were also frequently presented as significant for the ideational possibility of change for South African political theorists. My comparative focus here is not on a narrow binary of an identarian nature. Rather, it stems from a genuine interest in revealing how different contexts, which include Turner's and Nolutshungu's varying racial realities and historical contexts, may have contributed to producing different theoretical accounts and, more importantly, differences or similarities for the politics of change. The utility of comparative political theory, then, is also structural. It is born from the recognition of why it is difficult to overcome deeply rooted practices in the academy and in political theory in particular, from the common and sound intuition that in a globalised era we need to globalise our understanding of political thought and integrate a myriad of perspectives (Williams 2020, 2).

Perhaps one apparent place of initial, comparative inquiry, for an account such as this one, is an investigation into the direct use of texts and ideas. In other words, given that both Turner and Nolutshungu theorised on questions of race and liberalism and responded to Black Consciousness literature, it is not implausible to suggest that they would have encountered and possibly read and cited each other's work. As academics, radical thinkers and contemporaries, is there any evidence of citation or meaningful use of each other's work? A close inspection of Turner's and Nolutshungu's main texts does not disclose evidence of direct intellectual dialogue or theoretical cross-citation. That said, it is interesting that, in his main text *Changing South Africa*, Nolutshungu makes direct reference to Turner's life and broader intellectual project in a footnoted discussion. This discussion deals with the BCM and the strategies of its curtailment by the apartheid regime. In this regard, Nolutshungu states:

> The state response may, however, be seen as operating at two levels: that of the highest official policy, which did not recognise a need for the whole suppression of BCM, and that of functionaries at the middle and lower levels of security policy, and right-wing militants, who 'unofficially' had recourse to terror and intimidation against militants. Two particular episodes of right-wing terror relating to the student scene stand out: the murder of Dr Turner, a radical white lecturer at the University of Natal, and the assassination by parcel bomb of Tiro in Botswana. (Nolutshungu 1982, 177)

While there is no bibliographical reference to Turner's book *The Eye of the Needle* in any of Nolutshungu's bibliographical references, it suggests that Nolutshungu was aware of Turner's radical politics, academic contribution and the extraordinary measures of state-sponsored violence that were enacted to carry out his assassination.

INTELLECTUAL AND HISTORICAL CONTEXT

Turner and Nolutshungu are important intellectual figures, at significant inflection moments during the apartheid period. Turner's *The Eye of the Needle*, published in 1972, follows the Sharpeville massacre of 1960 and precedes the 1976 Soweto student uprisings. Racial oppression, institutionalised segregation and state-sanctioned force were the normalised tactics of the apartheid government of this era. Turner witnessed these forms of ongoing brutality and sought to respond by combining critical thought with action. The scholarly training he received at the University of Paris was critical to his approach. Sartre's existentialist political philosophy formed the basis of his doctoral dissertation and influenced the radical trajectory of his thought. The University of Natal, where Turner joined the Department of Political Science in 1970, provided a valuable backdrop from which Turner could – through his research, teaching and activism – stage his resistance to apartheid injustice. As Tony Morphet (1980, xviii) suggests, 'Turner's interests lay in analysis, shared understanding and organisation.'

In January 1978, Turner was murdered at his home by an unknown assassin. The South African state of the late 1970s was in profound political crisis. Violent tactics were used to quell political resistance, widespread protests and public defiance against apartheid. A few months earlier, on 12 September 1977, the Black Consciousness activist and political philosopher, Stephen Bantu Biko, had died in police custody. Biko and Turner were friends, with a shared intellectual and political vision for radical change. Turner's ideas reflect on the meaning of Black Consciousness and the utility of its ideas for South African reform.

During this period, Nolutshungu was working as a university academic in the Government Department at the University of Manchester, having completed a PhD on South African politics in the same department in May 1972. Nolutshungu was a remarkable black intellectual thinker, professor and theorist. Trained at Keele University, where he sought political exile, Nolutshungu's doctoral thesis, concerned with 'African Policies of the Governments of South Africa (1945–1971)', represented his abiding interest in apartheid and South African politics, and the theoretical and interpretive possibilities for radical change. This sustained interest in South Africa and Africa reflects in his wide-ranging research publications. Nolutshungu worked as an academic in various departments around the world, in the United Kingdom and the United States, where he produced a significant number of academic articles in addition to publishing five books in the fields of international relations, foreign policy and political theory. His most significant scholarly contribution to political theory is contained in *Changing South Africa*. This book, written during a period of heightened political pressure against the apartheid establishment, offered a refined and clearly developed analysis on understanding apartheid South Africa, in terms of both the prevailing political and economic system as well as the nature of its structural realities and the political terrain which conditioned it. It is thus hardly surprising that Nolutshungu refers to his method as reflective, as much of the documented primary research is complemented with careful and critical reflective insights.

Nolutshungu describes his book as a three-part essay that undertakes a theoretical analysis of what political change in South Africa would constitute, in light of two major considerations. First, that the 'objective material inequalities between Blacks and Whites' impede the process of resolution insofar as it continues to be a process conducted by elite actors (Nolutshungu 1982, 11). Second, that an analysis for change ought to consider and appreciate black responses, in particular, 'political and ideological resistances' to domination under apartheid, especially those black voices which favour radical change as the primary method of reform (Nolutshungu 1982, 11).

Turner's rationale for writing *The Eye of the Needle* is somewhat different. Although, like Nolutshungu, he is invested in theorising social change, he turns to the possibilities of utopian thinking. His focus is not on evaluating actors, agents or black responses to resistance, but on persuading his white audience to think in 'long-range utopian terms' about theorising the ideal, just society (Turner 1972a, 1). Turner is also less consumed by the rigours of academic writing and develops his account for a non-academic audience. Turner proceeds with a set of premises about the importance of utopian thinking, the first theological, the second, social: 'We may find that Christianity is incompatible not only with racism but also with many of the other norms regulating our behaviour, and that in order to live in a Christian way we will need radically to restructure our society' (Turner 1972a, 2).

More fundamentally, Turner is concerned with how utopian thinking addresses two important sets of problems: (i) why society works in the way it does, and (ii) what the moral justifications for its ethical imperatives are (Turner 1972a, 2). Contrastingly, Nolutshungu's reflective approach to social and political change hinges less on utopian thinking and more on understanding the alignments of domination and submission which are conditioned by 'political rather than economic relations' (Nolutshungu 1982, 12). This is because, for Nolutshungu, alignments are produced in politics and are never empty of economic content. As such, dominance and exploitation are integrally connected, 'if conceptually and operationally distinguishable', which is why they need to be carefully theorised when considering radical change (Nolutshungu 1982, 12). It is thus evident that Turner and Nolutshungu apply distinct academic approaches to how social and political change ought to be theorised. Both, too, signal their commitment to the positions articulated in their writings (Morphet 1980, ii; Nolutshungu 1982, 17). While both are interested in exploring the structural reasons for material inequality, power imbalances and domination, Turner sees utopian thinking as the path to evaluate these conditions and to critique and explore the possibilities of choice and moral judgement (Turner 1972a, 5). Nolutshungu, on the other hand, is concerned with making room for a political discussion of change that seeks to identify what is political by advancing a view of politics not merely 'instrumental to economic ends or passively reflecting economic determinations' (Nolutshungu 1982, 17). Nolutshungu surmises that such a discussion of politics, as a distinctive inquiry, provides a richer account of theorising questions of freedom, domination, repression and self-government.

In this sense, Nolutshungu engages more closely with the race/class debates which dominate the intellectual discussions of this period. Conversely, Turner is not explicitly interested in the contours of the primacy of race or class, but is drawn to a larger set of theoretical concerns about human freedom and behaviour rooted in utopian possibilities for radical change. Saul Dubow thus correctly points out that, as a 'non-doctrinaire' intellectual, Turner might have agreed that, in an ideal South African society, race and class could be transcended (Dubow 2014, 169). That said, Turner's voice of radicalism engages with the race and class debate insofar as he combines a Marxist analysis with the practical concerns faced by black workers (Dubow 2014, 169). This interest in combining theory and practice enables Turner to exert a profound 'new left' influence on radical white students at the University of Natal (Dubow 2014, 169).

Nolutshungu engages with the race/class debates in an equally radical way. As a black intellectual, he recognises race as a key source of domination and is critical of Marxist positions that simply reduce race to a vehicle of capitalism (Omar 2021, 90). Nolutshungu perceives that many Marxist intellectuals ignored the critical racial dimension in their analysis of apartheid and that instances of resistance to domination and exploitation ought not to be viewed as a form of false consciousness but, first and foremost, as reactions to the terms of domination (Nolutshungu 1982, 13). Nolutshungu viewes race as critical to the narrative of political change. He broke free from a dominant discourse during this period, by placing a considerable measure of emphasis on racial domination as a fundamental driving force of apartheid and as central to theorising political and social change (Omar 2021, 91).

LIBERALISM AND THE CRITIQUE OF CAPITALISM

Both Turner and Nolutshungu offer excoriating critiques of liberalism and capitalism in their analysis of political reform in late-apartheid South Africa. To begin, both Turner and Nolutshungu cite John Locke as a foundational thinker of liberal ideas (Turner 1972a, 22; Nolutshungu 1982, 8). They also view Locke as a thinker bound by the exigencies of his own historical context. In this regard, Nolutshungu argues that political thinkers are products of their age and need to be interpreted as responding to their own contexts (Nolutshungu 1982, 13). Similarly, Turner contextualises Locke as a seventeenth-century European philosopher, arguing that Locke's somewhat bizarre views on medicine and astrology are informed by the historical context of a seventeenth-century England 'riddled with superstition' (Turner 1972a, 25). Whereas Turner does not comment on the utility of Locke's liberal ideas, Nolutshungu does. He describes Locke's defence of property in his account of liberal government as an 'odd notion' (Nolutshungu 1982, 8). He further suggests that Locke's liberal defence of property is based on unalterable principles which include rights, human nature and divine will (Nolutshungu 1982, 14).

Nolutshungu views liberalism as an outcome of major developments in the nineteenth century, when industrial capitalism prompted large-scale social change and the crisis of class inequality. The struggle of the working class stood constantly at odds with the liberal, capitalist order, which sought to ameliorate inequality through democratisation. The teleology of liberalism, Nolutshungu argues, emphasises the beneficence of material progress and economic growth: 'a progress of capitalism from a crisis-ridden order of class inequality and exploitation to a more egalitarian, beneficent dispensation' (Nolutshungu 1982, 15). The problem, however, is that the idea that economic expansion could provide liberal democracies scope for social change and reform is somewhat obfuscated by its illiberal goals for territorial expansion and imperialism. Locke, Nolutshungu points out, recognised the paradoxes of unlimited accumulation, but nonetheless legitimated colonial expansion as the key to class antagonisms waged by the propertyless working classes (Nolutshungu 1982, 16).

Turner does not critique Locke in exactly the same way, but is acutely aware of the illiberal foundations of modern political liberalism. As such, Turner provides a historical critique of the foundations of liberalism in legitimating colonialism and conquest in the context of South Africa. This critique of liberalism was prominent in inspiring a form of radical politics, which, as Steven Friedman suggests, 'reshaped white resistance in the 1970s' (Friedman 2017, 10). While Turner's conception of a 'post-racial society' founded on egalitarian principles and equal citizenship suggests a liberal orientation, a close reading of *The Eye of the Needle* reveals that Turner was concerned with how liberalism had been appropriated in particular ways in South Africa in order to legitimate white settler colonialism and domination. As Turner argues: 'The term "liberal" has a long tradition. It is normally understood as referring to a set of beliefs about the limits of government, the importance of the rule of law, the rights of freedom of speech and assembly and so on. The problem here is whether to accept the traditional meaning of the word or the meaning which has tended to become associated with the word in South Africa' (Turner 1972a, 429).

In chapter 7 of *The Eye of the Needle*, Turner shifts his attention to liberalism in the context of structural inequality. Liberalism, for Turner, had produced profound inequality of power, wealth, education and status. Such inequality, 'a function of its past', disclosed the origins of settler colonialism and capitalist accumulation (Turner 1972a, 22). Turner argues that inequalities are the result of the skilful use of power in the interests of whites, 'who acted thus because they had internalised the capitalist human model, a model incompatible with Christianity' (Turner 1972a, 76). In this way, one can argue that Turner viewed social inequality in historical and structural terms. In this historical overview of white settler domination, Turner cites military power and the threat of military force as instrumental in laying the basis for the inequality of South African society (Turner 1972a, 26–27). What is most striking in Turner's theory of culture and conflict is his concern with the overlapping interests produced by capitalist accumulation. Here, Turner contends that what is characteristic of 'white culture' is the desire to accumulate wealth and 'the drive to seek personal satisfaction in the consumption of material goods' (Turner 1972a, 33). For Turner, these impulses, indicative of the pernicious capitalist human model, come at the expense of building healthy relations with other social groups and forging a just and egalitarian society. Furthermore, interpolated in this model are racial dichotomies of black inferiority and white superiority, the conquest of land, settler occupation and dispossession of indigenous people (Turner 1972a, 23–24).

Like Turner, Nolutshungu identified a similar problem with structural inequality. The enduring legacy of settler colonialism, Nolutshungu noted, is most 'often expressed in racial terms', as domination produces a hostile division between coloniser and colonised, generating a persistent inequality of power relations (Nolutshungu 1982, 205). This occurs long after the initial period of colonisation. Nolutshungu's critique of liberalism is equally sceptical of claims that advanced the liberating power of capitalism. Nolutshungu contends that capitalism in South Africa, conditioned by existing colonial political institutions, was unlikely to deliver black material prosperity and political freedom. For Nolutshungu, 'reform from above faces a major problem of legitimation, a dual problem of ideology and politics, which is structural' (Nolutshungu 1982, 204). The liberal, capitalist class structure, Nolutshungu argues, delimits the possibility for real democratic change. This is because political liberalism, which is often justified in its own right, is deeply tied to economic liberalism, where it is difficult to dislodge grand political ideals from the problem of possessive individualism (Nolutshungu 1982, 16).

Moreover, liberal debates, like the ones promulgating liberal political reform in South Africa, neglect to take seriously the paradox of liberalism. In a capitalist structure, wealth taxes, a planned economy and social welfare are frequently viewed as anathemas to economic growth and free market enterprise (Nolutshungu 1982, 16). The belief in a kind of tendential law of capitalist liberalisation as the harbinger of political and social emancipation for the majority of South Africa's people, Nolutshungu asserts, must therefore be thoroughly critiqued (Nolutshungu 1982, 17). Admittedly, one can argue that Nolutshungu is conservatively optimistic about the emancipatory potential of a liberal state and of a capitalist model creating the conditions for a just and free future democratic order. This has particular contemporary relevance for South Africa three decades into democracy, where the capitalist order has further entrenched inequality.

Turner was likewise critical of the emancipatory potential of a liberal state in a future dispensation. He argued that a conversion to a liberal state that ended racial discrimination would not fundamentally alter the position of black people: 'Real change can be brought about only by a fundamental redistribution of wealth and power.' Moreover, Turner envisaged that real social and political change could be generated in a utopian ideal of participatory democracy (Turner 1972a, 76). For Turner, both whites and blacks were oppressed, but in different ways. The apartheid social system perpetuated itself 'by creating white lords and black slaves, and no full human beings' (Turner 1972b, 22). Nolutshungu, too, recognised the insidious nature of this social system. Unlike Turner, his immediate solution was not a radical theoretical model for confronting this dreadful condition. Instead, he proffered practical implications: the contingency of large-scale revolt and revolution. For Nolutshungu, the stability of the entire order rested on the complete abandonment of racialism, political as well as economic. In this sense, Nolutshungu viewed political movements such as the BCM, and black nationalist organisations such as the African National Congress (ANC) and the Pan Africanist Congress (PAC), as generative of a remarkable form of resistance politics that promoted a distinct form of armed rebellion and social radicalism (Nolutshungu 1982, 206).

THE BLACK CONSCIOUSNESS MOVEMENT

A third overlapping area of intellectual inquiry is undergirded by Turner's and Nolutshungu's interest in the BCM. This is hardly surprising, given their profiles as radical academics and as intellectuals concerned with theorising South African political and social change. As a newly appointed lecturer at the University of Natal, Turner struck up a close friendship with Steve Biko, the founder of the BCM, a medical student and an activist in the non-European section of the same university at the time (Dubow 2014, 169). Biko and Turner had a set of interests in common: existentialism, dialectical analysis and a vision for a radical reform (Macqueen 2018, 58). Turner's account of the BCM is discussed in *The Eye of the Needle* and later found in a set of important written interventions which foreground the place of the Black Consciousness philosophy in relation to white liberalism (Turner 1972b). Turner sees in the BCM a common radical agenda, concerned with transforming the inherited structures of an oppressive society (Dubow 2014, 169). This form of liberatory radicalism hinged on reconfiguring the idea of socialisation. Turner's political orientation, profoundly influenced by the work of Sartre, valued the 'self-reflective quality of human consciousness' (Macqueen 2018, 4). Consciousness enabled people to make choices that could mitigate against narrow and unproductive forms of socialisation. This, for Turner, provided unlimited potential for future utopias and societal forms. As such, Turner argued that social change depends on a deliberate path of avoiding the vicious cycle of defective forms of socialisation, created, for example, through the capitalist model. While individuals are created by the socialisation process, there are instances of transcending its limitations. These include new socialising forms of radical, political agency which encourage 'ways of behaving which [are] opposed to the social structure' (Turner 1972a, 84).

Turner shifts his attention to surveying examples of these possibilities. He singles out the development of the philosophy of Black Consciousness among students and intellectuals. The BCM, for Turner, 'indicates an important breakdown of the socialisation process' (Turner 1972a, 87). It harbours the potential for radical change by black subjects, infused with a sense of consciousness and with a desire to 'create a new type of society embodying new values' (Turner 1972a, 87). Socialisation is a critical aspect of Turner's utopian vision for social change. The BCM, for example, involves individual conscientisation towards the needs of countering an oppressive social system. It is interested in developing a powerful set of social values in order to bring a new society into existence, or at least envisaging what an ideal society could look like. Turner challenges the liberal claim that the BCM's emphasis on race can be deemed racist: 'The refusal of blacks to want to be "like whites" is not racism. It is good taste' (Turner 1972b, 20). The BCM, for Turner, united the shared purpose and interests of many blacks living under the unjust conditions of apartheid, experiencing political powerlessness and suffering from racial discrimination (Turner 1972a, 89).

Yet Turner questioned the notion that asserting black dignity was enough. In this regard, he argued that the BCM must be accompanied by a political analysis which theorised the complex fissures amongst black people and the possibilities of orienting a future society (Turner 1972a, 89). This, as the BCM had routinely argued, included a rejection of capitalist society, 'for in South Africa it is the acceptance of such values that is the most potent threat to the unity of black people' (Turner 1972a, 90).

Like Turner, Nolutshungu saw the emancipatory potential of the BCM. The political development of the BCM up to 1976, he argues, vividly captures a remarkable form of social radicalism, specifically created by blacks under apartheid and instantiated by a tradition of national struggle and nationalist assertion (Nolutshungu 1982, 206). Nolutshungu's historical and interpretative method in presenting the development of the BCM from the period 1967 to 1976 is particularly compelling in revealing the internal logic of the movement, its ideological and organisational ambiguities, its key philosophical imperatives, the success of its conscientisation project and, above all, that black oppositional responses were rooted in deliberately political rather than economic terms. In other words, Nolutshungu foregrounded his theory of political change by according race its proper place (Omar 2021, 102). He maintained that the significance of racial consciousness and action was not a mere peculiarity requiring education and transformation through a universalist socialism or liberalism. Rather, it was inextricable from the political terrain of colonial heritage in South Africa and, as such, an 'integral component of the relations of domination and exploitation at the most fundamental level' (Nolutshungu 1982, 62–63).

For Nolutshungu, the philosophy of Black Consciousness was a valuable example of how the question of race, if constructively approached, would move beyond discussions of ideology, economic exploitation and other false precepts (Nolutshungu 1982, 62). The BCM, Nolutshungu asserts, was activated by political rather than economic aims, reiterating the idea that black nationalism is primarily related to the terms of domination rather than any economic aims. In the course of its development, however, the BCM, for Nolutshungu, espoused a more expansive form of social radicalism, reflecting both political and economic aspirations.

In Turner and Nolutshungu, there is some discussion about the attitude of the BCM towards white liberalism. Turner believed that discussions on Black Consciousness and white liberalism were mired in confusion and that common questions of strategy were obscured by misconceptions and semantics (Turner 1972b, 20). For Turner, two arguments are significant in disentangling the BCM and the place of white liberals. First, on the strategy of appealing to white sensibilities to fight the case of black domination, Turner argues, Biko and others rightfully critique white liberals. Blacks cannot rely on white liberals to argue their case in the context of white institutions and apartheid domination (Turner 1972b, 20). Second, Turner acknowledges the critique of white

supremacy and the charges of black assimilation levelled at liberal thinking. Some liberals are arrogant, paternalistic and insulting towards blacks
in their acceptance of the 'civilising mission' of whites. This idea proceeds
from the logic that blacks are not biologically but culturally inferior:
'They may be educable, but they need whites to educate them' (Turner
1972b, 20).

Like Turner, Nolutshungu recognises that the strategies of the BCM
evoked a wide range of responses. But for him, its main commitment
was to undeniably lead and issue the terms for the liberation project
of raising political consciousness. This was important for black people in preparation for the future phases of the liberation struggle
(Nolutshungu 1982, 170). Such a task, he acknowledged, would cause
the project to sit at odds with white liberal activists, many of whom,
home-grown or foreign, preferred a more congenial version of its mission (Nolutshungu 1982, 173). This attitude ought to be interrogated.
In Nolutshungu's view, white liberals should not reject or appropriate
versions of the Black Consciousness philosophy for their own ends.
This would lead to a distorted understanding of the Black Consciousness
philosophy, based on preformed visions, and would empty the movement of the radical political agency it was seeking (Nolutshungu 1982,
173). Yet more importantly, liberals who critiqued the BCM for mili-
tancy hardly understood that striving for such a radical programme for
social political change, in the face of state repression and ruthless brute
force, was an admirable if not remarkable ideal: 'To believe as they did
that a black national students' organisation could be set up and made to
work in South Africa and that it could, moreover, encourage the formation of other organisations actively opposed to government policy
was a heroic view' (Nolutshungu 1982, 175). The rise of the BCM and
the response of young people to police measures between 1976 and
1978, which stood in sharp contrast to earlier acts of mass protest, were
thus, for Nolutshungu, intricately connected and a practical instance
of the utility of its mission. Turner's account of the Soweto uprising
is interrupted by his assassination in 1978. It might be plausible to

suggest that the two may have agreed on the link between the BCM and the Soweto student uprising.

Finally, one last point is important to emphasise. Turner was critical of the BCM for its generalised attack on white liberals. He argues that while many of its attacks on liberals were justified, some were 'too sweeping' (Turner 1972b, 22). There is a place, he believed, for white liberals to exert their political efforts: 'in the area of changing white consciousness' (Turner 1972b, 22). In this, Turner brings his theory for radical change full circle. Having provided a theory that critiques white liberalism and capitalism, he now uses the idea of Black Consciousness to set forth his vision for radical social change. This requires whites to understand how they oppress themselves by pursuing material self-interest, which 'empties their lives of meaning' (Turner 1972b, 22). In this sense, Turner and Nolutshungu converge on the importance of Black Consciousness in activating a new form of social radicalism. Both, too, highlight the productive tensions within its philosophy, reflecting a willingness to deeply engage with the complex nature of these debates. Perhaps where they might have differed is in Turner's final statement that the time had come 'for both sides to bury the argument' (Turner 1972b, 22). Nolutshungu is unwavering in his prioritisation of the question of racial domination and its particularity. For him, the foremost ideological intentions of the BCM, in the creation of a broad-based unity of black solidarity against the apartheid system, might not loosen the hold of liberal caution but did fill a very important void. Ultimately, Nolutshungu's normative mode of analysis discloses that the ideals of the BCM are hardly 'utopian'. On the contrary, they are 'more faithfully reflective of objective characteristics of the political, economic order and correctly apprehend the unworkability of neo-colonial or elitist solutions' (Nolutshungu 1982, 17).

CONCLUSION

In this chapter, I have drawn from the methodological presuppositions of comparative political theory to bring into conversation two extraordinary South African thinkers that have theorised radical social change. Turner's ideas have not remained the 'esoteric preserve of academics', as Friedman (2017, 10) suggests, but enjoy a popular reception, with a continuing resurgence of interest in his political theory in contemporary South Africa (Macqueen 2018, 1). After all, Turner himself composed the text with the intent to persuade his broader, white audience that 'whatever its other faults [it is] cheap, short, non-academic and free from philosophical name dropping' (Turner 1972a, 1). The lack of visibility of Nolutshungu's ideas, beyond the realm of limited academic citation, requires further explanation. Neither thinker pursued party politics or openly aligned themselves with the activism of a political movement. Yet, as I have demonstrated through this comparative inquiry, their ideas on political change, race and liberalism offered prescient critiques which have enduring contemporary relevance. Radical thinking has enriched, and continues to enrich, our understanding of contemporary South African politics and society. More importantly, however, both Turner and Nolutshungu offer a valuable lesson for the imaginative potential of political theory and value judgement. Normative thinking, with an acute awareness of political context, can continue to offer pathways to imagining bold, different and alternative futures, however radical they may be.

REFERENCES

Dubow, Saul. 2014. *Apartheid 1948–1994*. Oxford: Oxford University Press.

Fluxman, Tony and Peter Vale. 2004. 'Re-reading Rick Turner in the New South Africa'. *International Relations* 18 (2): 173–189.

Friedman, Steven. 2017. 'The Nemesis of the Suburbs: Richard Turner and South African Liberalism'. *Theoria* 64 (151): 10–19.

Keniston, Billy. 2013. *Choosing to be Free: The Life Story of Richard Turner*. Johannesburg: Jacana.

Macqueen, Ian M. 2018. *Black Consciousness and Progressive Movements under Apartheid*. Pietermaritzburg: UKZN Press.

Morphet, Tony. 1980. 'Biographical Introduction'. In *The Eye of the Needle: Towards Participatory Democracy in South Africa*, by Rick Turner, vii–xxxiv. Johannesburg: Ravan Press.

Nolutshungu, Sam. 1982. *Changing South Africa: Political Considerations*. Manchester: Manchester University Press.

Omar, Ayesha. 2021. 'Sam C Nolutshungu: Race, Reform, Resistance and the Black Consciousness Movement'. *Journal of Comparative Political Theory* 1: 81–105.

Piper, Laurence. 2010. 'From Religious Transcendence to Political Utopia: The Legacy of Richard Turner for Post-apartheid Political Thought'. *Theoria* 57: 77–98.

Turner, Richard. 1972a. *The Eye of the Needle: An Essay on Participatory Democracy.* Johannesburg: Spro-Cas Publishers.

Turner, Richard. 1972b. 'Black Consciousness and White Liberals'. *Reality* 4 (3): 20–22.

Williams, Melissa. 2020. *Deparochializing Political Theory.* Oxford: Oxford University Press.

3

On Biko's Turn on Turner

Tendayi Sithole

There are manifold commonalities between Rick Turner and Steve Biko. Both were brilliant and uncompromising radical thinkers who insisted on thinking critically and clearly. They met and formed a dialogic relationship which always meant a profound sense of sharing ideas.

Having criticised white liberals and broken away from their political clutches, including those of the National Union of South African Students, Biko continued to work with some of them. He even still maintained a close friendship with some white liberals who felt aggrieved by the so-called 'separatist stance' which Biko took. The formation of Black Consciousness compelled Turner to participate in a critical engagement with Biko. Biko stood his ground, maintaining an ethico-political position and being unreserved, wayward and combative with respect to white liberal tendencies. It had to be clear that Biko had committed to a cause, and the relationship he had with white liberals was not that of appeasement, but a genuine working relationship. More pointedly, the time of blacks being dependent, or being made to be so, was over. The terms were different, and it was not business as usual.

Turner and Biko were, more importantly, revolutionary contemporaries who dedicated most of their valuable time to their calling. Both have a footprint in what is famously known as the 'Durban Moment', a moment where their interlocutory relationship was clearly manifest. In short, Turner and Biko were in the same struggle against apartheid.

Turner and Biko were possessed by that unyielding political commitment which has always meant that their radical demands should be actualised, and they dared to dream in the belly of a nightmare intent on shattering revolutionary dreams. They lived, by way of risking their lives, to combat apartheid. Both Turner and Biko were impassioned, determined figures who did not let anything deter them from their struggle for a life of freedom. This obviously shaped them in profound ways to be courageous, ingenious and loving. They did not compromise and refused to prostitute their souls in the service of apartheid or any other form of injustice. Biko and Turner led the life of struggle and that came at a cost (their lives were both cut short by the lethality of apartheid). Both were extensively and intensively surveilled and condemned by the racist state at the hands of which Biko, aged thirty, died in 1977, and Turner, aged thirty-six, died in 1978. And, more tellingly, their deaths were not accounted for. They fought for freedom and a different South Africa, which they did not live to see. In their existential struggle, Turner and Biko did not seek any form of martyrdom; they engaged in the radical pursuit of freedom – for each, a necessity.

OF (DIS)SIMILAR FIGURES

It would be incomplete to say that Turner and Biko were seasoned radicals. They were philosophers of struggle and they lived the life of struggle which, then, demanded that they think through that struggle in evocative ways. Both were existentialists concerned with the human condition and thus the lived experience of the apartheid world, which they confronted in intentional and intense forms. The existential mode of both figures was concerned with living a life of freedom, and that would mean being responsible for their freedom and acting on their concerns.

Further, they had to set their own terms and determine what this freedom meant to them. A life of freedom was structurally denied, which prompted Turner and Biko to wage their existential struggle to be free. Neither could be deterred in their radical pursuit of freedom because, as Frantz Fanon (1969) states, everything depended on it. Theirs was a freedom that cannot be given, but must be fought for. This is the lived reality of Turner and Biko. However, they were not on the same ontological side. Turner was white and Biko was black. This matters, and it is this that cannot be overlooked because apartheid defined the existence of blacks and whites along racial and racist fault lines.

For Biko (1978), the problem was apartheid. Mabogo More (2017) notes that Turner paid the ultimate price by fighting against apartheid. Yet Biko pointed to the homogeneity of white people and, even as More notes the exceptions of those who sacrificed their lives for the 'anti-apartheid cause', this does not mean that white paternalism and arrogance were not pervasive. So, Turner was no different from the whites that Biko criticised. Turner was responsible for his own freedom and that means what he was doing was necessary. He had to, without any form of exceptionalism being extended to him, fight against apartheid; it was his moral obligation. In short, what Turner did was the right thing to do. It was nothing pious; he had a duty to do it. As More notes, Turner was even responsible for the system he fought against.

Turner and Biko were both banned by the apartheid regime. They were confined, subjected to a life of unfreedom and that really meant that everything that was in the name of freedom would become costly. Therefore, the hazards of freedom were more apparent than it being an inalienable right. To live freely, under antiblackness, meant that the stakes were much higher for Biko than they were for Turner, since Biko's ontological standing was more precarious than that of Turner. Certainly, the banning order, which was implemented under the draconian Suppression of Communism Act, had the same absurd stipulations to all those who were confined by its red line. Everything under this red line was arbitrary and even, by shape, amoebic. For, it was made easy to cross this line. By marking its crossing as a seditious act, apartheid found itself justified even though it was a well-known truth that it was an unjustified regime – say, unjust.

Turner and Biko, as banned beings, were considered to have stepped on and over the red line. This red line, in its arbitrary and amoebic form, was what Turner and Biko did not fear to step on or step over. Their radical refusal to be subjected to the absurdity of its unjustness and to be cowed by the fear that serves as the inscriptive marker of the Suppression of Communism Act, their lives consequently being confined and contained within unfreedom, Turner and Biko made freedom the possibility that comes from the limits of impossibility. They neither succeeded nor failed in their freedom struggle, but the very intention of having to act and stand by their principles meant they did not fear the life of freedom.

What did it mean for Turner and Biko to be subjected to the banning order of the Suppression of Communism Act? The answer is simple: Biko's and Turner's freedom of speech, association and movement were severely truncated. Apartheid applied the power to ban as an absolute and whoever was banned under the Suppression of Communism Act had no juridical standing. That is why the draconian nature of this injustice was nothing but juridical excess. The system of banning as deployed by apartheid had nothing to do with the rule of law. The restrictions on the liberties of individuals were to create, according to the Act, the banned person who, in reality, could not enjoy any form of participatory existence. The banned person was a redacted being.

Death has always been the marker of Turner and Biko. The fear of death had been the way apartheid operated, but Turner and Biko did not flinch or fear. It could be said that they lived in the shadow of death. The way apartheid operated implanted death into their consciousness so that they would not act and they, subjected to draconian restrictions, had to be silent. To ward off this silence, and for them to speak and act, neither Turner nor Biko feared death. Apartheid is known for using the law to decimate those who were against its policies. With the Suppression of Communism Act being one law amongst a plethora of laws, the might of the state, its policies being racist to the core and its rule being excessive, there was no way that there would not be any form of resistance. The hyper-juridical nature of apartheid made it impossible for there to be any form of civil liberties. The law is absolute – that is, the last word. There was nothing that could be said after the last word had been spoken. With this as the basis on which apartheid fabricated its polity, it was a given that not everyone would subscribe to this absurdity. Turner and Biko would not bow down to the law that was unjust. They would not submit to the silence that apartheid imposed, and they dared to speak in their own name. This, then, made them targets of apartheid's lethality and ultimately caused their tragic and premature deaths.

APARTHEID IS EVIL

Biko (1978, 27) emphatically states: 'Apartheid – both petty and grand – is obviously evil.' There is no exaggeration in this emphasis. The ethical stance of calling apartheid what it is and without any form of fear is what Biko felt to be bound by. This is the duty he had to fulfil: calling things what they are was the imperative. By calling apartheid evil, Biko is not engaging in moral painting. He is seeing through to the root of apartheid and there was no form in which he could paint it rightfully other than as evil. That was the reality he had to lay bare. And that, for him, was the thing that he had to do because there was no way he would lie to himself.

The dehumanisation that blacks were subjected to produced a hellish existence. To elaborate, it is worth clarifying Biko's position in this regard:

> Nothing can justify the arrogant assumption that a clique of for-eigners has the right to decide on the lives of a majority. Hence even carried out faithfully and fairly the policy of apartheid would merit condemnation and vigorous opposition from the indigenous peoples as well as those who see the problem in its correct perspec-tive. The fact that apartheid has been tied up with white supremacy, capitalist exploitation, and deliberate oppression makes the prob-lem much more complex. (Biko 1978, 28)

At the height of apartheid, Turner (1972a, 76) wrote: 'South Africa is an unequal society.' This is the truth. It is, however, only the half of it. Because of this inequality, Turner (1972a, 76) calls for change: 'Political and economic power is concentrated in white hands. The result is a situation in which merely removing the apartheid brakes on mobility and ending racial discrimination will not fundamentally alter the position of the black people of South Africa. A real change can be brought about only by a fundamental redistribution of wealth and of power.'

For Turner, at least, this was the right path. However, it was the wrong path for Biko (1978, 29), who retorts: 'The first step therefore is to make the black man come to himself; to pump back life into his empty shell; to infuse his life with pride and dignity, to remind him of his complicity in the crime of allowing himself to be misused and therefore letting evil reign supreme in the country of his birth.' What Biko puts as a matter of importance is not of the same nature as what Turner considers important. Biko talks about something deeper and more profound in evoking the concept of evil. There is nothing of inequality or having to address it by the redistribution of wealth and power; this will not exorcise the evil. Apartheid is evil for Biko and for Turner it is only unjust. Uprooting this evil is not what Turner intends. What is evil if not dehumanisation itself? The focus is not only apartheid, but the long historical arc of South Africa's settler-colonial project. Even in contemporary South Africa, what is the country if not a settler-colonial polity? That, as a formulation, confronts the evil that apartheid is; it has only been the sophistication and perfection of the original settler colonialism.

Turner sees inequality as the foundational problem, caused by moral corruption and the 'ethical vices' of whites; to him, this is akin to the continued pain of seeing evil. But a discussion of the ethical comes to nothing when evil is the perverted and prevailing logic or sphere of life. For Biko, to declare apartheid evil, in its petty and grand scale, is to point to the quotidian nature of things. The evil of apartheid haunted the everyday life of blacks. That is why evil has been lurking over blacks to make them 'empty shells' which, for Biko (1978), is a condition that must be obliterated.

Turner (1972a) has the right idea(l)s which, in their utopic register, put the emphasis on solutions as opposed to the diagnosis of the problem: evil. Turner argues for a society which should freely express love. There is no indication from Turner that love trumps evil. Simply put, for Turner, there is no category of evil at all when it comes to apartheid. The creation of a society that freely expresses love, a just society, is what is a matter of concern. For Turner, such a society is sorely needed in order to create a participatory democracy. Here is the evil that is apartheid and, Biko, putting it out there, sees it as something that cannot be remedied by the participatory democracy which Turner proposes. There cannot be a push for participatory democracy when blacks are closed out – 'or blacked out'. It is not that Turner has no basis for advocating a participatory democracy; the necessity of utopian thinking is the foundational basis of the critical project. At the beginning of his book, Turner (1972a, 1) remarks: 'We need therefore to explore, and, if necessary, to attack, all the implicit assumptions about how to behave towards other people that underlie our daily actions in all spheres.' The emphasis is on change and that it is rooted in behaviour. Turner's insistence on individuation does not, in any way, look at the infrastructure of racism which underwrites apartheid. This disavowal is based on Turner (1972a, 2) arguing that 'an institution is nothing but a set of behavior patterns'. Perhaps there is something deterministic about this, and what if evil has been the grit of this behaviour? Turner (1972a, 2) goes on to say: 'It is the way in which people behave towards one another.' If apartheid is reducible to that, then there is the problem of what is at stake.

The issue of white ignorance is valorised by Billy Keniston (2013) and thus the benevolence that is extended to whites has to do with their lack of imagination. This does not, at all, reveal the extent to which racism is part of the white unconscious which, for Biko, needed to be exposed by a dose of Black Consciousness. In the manner that Keniston (2013, 60) articulates Black Consciousness it is clear that it means 'a fundamental shift in the relations between white liberals and blacks'. This is the radical change. Its fundamental basis is 'primar[ily] with fostering an autonomous and unified black viewpoint' (Keniston 2013, 60). This is a viewpoint that Turner would not agree with. Instead, Turner wanted to clarify what white liberals and Black Consciousness meant in their political projects. But this has been nothing but a fuss. The white ignorance that begets white benevolence is, ruling out any form of antagonism as Keniston details, a concern. In fact, Turner emphasised that whites need a new consciousness and new culture (Keniston 2013).

White ignorance is what Turner (1972b) points to as the problem of blacks being treated as inferior. It is this inferiority that is intensified by evil. This creates a situation where blacks have no standing, to such an extent that they can be eliminated as human beings, and thus not be accounted for in ontological terms.

Still, on that note of white ignorance, Turner (1972b, 22) insists: 'The structure of South African society today is a function of its past.' Looking at the origins of inequality, as if that is the problem that stems from 'naturalistic accounts', has led Turner to misdiagnose. This is what Turner (1972a, 32) says: 'Race prejudice, although a real factor, is based on ignorance and irrationality.' This is what causes Turner not to take notice (wittingly or unwittingly) of what Biko rates as the higher stake – apartheid as evil. By reducing the stakes to ignorance and irrationality, Turner buttresses reality. What Biko exposes as evil, Turner sanitises as ignorance and irrationality. This emphasis on behavioural change will likely have no effect in dealing with the exorcising of evil. If Turner sees the functioning of South Africa as the problem, he does not, in absolute terms, seek the spirit of evil but places emphasis only on inequality.

If the laws are the structure of South Africa, they are levers and levels that calibrate this evil that Biko bemoans. These laws are evil. They create a situation where evil can reign supreme.

ON THE MATTER OF POLITICS

Under apartheid, in an antiblack world, which is the perfection of the long settler-colonial arc, the black and white ontological distinction has not only been politicised but hyper-politicised. The latter means, as Lewis Gordon (2008) states, that war is declared on politics. Blacks are not allowed to be engaged in politics as this is considered sedition. With this criminalisation of politics, and that being the ethical imperative of blacks, there is no way that Turner's discursive undertaking accounts for the stakes that Black Consciousness philosophy is engaged in. By not taking politics as the imperative, Turner is outside what Gordon insists on as Biko's phenomenology (2008, 83), outside the reality through which the lived experience of the black is articulated, expressed and acted upon.

It is through the radical distinction of the infrastructure of antiblack racism that apartheid is found, lived and re-engineered. Therefore, even though both Biko and Turner were on the offensive insofar as apartheid was concerned, they inhabited different worlds.

The problematic that has been the idea of South Africa, and its being founded on conquest, dehumanisation and death is what is clear in Biko. The philosophy of Black Consciousness is very pointed in diagnosing this problematic and, more fundamentally, it agitates for liberation. The birth of Black Consciousness has meant that blacks identified and diagnosed the problem and began to become attuned to their lived experience.

The radical politics of Turner in critiquing the idea of South Africa has had a profound impact that cannot be overlooked. It is this radicality that means taking a stance and not being complicit in oppression. Turner died for his idea(l)s and his cause was the right one. The same is the case with Biko.

In his interlocutory intervention and invention, Ian Macqueen (2018) argues for what he calls the avenue for progressive thought. In this space, Macqueen (2018, 58) argues that Black Consciousness has been anti status quo, and the aim has been 'to carve a discursive space as part of the process of [black people] liberating themselves from the dominance of white voices'. Thus, framing it properly, Macqueen (2018, 14) writes: 'Black Consciousness sought to challenge both the physical system of white racism and the psychological dimension of a crippling inferiority complex among black people as a consequence of that system.'

For Macqueen, Turner is the figure of the progressive movement and that, more predictably, makes Turner somewhat exceptional (him being a white radical against apartheid). However, Turner cannot be exempted from being a part of the camp of dominant white voices. For he was a white radical who criticised the decolonial path that Black Consciousness took, although he partly agreed with it from within his undisturbed whiteness. Even though the utopic registers were intact to create the 'progressive future', what is amiss in Macqueen and in Turner before him, is the instant critique that expels whites from matters that have to do with blacks. Macqueen's 'progressive space' does not account for the ontological scandal of antiblackness that Biko criticised, calling for its obliteration. Biko makes it clear that he was not taking the path of 'progressive radicalism' which, for Macqueen, champions liberation in its interlocutory position, but for Biko, fails dismally to take seriously his spirited critique. By expecting nothing from blacks, Macqueen notes what is well known, and that is the fact that white liberals were surprised by Biko's turn. It is in this turn that blacks changed things radically. Progressive movements were driven by the liberal consensus and that is what Black Consciousness stood against, because what Macqueen saw as purposeful and positive, and yet remained silent on, was the perversity of paternalism. Even though Macqueen identifies the paternalistic thinking within the white liberal circles, he does not mention the racist fabric that Biko tears apart. Biko (1978, 63) says: 'The Progressive have never been a black man's real hope.' The impression that Macqueen creates is that, in the interlocution of Turner and Biko, Biko needed white liberals: 'In this context, Biko saw liberals as playing a mitigating role in facilitating change, but this role would always, of necessity, be supplementary to black leadership' (Macqueen 2018, 110–111).

Turner (1972b, 20) defines Black Consciousness thus: 'The major misperception is to see "Black Consciousness" as essentially an attack on "white liberalism", and nothing more.' By stating that this is a distortion of Black Consciousness, Turner is also distorting white liberalism. Black Consciousness is what blacks determine *for-themselves* and *in-themselves*.

This is what white liberals will not allow because they want to have absolute control of blacks. Turner notes that the attitude, amongst white liberals, is that blacks must do and become what whites want. Here is Turner's reply (1972b, 20): 'The refusal of blacks to want to be "like whites" is not racism. It is good taste.' What is clear from Turner is that it is right for blacks to be on their own. He does not accuse Black Consciousness of being racist in its separatist take and its criticism of white liberals as being something disavowed.

Turner (1972b, 20) states clearly that blacks have always been expected to 'make appeals to the moral sensibility of the whites'. This is what Biko would not do. What blacks are is not determined from the outside.

Whites will fight against change because, as Turner states, they are wedded to their material interests. Turner (1972b, 22) sees this as resolvable through change which comes from 'co-operation with all their fellows in changing South Africa'.

The fact is that Turner and Biko view white liberalism in unique and divergent ways. This divergence does not mean Turner and Biko are wrong. Turner sees white liberals from a white point of view and Biko from a black point of view. Biko might be accused of overgeneralising white liberals, but it is Turner who ignores the fact that Biko deliberately stated that he lumps whites together. For Biko, whites are a homogeneous group. That, in fact, comes from the black existential condition. White liberals, even for Biko, include the white left that Turner belongs to. Biko argues that whites are who they are in terms of the ways in which blacks are oppressed. Even though Turner claims that whites and blacks are oppressed, this does not translate into equality. There is white privilege and there is black dispossession. When Turner mentions different ways in which white liberalism must be understood, he insists that there has been little thought about how white liberals should be understood.

Biko refused to overlook white liberal tendencies to undermine blacks. Blacks had to do for themselves what they needed to do, and, more obviously, there was no good that white liberals could do for them.

Biko distinguished himself as a critic of white liberals because he did not concede; he maintained his position on white liberals.

Here is a claim by Macqueen (2018, 115): 'It is evident how much Turner and Biko agreed in their assessment of South African society.' This sedimentation of the liberal consensus is problematic, for Turner did not see race as the base on which South African society was constructed, whereas Biko saw it as such. For Biko, the problem is white racism and Turner knows this, but chooses to downplay what Biko foregrounds. Turner and Biko did not see South Africa the same way nor did they conceive of elements of a 'progressive future' in the same way. Macqueen quoted socialism as the link, but this is not true because each thinker had a different conception of what socialism is. Biko only referred to Turner when he was citing socialism because of the changed distribution of wealth that the future black government would bring. There was no common ground between the two on what the future of South Africa would be, because the utopic registers of Turner and Biko do not come from the same world.

Biko's political practice is, according to Gordon (2008), based on its 'phenomenological significance'. This stems from the understanding that Biko's thought is informed by his lived experience and it is from this that his consciousness manifests. His political formation is a result of this reality. Gordon points to the significance of Biko's political and social formation in apartheid South Africa, which led to his critique of the naturalism of apartheid categories. By doing things differently, the fibre of the political always means the emergence of the self, the radical unfolding, the remaking of the world as it were. 'The self, so to speak, is always struggling with its own fragmentation and incompleteness in relation to a world that resists it and through which other selves emerge through such struggle' (Gordon 2008, 84). There is a struggle to be free and there is the self that is not according to the desires of the oppressor. Biko's definition of Black Consciousness also comprises the creation of a different self – that is, the self that must come back to itself. This does not mean the enclosed self, but the self that is in relation to other selves in the existential struggle to be free. The envisioned self, as Biko calls it, is one that is made and shaped by the existential struggle and thus upholding of Black Consciousness philosophy:

> Black Consciousness is thus identical with political life, and those who are willing to take on the risk of politics in a context where a state has waged war on politics are, as their opposition mounts, blackened by such a process. As a political concept, this makes the potential range of Black Consciousness wide enough to mean the collapse of the antidemocratic state. The moving symbol of this was the expansion of that consciousness in apartheid South Africa and its spilling over into the international community with the consequence of a response that required more than the question of inclusion instead of the construction of *a different state*. (Gordon 2008, 89, original emphasis)

Politics is what Turner and Biko were engaged in and it can be said, without exaggeration, that these were politics of a radical kind. Apartheid did not want politics. The self in politics is the one that apartheid sees as the enemy to be eliminated. Turner and Biko were treated as such. Politics, for Gordon, is the 'discursive opposition' and this is where the self is reshaped and lives in a radical form.

THE LIVED EXPERIENCE

The lived experience of being-in-the-world and being-black-in-an-antiblack-world is not the same. The former is what Turner inhabits and the latter is what Biko inhabits. Also, the ontological questions of both figures do not come from the same site of the lived experience. The urgency that generates and expresses these ontological questions will ultimately differ. Turner's and Biko's urgencies cannot be reduced to the singularity or similarity of being cut from the same cloth. Even if they are comrades, they are not on the same side of the racial divide.

This creates a distinction between Biko and Turner and fundamentally foregrounds what is urgent and what is insisted upon, for each. Even if Biko and Turner confronted apartheid, their stakes were different, and that is at the core of what Black Consciousness and white liberalism are. Biko and Turner are not on the same ontological plane and the questions that animate their oppositional thought to apartheid are not the same.

The reality of apartheid, its facticity, its lifeworld – say, the lived experience of being under apartheid – means different things for whites and for blacks. Whites are not racially marked, and blacks are – that is, they are dehumanised as non-beings and if they live, they are subjected to the lethality and pathology of apartheid. What blacks are faced with, then, is the reality of having to live in the death-world of apartheid. Here, it is important to argue that the racial mark of the black is the subjection to the death-world.

The life of the black has been subjected to the denied existence. To live freely, as the black, under apartheid, meant something of a crime if not, by way of absurdity, sedition.

The racial marker that burdened Biko did not burden Turner. The definitional inscription of being black, which is to say, Biko as racially marked, is not the lifeworld of Turner. If there is such a thing as being fully human, and being exempted from the wrath of apartheid, Turner is advantaged by his whiteness. Biko's burden of being black, thus blackened by apartheid, is the mark that dethrones him from anything that has to do with the human status. In an antiblack apartheid world, as More (2012) states, anything can be done to blacks without any form of consequence. That, as the matter of fact, did not leave Biko untouched, and his death came as the result of his not being considered human; the honour and dignity he fought for and asserted were erased. The might of apartheid, the marker of Biko, did not mark Turner in racist terms (even though he was regarded as the 'kaffir lover/apologist') at all.

When the apartheid regime loathed Turner, he did not care and went on to radically pursue his freedom and to fight for it. His freedom meant, in principle, fighting against apartheid and standing for his own truth. For him, at least, being a beneficiary of apartheid was not something he could live with. Turner's freedom, indeed, meant the freedom of blacks and, in general, the freedom of all races. It meant that life had to be lived differently, and not the way apartheid imposed it.

The whiteness of Turner and the blackness of Biko is what apartheid makes clear, and this is the facticity that still animates the politics of criticism in accounting for what Black Consciousness is and what white liberalism is. Turner and Biko do not depart from the same place. The struggle against apartheid, calling for its end, was forever forceful in both these figures' lives. But this does not mean the commonality of the same means and ends. What makes things radically different is mainly the question of the racial mark.

Apartheid was an unfriendly world for blacks. The idea of extending hospitality to blacks as citizens in the territory named South Africa did not pertain to blacks. What remains is the fact that they were exteriorised by the racist-settlerist machinations of apartheid. But the hostility extended to Turner and Biko was not experienced and lived in a similar way. By design and intention, the hostility was directed at blacks and this was done to ensure that the life of whites was protected at all costs by way of violating the everyday lives of blacks. Then, what was directed to blacks was violence that was structural in making the very idea of living unbearable, if not unlivable. The life of dispossession and the life of privilege are what remains as the marker of apartheid, which makes the lived experience of being white and being black different. That is why it cannot be said that Turner and Biko dealt with the same problem from the same ontological position.

In his tireless critique of apartheid, working out ways to be free and figuring out utopic registers, Turner had a clear idea of what South Africa should be. And, far from liberal paternalism and its racist desires, the holding onto settler-colonialist privileges and scandalous silence on black dispossession, the socialist vision was, for Turner, the reality that could be mapped.

It would be wrong to classify Turner as a liberal. Peter Hudson (2017, 1) echoes this: 'Rick Turner was not, in other words a liberal.' He did not even refer to himself as a liberal. However, the fabric of the egalitarian society and the utopic register of Turner, being social democracy, is what is not concerned with the pressing question of antiblackness. This question, instead, falls into Biko's domain and it is taken up lucidly and rigorously. More to the point, Turner is not far from the liberal consensus which he criticises.

Turner puts forth his utopic register. In pushing for participatory democracy, Turner (1972a, 35) gives this diagnosis: 'The essential problem in South Africa is this: How can we design a set of institutions that will give all individuals power over their own lives without permitting them to exercise power over other people? How can we design political institutions that will give people maximum freedom to choose what to do with their own lives?'

This is the scandal of apartheid and it is not controlled as the form of power whose evil is to make black life unlivable. The infrastructure of antiblack racism is what Biko (1978, 28) boldly confronts: 'One should not waste time here dealing with manifestations of material want of black people.' This, as Biko shows, is futile. Biko is concerned about something else. He does not fall for the utopic ideal that Turner presents which, when it comes to what Black Consciousness is dealing with, is irrelevant. Biko (1978, 32) goes on to insist: 'Thus in all fields "Black Consciousness" seeks to talk to the black man in a language that is his own. It is only by recognizing the basic set-up in the black world that one will come to realise the urgent need for a re-awakening of the sleeping masses.'

This is what, according to Biko, serves as the basis of Black Consciousness. Clear and sophisticated, Turner does criticise Biko's Black Consciousness. What Turner takes on is the criticism against white liberals. This, for Turner, becomes what is somewhat misunderstood because, for him, the criticism is against the white racist society. Here is Turner (1972a, 125) on Black Consciousness: 'The idea of Black Consciousness has certainly made considerable impact in South Africa in the last few years. However, both the ideological work of articulating and propagating a new black culture and organizational work of developing community organisations seem for the moment not to have progressed very far.'

THE TURN AND THE WHITE LIBERAL FUSS

It is the work of Black Consciousness that Biko expresses and embodies. What remains as something that progresses, even within the limit, is the very commitment of making sure that things will be done even if apartheid denies them. The work that does not rely on outcomes but on the very effort of radicalising politics, advocates fundamental change. This is what Turner does not recognise only because there is no 'progress' which is something that is marked by the outcomes of the community organisations. In this light, Turner (1972a, 127) reduces Black Consciousness to 'a relatively small percentage of predominantly middle-class blacks'.

Turner is correct to note that Black Consciousness furthers black solidarity. However, Turner still insists on the idea that in the politics of progressive movements as Macqueen (2018) suggests, Black Consciousness is characterised as not having any numerical potency, and is therefore deficient.

The liberal consensus refuses blacks the right to see things from their own perspective. As such, the call for fundamental change by blacks is something that is seen in offensive terms if it is not structured according to liberal sensibilities. 'Apparently it's alright with the liberals as long as you remain caught by *their* trap' (Biko 1978, 25, original emphasis). This means that blacks cannot think, know and feel on their own. All must be in accordance with liberal sensibilities and that is the thing that determines, absurdly so, how blacks should be. 'Somehow, however, when blacks want to do their own thing the liberal establishment seems to detect an anomaly. This is in fact counter-anomaly. The anomaly was there in the first instance when the liberals were presumptuous enough to think that it behooved them to fight the battle *for* the blacks' (Biko 1978, 25). Seldom will the liberal consensus be about the ending of the evil of apartheid. Biko called apartheid for what it was.

Things cannot go according to Turner's way. It is the turn of Biko that is being argued here. Biko's turn cast aside an old approach, which meant, for blacks, doing things on their own, for themselves. 'A definitive spirit of independence and an awareness of ourselves as a group with potential strength is beginning to manifest in many ways' (Turner 1972a, 17). This, as a turn, is blacks, as Biko states, having faith in themselves: they could not and must not outsource their faith to others at all. They are responsible for themselves and cementing their forces to be their black envisioned self that Biko argues for. It is Biko (1978, 18) who warns: 'Hence our originality and imagination have been dulled to the point where it takes a supreme effort to act logically even in order to follow one's beliefs and convictions.' The situation that blacks are in is what Turner cannot fully grasp. Where Turner is coming from is the white world, which Biko calls the 'white community': 'Basically the South African white community is a homogeneous community. It is a community of people who sit to enjoy a privileged position that they do not deserve, are aware of this, and therefore spend their time trying to justify why they are doing so. Where differences in political opinions exist, they are in the process of trying to justify their position of privilege and their usurpation of power' (Biko 1978, 18).

Biko criticises what Turner will be against. It is as if what Biko says above borders on the erroneous and glosses over the complexities among whites. But Biko's judgement of the white 'community' as homogeneous is justified. Turner wants to distinguish between Black Consciousness and white liberals, and that does not go far in confronting the scandal that Biko exposes. Biko exposes the liberal scheme of things; he does not flinch in exposing white liberals for who they are and what they do:

> So, while we progressively lose ourselves in a world of colourlessness and amorphous common humanity whites are deriving pleasure and security in entrenching white racism and further exploiting the minds and bodies of the unsuspecting black masses. Their agents are ever present amongst us, telling us that it is immoral to withdraw into a cocoon, that dialogue is the answer to our problem

and that it is unfortunate that there is white racism in some quarters but you must [know] that things are changing. (Biko 1978, 50–51)

Blacks are undermined and they are subjected to paternalism which has, at its core, the view that they cannot do things on their own or in the way they deem fit. It is as if they do not know what they want. This, for Biko, other than being paternalistic, is the view of those people who do not take blacks seriously. Indeed, it would be naïve to expect them to take blacks seriously. The provocation and the response that determine Black Consciousness is what Biko takes as an important coordinate for dealing with the situation of being black.

Because they insist on criticising white liberals, blacks are 'accused of being ungrateful, disrespectful and militant' (More 2017, 194). All this comes from the silliness of claiming that blacks cannot be anything without white liberals. Blacks are, therefore, not allowed to have inherent qualities of 'seeing for themselves, hearing for themselves, thinking for themselves and talking for themselves' (More 2017, 194). It means that blacks cannot be on their own and thus, they must be subjected to white tutelage and paternalism. More goes on to note that white liberals fear that blacks will become something that they will not be able to deal with. That is why they are interested only in having supreme control over blacks.

Biko's Black Consciousness, as what is done by blacks, for blacks and from blacks, is predicated on what Nelson Maldonado-Torres (2006) terms the decolonial turn. In his definition, Maldonado-Torres (2006, 114) says that the decolonial turn 'refers to the decisive recognition and propagation of decolonization as an ethical, political, and epistemic project in the twentieth century'. The project of decolonisation is what dismantles the colonial infrastructure. It is a pathway to liberation, and it is, according to Maldonado-Torres, a sophisticated anti-colonial discourse and, essentially, the generative site of the decolonial turn as the charting of freedom. This is the disenchantment of unfreedom.

For blacks to take the decolonial turn becomes a nightmarish affair for white liberals. That, predictably and banally so, is touted on the myth that whatever blacks do will become disorder, with the cause for concern being that there is no dose of rationality. Black Consciousness, when it is orchestrated along the lines of the decolonial turn, becomes labelled and libelled as racism. This, it is known, is nothing but absurdity.

These are the odds that Black Consciousness had to face and in taking the decolonial turn, a radical effort was made to rewrite the ontological script and to invent a new conception of the black being. White liberals would still insist that blacks are human and all they needed was just to lower the bar of civilisation so that blacks can be ontologically incorporated. By rejecting the liberal consensus and taking the decolonial turn, Biko asserts the black being and that means the reworking of the ontological script. It means, then, a new conception of being will come about in the terms that are defined, determined and dictated by blacks. This is what informs the decolonial turn insofar as Biko is concerned, because politics are conducted through other means. That is why Gordon (2008, 87) illuminates 'the role of politics in the context of political formation'. It is the discursive opposition, insisting on possibility by way of the decolonial turn, that ruptures the discursive enclosure to release potentiality. Black Consciousness, as Biko radically refuses to be bound by the liberal consensus, is a way of breaking a shell and emerging with a different conception of being. The refusal to be an obliging shell, being turned into an object, a thing that can be misused and abused, the rapturous nature of politics as a discursive opposition is what brings possibility alive. The decolonial turn will not, therefore, be reducible to an event, but the evidentiary critique that is the quotidian fabric of black radicality whose philosophy of Black Consciousness is based in black reality, the experience of which cannot be mediated. This is what Biko brings to the fore and what Turner, explicitly so, cannot take because there is too much at stake.

What Biko wants is not what Turner wants. Turner's and Biko's disenchantment with unfreedom is not the same thing. The point of divergence between these two figures is what is conceptualised as 'spatial rupture,' as Maldonado-Torres (2006) notes; in telling reality as it is, Biko underlines the fact that there are different lifeworlds. At the discursive level, Biko undertakes what is 'a decolonial strategy' (Maldonado-Torres 2006, 125). Biko excavates what is not supposed to be on the surface. And, this he does without any form of soliciting consent.

The decolonial turn, as done by Biko, can be said to be eruptive because it emerges from the annals of what has been entombed in the name of black passivity, something which Biko rudely awakens through Black Consciousness. The access point, which exists as the result of a radical puncture, a force that animates the protocols of radical critique, is what is radically distinct in the sense that challenges what closes other domains of possibility.

As rupture and eruption, the decolonial turn is beyond what Turner can withstand in that the political risks that Biko takes fall way outside his discursive grasp and frame. What Biko does is what is easily dismissed by Turner because the utopic registers of a radical social democratic South Africa are not what Black Consciousness advances. In the case of the latter, there is nothing to lose and everything to gain from having lived the life of dispossession and want. By taking the decolonial turn, Biko pushes the levers high and the shift that occurs at those levels is radical because the decisiveness of Black Consciousness makes it a responsibility of blacks to determine freedom in their own terms. The modes of the existential struggle that Black Consciousness inaugurates and enacts show, more explicitly and with much lucidity, that blacks are doing it on their own and they do not need any white liberal caution and corrective. The way blacks have been undermined in determining their own freedom is a cause of strain for white liberals, and thus even Turner experiences traces of wanting to accept that blacks have to end apartheid in their own way. This is because the responsibility for claiming the freedom they are fighting for is theirs.

CONCLUSION

What cannot be discounted is the fact that Turner engaged Black Consciousness in a responsive way. Truly, he did not have to agree with Biko's Black Consciousness. Not because he was white – Turner was a revolutionary thinker, a contrarian. Both Turner and Biko called apartheid into question and called for the radical and fundamental change of South Africa. In different ways, their dialogue became an imprint of the liberatory horizon but, as it is known, from divergent routes. The commonalities and differences between Turner and Biko do not count to the same degree. In fact, the white world of Turner and the black world of Biko, the latter as created by settler colonialism and its perfection by apartheid, made the political projects of these impassioned figures distinct. There is no moderate ground here. The protocols of radical criticism, even pointed towards apartheid, do not hold the same existential impetus for what can be termed being-in-the-world for Turner and being-black-in-an-antiblack-world for Biko. The givenness and abstraction of being-in-the-world in Turner and the concreteness and particularity of being-black-in-an-antiblack-world in Biko show that they are in different existential planes. These worlds are irreconcilable.

What Turner is privileged with is what Biko is dispossessed of. The existential nightmare of Turner is not that of Biko. In apartheid South Africa, the whole world is against Biko, and Turner is exempted from its cruelties because he is white. This, however, does not discount the fact that his standing was just: Turner acted (and rightfully so) against such a world instead of being complicit in the system that yielded its spoils. But, in the main, Biko's Black Consciousness could not be subjected to Turner's discursive levers. Biko's critique of white liberals implicates Turner because his intervention in Black Consciousness bears the trace of the things that Biko strongly criticised.

REFERENCES

Biko, Steve. 1978. *I Write What I Like*. Oxford and Johannesburg: Heinemann.
Fanon, Frantz. 1969. *The Wretched of the Earth*. Translated by Constance Farrington. London: Penguin Books.
Gordon, Lewis R. 2008. 'A Phenomenology of Biko's Black Consciousness'. In *Biko Lives! Contesting the Legacies of Steve Biko*, edited by Andile Mngxitama, Amanda Alexander and Nigel C Gibson, 83–93. New York: Palgrave.
Hudson, Peter. 2017. 'Let's Talk about Rick Turner'. *Theoria* 64 (151): 1–9.

Keniston, Billy. 2013. *Choosing to be Free: The Life Story of Richard Turner*. Johannesburg: Jacana.

Macqueen, Ian M. 2018. *Black Consciousness and Progressive Movements under Apartheid*. Pietermaritzburg: UKZN Press.

Maldonado-Torres, Nelson. 2006. 'Césaire's Gift and the Decolonial Turn'. *Radical Philosophy Review* 9 (2): 111–138.

More, Mabogo P. 2012. 'Black Consciousness Movement's Ontology: The Politics of Being'. *Philosophia Africana* 14 (2): 23–39.

More, Mabogo P. 2017. *Biko: Philosophy, Identity, and Liberation*. Cape Town: HSRC Press.

Turner, Richard. 1972a. *The Eye of the Needle: An Essay on Participatory Democracy*. Johannesburg: Spro-Cas Publishers.

Turner, Richard. 1972b. 'Black Consciousness and White Liberals'. *Reality* 4 (3): 20–22.

PART II

TURNER'S THEORETICAL LACUNAE

4

Women in the Frame: Reading Turner's *The Eye of the Needle* through Simone de Beauvoir's *The Second Sex*

Paula Ensor

I n *The Eye of the Needle* (1980) Rick Turner challenges us to confront the proposition that human beings can choose the lives they wish to live, and that there are, theoretically, no limits to the exercise of this choice. His injunction for us to choose, our freedom to do so, the choices he places before us for deliberation and the utopia of participatory democracy he describes, shape the argument of his book. For Turner, through reflection, choice and action we are able to transcend the chains imposed by socialisation (family, education, the media, religion and so forth) and craft the identities we wish to embrace. Each of us has the capacity to exercise free choice, and we augment ourselves as rational, authentic independent beings through a distanced reflection on the world, examining and evaluating the pressures of everyday life, and thereby rising above them. This notion of self-betterment, of self-actualisation, of movement towards selfhood through transcendence, away from the facticity of everyday life so profoundly shaped by the processes of socialisation, emerges from Turner's existential commitments. Freedom to choose, and choosing to be free, animate Turner's book, as it did his life.

This chapter is concerned with two aspects of Turner's utopia: the way in which he theorises the position of women and, linked to this, how his insistence on our freedom to choose might be viewed from the standpoint of women, and African women workers in particular. Both aspects are opened up for discussion here using Simone de Beauvoir's *The Second Sex*. Her work, first published in 1949, provides a lens through which to critique what Turner says, and does not say, about the position of women, and most especially African working-class women in the early 1970s in KwaZulu-Natal, where Turner lived and wrote his text. I will explain below why I have chosen this lens.

Three themes are drawn from Beauvoir to illuminate this discussion: freedom, work and the body. Freedom and work form key organising ideas in Turner's utopia, as they do for Beauvoir, but she goes further to argue that the body (in her case the female body) constitutes a critical impediment to the work of transcendence. Only by addressing the obstacles that patriarchal society has inscribed on women's bodies will opportunities for work, self-realisation and freedom become possible. More recent commentators on Beauvoir's work have pointed to its resonance with Frantz Fanon's *Black Skin, White Masks* (1968) in their exploration of the particular plight of black women. Drawing these themes together – freedom, work and the black female body – I draw attention to what I have termed the 'unrecognised Other' at the time of Turner's writing: the African woman textile worker. Her positioning raises profound questions about Turner's utopia and the freedom he claims we can and should exercise. She also calls into question Beauvoir's rather scant consideration of women's agency in struggle.

In elaborating his utopia in *The Eye of the Needle*, Turner provides limited scrutiny of the position of women and I underscore my argument in this regard by referring to two other texts with which Turner was closely associated at the time: one on the Durban strikes (Institute for Industrial Education 1976) and another on the question of class consciousness among colonised workers (Fisher 1978), both of which give limited, if any, attention to the position of women, and black women in particular.

TURNER'S *THE EYE OF THE NEEDLE*

In the preface to the 1972 edition of the *The Eye of the Needle*, Turner states his intention: to examine orthodox thinking about South Africa and the assumptions made about human nature, how societies work, and the meaning of freedom. He indicates that his mission is to sketch out 'an ideally just society' (Turner 1980, 1) and offer an invitation to his readers to engage in utopian thinking that will enable them to explore and critique 'all the implicit assumptions about how to behave towards other people that underlie our daily actions in all spheres' (Turner 1980, 1). Turner identifies the central problem as follows: 'How can we design political institutions that will give people maximum freedom to choose what to do with their own lives?' (Turner 1980, 35).

Turner finds the answer in what he terms a 'Christian human model': participatory democracy under workers' control of production. The workplace is central to his utopia as this is where, in his argument, most adults spend most of their lives. Here, workers themselves should decide on wage levels and hierarchies (race, gender and ethnicity are not invoked at all as possible threats to this), working hours and other conditions of work, mediated through democratically elected workers' councils. Extending beyond the single factory to consider its interaction with other productive units, Turner turns to the wider challenges and dilemmas to be confronted in governing society and planning and running the economy. While brief consideration is given to the role of the market, investment, taxation and the collection and distribution of information across enterprises, the account stops short of mapping out the implications for state formation. In his review of South African history, Turner concludes that conflict and tension in apartheid South

Africa stemmed largely from extreme inequality and that a just society in South Africa could not be achieved without a significant redistribution of wealth. In South Africa, then, participatory democracy for Turner meant 'replacement of private ownership of the means of production by workers' control in industry and agriculture' (Turner 1980, 82), universal franchise and maximum decentralisation to local and provincial authorities.

Turner encourages us to exercise our capacity to choose which societal model we wish to live by. For him, the only impediments on this journey of transcendence are prejudice and the socialising effects of the media, education and the family. In order to achieve this utopia, Turner suggests a number of approaches: learn to live our individual lives differently (for example through communal living and the sharing of material possessions); criticise South African materialistic values; and ensure that all organisations in which we work prefigure the future in their day-to-day practices.

ADDRESSING THE POSITION OF WOMEN

Turner's utopia has been praised and criticised on many grounds – political, economic, strategic and other – especially with the hindsight gained these fifty years on. My focus here is on his treatment of gender and the position of women. Early on in *The Eye of the Needle* Turner addresses the issue of gender inequality, challenging the common-sense assumptions that women are necessarily confined to duties of domestic labour and child-rearing, and excluded from important and fulfilling roles in society. He stresses the importance of thinking in a utopian way about the position of women in society, posing the question: 'How should men and women relate to one another, and what social institutions should we strive for in which to embody these relationships?' (Turner 1980, 5). These questions are posed but not addressed further in the text.

Gender issues are raised explicitly, briefly, on five further occasions in *The Eye of the Needle* (Turner 1980, 8, 10, 92, 93 and 98), covering text that, taken together, constitutes just over two pages of the book. Turner discusses gender in the course of discussing the effects of socialisation processes and the associated alienation which results from reified and stereotypical social relationships. Socialisation into male and female roles takes place from birth, with the consequent reduction of human interaction to stereotypical roles and alienation for both men and women. His interest is exclusively with stereotyping in the domestic sphere: who makes coffee, feeds and cares for children and washes dishes; who participates in the torpor of tea parties (white middle-class women); and what the implications for intimate male–female relationships are. Apart from the comment about white women and their tea parties, he does not differentiate between black and white women or between middle- and working-class women, nor does he address the particular challenges confronted by women simultaneously oppressed on the basis of race and class.

In describing his utopia of participatory democracy and workers' control, Turner does not elaborate upon the position of women at all. Rather, we are presented with a generic 'worker' whose identity has been radically depoliticised: the workers in the model of participatory democracy are without gender, race, ethnicity, religion, sexual orientation or family, an issue to which I will return later. This is striking, for two reasons: firstly, because of the extraordinary role played by African female textile workers in the Durban strikes of 1973 and, secondly, because Turner's relative silence in relation to women renders his utopia unusual within radical utopian traditions. For example, those whom Frederick Engels described as the 'three great Utopians' (Engels 1968, 396): Henri de Saint-Simon (1760–1825), Charles Fourier (1772–1837) (see Goldstein 1982) and Robert Owen (1771–1858) (see Donnachie 2011), all placed the liberation of women centrally within their vision of a new society. While these utopians differed amongst themselves, they shared a common concern to change the legal, political and economic position of women in society, addressing rights of access to equal education with boys, rights in terms of relationships with men, rights to divorce and birth control, access to childcare and so forth. These demands formed central planks of their various platforms. According to Engels, it was Fourier who 'was the first to declare that in any given society the degree of woman's emancipation is the natural measure of general emancipation' (Engels 1968, 400).

To provide empirical evidence in support of his argument for a utopia of participatory democracy and workers' control, Turner reviewed attempts at workers' control in Israel, the Soviet Union, Ujamaa villages in Tanzania, Eastern Europe and China. A useful litmus test to measure the depth of participation and control in these sites would have been to consider specifically the degree of involvement in these projects of marginalised groups, including women. Carole Pateman (1970), for example, upon whose work Turner partly relies in his discussion of participatory democracy in Yugoslavia, reports on the fact that women and semi- and unskilled workers were significantly underrepresented on Yugoslavian Workers' Councils (Pateman 1970, 99). Turner's concern seems to be overwhelmingly with the threats to participatory democracy posed by the rise of oligarchy, the sedimentation of new elites and measures required to prevent their emergence.

In the final postscript to the book, written in February 1973 as the Durban strikes were drawing to a close, Turner engages in an extended exploration of the potential for change in South Africa, in which gender issues do not surface at all.

In reading the many commentaries on *The Eye of the Needle* over the past fifty years, the only reference I have been able to find which remarks on the relative absence of women in Turner's utopia is by Alex Lichtenstein, who notes that Turner's 'workplace democracy offers little to women and others excluded from collective forms of factory labour' (Lichtenstein 2017b, 50). While this is true in relation to women outside of the workplace, I argue below that it is equally true for those within it.

Two other influential texts with which Turner was associated reveal similar lacunae in relation to women: *The Durban Strikes 1973: Human Beings with Souls* (Institute for Industrial Education 1976) and a book chapter authored by Foszia Fisher, widely considered to have been influenced by Turner, on class consciousness amongst colonised workers in South Africa (Fisher 1978).[1] *The Durban Strikes* was published by the Institute for Industrial Education in 1974 and then again in 1976, and has served as the key reference text on the Durban strikes over the past fifty years. There is not space here to analyse this book in depth, but it is important to mention that, as is the case with *The Eye of the Needle*, only one commentator over the past decades has commented on the minimal attention paid in the *Durban Strikes* book to women, their conditions of life and work and the very significant role they played in the strikes (Berger 1983). In neither *The Eye of the Needle*, nor *The Durban Strikes*, nor the Fisher/Turner paper on class consciousness, does gender emerge as a key category for analysis.

BEAUVOIR, TRANSCENDENCE AND THE BODY

Simone de Beauvoir (1908–1986) (and specifically her book *The Second Sex*) provides a productive vantage point from which to interrogate *The Eye of the Needle* because of her positioning within an existentialist tradition. This enables me to use an approach, in crucial respects common to both Turner and Beauvoir, in order to lift out those dimensions of *The Eye of the Needle's* argument which are of concern to me, to meaningfully identify the gaps and silences and make sense of what *The Eye of the Needle* actually says about the position of women. Also, importantly, Beauvoir was well known in France when Turner was a student there, and he was probably aware of the publication of *The Second Sex*, even if he did not read it. Beauvoir was a companion of Sartre for some fifty years, and in her own right a leading French intellectual in the postwar years. She wrote extensively – novels, essays, commentary and *The Second Sex* – and self-identified as a writer working within an existentialist tradition rather than as a philosopher.[2] The extent to which Beauvoir's work derives from Sartre's, or deviates from and exceeds him, has been the subject of extended debate (see for example Lloyd 1984; Moi 1994;

Kruks 1998; Lundgren-Gothlin 1998; Bauer 2001, 2004; Simons 2001). The secondary literature on her work, teasing out the theoretical influence of Beauvoir's antecedents and the significance of her contribution, commonly reverts back to the Master-Slave drama and Beauvoir's particular take on this. Beauvoir deploys the Master-Slave dialectic in much the same way as Fanon, in her case as a tool to understand what distinguishes the subordination of women from other forms of subordination, and to signal the forms that resistance to this oppression should take.[3] This is an important discussion but it is not possible here to consider the issues in depth. What follows is not a systematic discussion of her work but, rather, an appropriation of those aspects of it which enable me to throw light on my concerns with *The Eye of the Needle*.

Beauvoir's starting point is to pose the question: 'What is a woman?' and to make the claim that 'One is not born, but rather becomes, a woman' (Beauvoir 1949, 295). *The Second Sex* is then devoted to describing the condition of women, currently and historically, and attempting to provide an explanation of how their systemic oppression emerged over time.

Beauvoir argues that the self/other distinction is deeply embedded in human culture. 'Otherness is a fundamental category of human thought. Thus it is that no group ever sets itself up as the One without at once setting up the Other over against itself' (Beauvoir 1949, 17). Following Hegel, Beauvoir argues that self-consciousness develops through consciousness of the Other, in a reciprocal tussle between a transcendent self and an immanent self. These two dimensions of the divided self are dialectically linked: as the transcendent, creative self moves beyond the fixed, reified, local, immanent self, to a higher level of consciousness, this expanded consciousness emerges as its dialectical opposite, to constitute a new self/other dialectic, which in turn must be transcended. This potential for self-realisation, the ongoing imperative to make and remake the self through exploits or projects, constitutes the free being.[4] For Beauvoir, reaching out for transcendence and self-realisation constitutes freedom, which is intimately tied to the possibilities opened up by work.

But these possibilities for transcendence are impeded by the meanings society has ascribed to the female body, which Beauvoir posits not as a thing, but as a situation. 'Woman both is and is not her body; the fact of having a female body is what makes her a woman, yet this very fact also alienates and separates her from herself' (Moi 1994, 164). 'The more the woman wants to assert herself as an individual, the harder it is for her to accept her biological destiny' (Moi 1994, 165). In describing the body as a cultural situation, Judith Butler argues, Beauvoir places the body at the nexus of two pressures: cultural interpretations that subject the body to laws, taboos and restrictions on the one hand, and on the other, the possibilities for choice, for engaging with, and contesting, received interpretations (Butler 1998, 38–39).

Bodily functions such as childbirth, menstruation, pregnancy, lactation, menopause – draining physical events that 'tie women to their bodies and to immanence' (Donovan 1985, 123) – have impacted negatively on woman's ability to engage in work, in projects that would enable her to flourish as a transcendent self, and which continue to inhibit her today.[5] People relate to the world through their bodies as 'the instrument of our grasp upon the world, a limiting factor for our projects' (Beauvoir 1949, 66) and in the case of women, this grasp is significantly weaker than that of men. But Beauvoir is not arguing that women are determined by their bodily functions: rather, 'by the manner in which her body and her relation to the world are modified through the actions of others than herself' (Beauvoir 1949, 734). That is, by the symbolic significance attached to her body.

Transcendence, for women, lies in the rational and free choice of those exploits or projects that can serve as a mode of transcendence, in other words, through work. This work is only possible if the impediments society has placed upon her body, those which threaten to drag her back to immanence, are overcome. As Sonia Kruks puts it: 'Immanence is a condition which must be continuously inflicted on woman. As long as it is inflicted, it is, for her, her destiny' (Kruks 1998, 61). Kruks goes further to say that escaping immanence cannot be achieved simply through the exercise of individual choice, but through a systemic change in woman's situation (Kruks 1998, 62).

Beauvoir wrote *The Second Sex* in the immediate aftermath of the Second World War, a few years after French women were enfranchised, but when legal discrimination against women remained with regard to maternity leave, adequate childcare, contraception and abortion. Access to these rights would have reduced the burdens imposed by women's bodies. Beauvoir argued that, in addition to political freedoms such as the suffrage, women required economic independence through work and that working conditions should be improved significantly to ensure equality with men. But she went further, to argue that patriarchy in society more generally needed to be addressed, with a profound redefinition of notions of masculinity and femininity, indeed, 'nothing less than a revolution in our understanding of what it is to be human' (Bauer 2004, 130).

The Second Sex can be criticised for its focus on a particular range of female experiences located largely within white, middle-class European life. The historical, biological, cultural, anthropological and other sources it draws on emerge predominantly from European intellectual traditions. She does not reflect in detail on the conditions facing black women, or those of woman factory workers. Her emphasis on the male/female binary is silent on the range of queer identities we encounter today, but it could be argued that her analysis does not foreclose their recognition. Her female Other is commonly read as being predominantly European, white and bourgeois (see for example Moi 1994; Simons 2001; Tarver 2011) although Meryl Altman (2020) rebuts much of this criticism, arguing that race and class considerations are embedded in Beauvoir's analysis.

Whatever reading one makes of her work, we can identify the similarities Beauvoir discusses between sexism and racism, with women and blacks both being denied the freedoms enjoyed by white males. Yet for Beauvoir, there is a significant difference between them as subordinated castes: blacks 'submit with a feeling of revolt, no privileges compensating for their hard lot, whereas woman is offered inducements to complicity' (Beauvoir 1949, 300).

Absent in Beauvoir's account is the position of black working-class women, whose conditions of life throw into relief all dimensions of the foregoing arguments in relation to freedom, work and the body. We are compelled to ask ourselves what liberation from the enslavement of the female body, the quest for transcendence and for freedom through meaningful projects means for black working-class women, and in the case of the present discussion, African female textile workers in Durban in 1973. I have chosen to focus upon these women not because they constituted the most marginalised section of South African society in the early 1970s, but because of their intersectional status as African, female and working class, and because the central agent in Turner's utopia of participatory democracy is the worker. I want to suggest that these women constitute an 'unrecognised Other' within Turner's text, one whose conditions of life and work demand, then as today, to be addressed in any utopia offering emancipation. I believe Turner later acknowledged this in an editorial (most likely written by himself) introducing a special issue of the *South African Labour Bulletin* in 1975, devoted to women workers and entitled 'The Divided Working Class'. The editorial makes the point that '*a focus on "woman's demands" can clarify the needs of society as a whole*' (*SALB* Editorial Board 1975, 1, emphasis added), and further that: 'The African women workers, for example, constitute the most oppressed group of workers in our labour force. It has been said that the African women in South Africa are perhaps the most displaced and deprived people in any country not involved in open war. In every sphere, the African women's rights have been steadily eroded' (1975, 2).

In the next section, I sketch the position of these women at the time of Turner's writing.

AN UNRECOGNISED OTHER OF *THE EYE OF THE NEEDLE*

Describing the conditions facing African women workers in the textile industry in Durban in 1973 from the vantage point of the present has proved a challenging task, as little, if anything, was written about these issues at the time. I have had to rely on accounts written at different stages *after* the Durban strikes, many appearing in the *South African Labour Bulletin* between 1975 and 1980. Two texts have proved particularly productive in piecing together this picture: one produced by Jean Westmore and Pat Townsend (1975), who interviewed African women workers living in Clermont, Durban, residing in either single-women's hostels or in housing in the township; and the other produced by the Natal Labour Research Committee (NLRC) (1980), which provides a detailed account of the brutal labour regime in Frame factories at the time of the 1980 textile workers' strike. Although both these accounts were written after the 1973 strikes, they provide sufficient information to piece together a picture of the brutal conditions under which African women textile workers laboured. There is little to suggest that conditions facing women in 1973 changed dramatically for the better in the intervening years, even as the number of African women employed in the textile industry grew dramatically.

African women workers in the early 1970s in KwaZulu-Natal were oppressed by a complex set of measures intended to contain them as Africans, as African women, and as African women workers. As Africans, they were voteless subjects of a violently oppressive apartheid regime. Their rights to reside, to move around, and to live with their partners were severely circumscribed by a labyrinthine web of laws which are difficult to summarise here (see for example UNCAA 1971, 1975, 1978; Unterhalter 1983). In a nutshell, these laws were devised as part of the legislative framework that maintained the migrant labour system at the heart of South Africa's racial capitalist system, and regulated the movement of Africans to the urban areas. A key element in maintaining this system was the penning of women, children, the sick and elderly within the bantustan reserves and brutally obstructing the urbanisation of African people.

As African women, their rights to reside and work in urban areas were linked to those of fathers, husbands or other male elders. A woman could reside with her husband in an urban area only if her husband had legal rights to remain there. For those who gained permission to reside in a city the 'rights' were precarious, and could be revoked if a woman moved away for a period, lost her job or lost her legal status within the family. In Natal at the time, all African women, whether married or not, were subject to the Natal Code, which rendered all African women, except in exceptional circumstances, as perpetual minors (Unterhalter 1983, 888; McClintock 1991, 113–114). This meant they were legally subordinate to their fathers, husbands or male guardians, and as such were unable to enter into contracts such as rental agreements, marriages and divorce without male permission. This subordinate status meant that life for African women, in the urban areas particularly, was highly precarious. Anne McClintock (1991, 113) comments that marriage for African women in South Africa was a 'legal and political catastrophe, yet marriage [was] virtually the only means for a woman to have access to housing or residence rights'. For African women these restrictions on movement and settlement were combined with deeply patriarchal prejudices against women with regard to employment, childcare and their role in the reproductive functions of capitalism.

As African female workers employed in factories, domestic environments and rural areas, they faced conditions of great insecurity. Their precariousness enabled the payment of extremely low wages and the imposition of harsh working conditions. African women entering employment in industry (and in the case of this discussion, the textile industry) carried with them their reduced civic status to confront an array of discriminatory measures against them as black, as female and as workers. This affected their access to jobs, their wages, their freedom of movement within the work environment and their bodily integrity.

From the 1960s and early 1970s, African women were recruited in large numbers into the KwaZulu-Natal textile industry, which was automating and modernising rapidly, requiring labour that was 'plentiful, cheap and disciplined' (Hirsch 1979, 10). By the late 1970s, African women constituted about 70 per cent of the workforce (Hirsch 1979, 15). At the time of the Durban strikes, the Durban area had become the centre of the country's textile production, dominated by the Frame group factories. Many of the African female employees were migrants from the KwaZulu bantustan who lived in hostels or dwellings in the townships within commuting distance to the textile mills (Lichtenstein 2017a, 104).

Within the factory environment African women encountered a barbarous regime of control. Wages paid for African women were at least 20 per cent lower than those paid to African men. At the time of the Durban strikes African women in the textile industry were paid as little as R3.50 per week. Many of these women were heads of single-parent families with children and elders to support.

Black women shared with black men common grievances about low pay, autocratic supervisors and the lack of channels to express grievances. Strikes by African workers were illegal, and those trade unions that existed to represent African workers, while not illegal, could not be registered and were constantly harassed. But women endured additional burdens on account of their gender.

African men predominated in the more skilled and supervisory classes of work so there was little scope for women to rise to these ranks. There was no provision for maternity leave. A woman textile worker interviewed by S'bu Khwela recalls: 'Whenever you went on maternity leave that meant you had retrenched yourself. The manager could dismiss you whenever he liked for no reason' (Khwela 1993, 23). The NLRC, reporting in 1980, noted that when African women were taken on at Frame for the first time they received a pregnancy test, and if they were found to be pregnant they were not employed.

Menstruating women suffered particular humiliations. Those suffering from menstrual cramps were allowed to sit down to gain relief, but often only in return for sexual favours for their supervisors (NLRC 1980, 29). The company strictly rationed the provision of sanitary pads and women workers were not allowed to supplement this ration with toilet paper or cotton waste produced in the factory. They were searched on leaving the factory each day to ensure that no waste products had been 'stolen' (NLRC 1980, 30). Permission to go to the toilet had to be obtained from the supervisors and workers often waited for up to an hour before the request was granted (NLRC 1980, 30).

Women interviewed by Westmore and Townsend complained of sexual harassment by male workers, whom they felt had no respect for them. 'On the factory floor, men ill-treat the women, make fools of them, and become vulgar by touching women in embarrassing parts' (Westmore and Townsend 1975, 26). Others mentioned that men assaulted women that they worked with and that reporting them was futile.

On top of the pressures of factory work, those women able to live with their children carried the additional burden of housework, cooking and so forth, struggling to balance the demands of overtime and shiftwork with domestic responsibilities.

Westmore and Townsend (1975) reported that many of the women they interviewed lived in single sex hostels but revealed little about conditions within these hostels. We know from later descriptions of life in huge hostel complexes (NLRC 1980; Lichtenstein 2017a) that a ruthless system of 24-hour surveillance was in place. Security guards patrolled the hostels night and day and could enter rooms without permission. No smoking or drinking was permitted. Women were not allowed to have their babies or young children with them and visits were tightly controlled. The position of all women in the hostel was extremely precarious and they could be expelled from the hostel on flimsy and arbitrary grounds, which for migrant workers meant repatriation to the rural areas.

In the early 1970s, then, African women textile workers were locked into a system of extreme exploitation and oppression within the factory (through low wages, the shift system, discriminatory practices relating to supervision, movement within the factory, sexual harassment and so on), within hostels, and within the community, where they confronted deeply rooted patriarchal systems. The legal position of African women, together with the control exercised within and outside of the factory, exemplifies vividly the ways in which these power relationships intersected to regulate women's bodies, creating deeply gendered, discriminatory working and living environments.

In spite of all these impediments, by the end of January 1973, 8 000 textile workers in Durban were on strike, mainly Indian and African women. They formed a small cohort of the estimated 60 000 workers involved in the Durban strikes, but the largest number of strikes, and those of the longest duration, took place in the textile industry, mainly in Frame group factories.

RETURNING TO TURNER, BEAUVOIR, AGENCY AND FREEDOM

In introducing this chapter, I set out three interrelated themes – freedom, work and the body – highlighted for me through Beauvoir's theorisation of the position of women in society. Freedom is a fundamental aspiration of both Turner and Beauvoir: freedom to become the person we wish to be, in the society we wish to make. Work is central to both of their arguments: for Turner, work produces wealth and well-being for all in a society organised appropriately to achieve this, and for Beauvoir, work additionally enables transcendence. The ability to engage in meaningful work in non-alienating work environments is for her a necessary condition for female emancipation.

Turner does not deal systematically with gender in his analysis, nor in elaborating his utopia, and thereby, we might argue, diminishes his notion of freedom. Gender, for Beauvoir, is fundamental to understanding the present and imagining the future. Overcoming the burdens and limitations loaded by both society and biology upon women through their bodies is necessary for securing their freedom.

African female textile workers in Natal in the early 1970s bring these three themes into sharp relief, and speak back to both Turner and Beauvoir. Harshly disciplined politically, socially, economically and bodily, these women carried a burden which any meaningful utopia, then and now, must address. They demonstrate the insufficiency of Turner's proposal that women and men might share differently the domestic responsibilities of home-making and parenting. African women in the 1970s could not reside and set up home where they chose, or have their children living with them by right. Power relations and the weight of patriarchal discrimination stood mightily against them. Regarding gender oppression simply as the outcome of socialisation and something one could think oneself out of, fails to acknowledge the webs of power and authority in which African women workers were ensnared.

The vantage point of the African female textile worker begs us to ask what 'freedom to choose' meant for these women (or indeed any oppressed people) in the context of a utopia which did not explicitly acknowledge the barriers that prevented them from exercising choice in any meaningful way. In this sense, they challenge Turner's analysis and his utopia.

But they also bring into focus the importance of choice and agency, as manifest in the extraordinarily courageous strike action taken by these women in 1973 (and subsequently). In this way they expose the limitations which Beauvoir's analysis places on their capacity to act.

Barriers to women fully engaging in participatory democracy and exercising real workers' control require analysis and programmatic response. Policies are required to enable women to become equally involved in production – policies that end discriminatory wage policies, provide adequate parental benefits and childcare, access to good education, relief from sole responsibility for domestic work, equal opportunities for promotion and eradication of hierarchies based on gender in the workplace. In other words, a set of policies intended to lift the impediments placed upon women through their bodies. Since Turner wrote his book, substantial gains have been made in South Africa, but much remains to be done to open up opportunities for women to really 'become' anything they choose, in an environment free from patriarchy, misogyny, gender-based violence and sexual harassment.

NOTES

1   The chapter referred to here was based on a workshop paper that Fisher delivered in August/September 1974, at the time that Turner was banned in terms of the Suppression of Communism Act.

2   I have relied on the Parshley translation of *The Second Sex* which was the only translation available until 2009. This translation has been severely criticised by Margaret Simons (2001), Nancy Bauer (2004), Toril Moi (2004) and others for its misunderstanding of Beauvoir's philosophical references and for the removal of significant amounts of her original text. A subsequent translation has also been criticised, on somewhat different grounds, and is also deemed inadequate (see Moi 2010).

3   Beauvoir's take on Hegel's Master-Slave dialectic is the focus of a considerable amount of commentary on *The Second Sex*, which makes for fascinating reading. Whether Beauvoir aligned the position of men and women with that of the Master and Slave is hotly disputed. Commentators such as Eva Lundgren-Gothlin (1998) place this relationship outside of the dialectic, casting woman as the Absolute Other. The problem with this interpretation is that it cannot account adequately for female agency and social change. For Fanon, the political project is to disrupt the dialectic in terms of which the slave turns his attention away from the object towards the master, whom he desires to emulate; in Beauvoir's case, placing the man/woman relation outside the dialectic implies that change needs to come from outside in the first instance: 'a woman's *situation* must be altered before she can effectively struggle for her freedom' (Kruks 1998, 61–62).

4   Beauvoir follows Alexandre Kojève (1969) here, who describes a project as work which begins from an idea which does not yet exist (that is, it is not mere repetition) and which is simultaneously transformative of Nature and of the self (Kojève 1969, 48–49).

5   Female learners from disadvantaged backgrounds in South Africa continue to miss school days because of their inability to afford sanitary products. *The Guardian* newspaper (7 August 2021) reported that even in wealthy countries such as Britain, menopause continues to restrict the professional lives of women.

REFERENCES

Altman, Meryl. 2020. *Beauvoir in Time*. Leiden and Boston: Brill.

Bauer, Nancy. 2001. *Simone de Beauvoir, Philosophy and Feminism*. New York: Columbia University Press.

Bauer, Nancy. 2004. 'Must We Read Simone de Beauvoir?'. In *The Legacy of Simone de Beauvoir*, edited by Emily R Grosholz, 115–135. Oxford: Oxford University Press.

Beauvoir, Simone de. 1949. *The Second Sex*. Translated and edited by HM Parshley. Aylesbury: Penguin.

Berger, Iris. 1983. 'Sources of Class Consciousness: South African Women in Recent Labour Struggles'. *The International Journal of African Historical Studies* 16 (1): 49–66. https://www.jstor.org/stable/217911.

Butler, Judith. 1998. 'Sex and Gender in Simone de Beauvoir's *Second Sex*'. In *Simone de Beauvoir: A Critical Reader*, edited by Elizabeth Fallaize, 29–42. London and New York: Routledge.

Donnachie, Ian. 2011. 'Robert Owen: Reputations and Burning Issues'. In *Robert Owen and His Legacy*, edited by Noel Thompson and Chris Williams, 13–31. Cardiff: University of Wales Press.

Donovan, Josephine. 1985. *Feminist Theory: The Intellectual Traditions of American Feminism*. New York: Frederick Unger.

Engels, Frederick. 1968. 'Socialism: Utopian and Scientific'. In *Selected Works in One Volume*, edited by Karl Marx and Frederick Engels, 375–428. London: Lawrence & Wishart.

Fanon, Frantz. 1968. *Black Skin, White Masks*. Translated by Charles Lam Markmann. London: Paladin.

Fisher, Foszia. 1978. 'Class Consciousness among Colonized Workers in South Africa'. In *Change, Reform and Economic Growth in South Africa*, edited by Lawrence Schlemmer and Eddie Webster, 197–223. Johannesburg: Ravan Press.

Goldstein, Lesley F. 1982. 'Early Feminist Themes in French Utopian Socialism: The St-Simonians and Fourier'. *Journal of the History of Ideas* 43 (1): 91–108. https://doi.org/10.2307/2709162.

Hirsch, Alan. 1979. 'An Introduction to Textile Worker Organization in Natal'. *South African Labour Bulletin* 4 (8): 3–42.

Institute for Industrial Education. 1976. *The Durban Strikes 1973: Human Beings with Souls*. Durban and Johannesburg: Institute for Industrial Education with Ravan Press.

Khwela, S'bu. 1993. '1973 Strikes: Breaking the Silence'. *South African Labour Bulletin* 17 (3): 20–26.

Kojève, Alexandre. 1969. *Introduction to the Reading of Hegel*. Assembled by Raymond Queneau, edited by Alan Bloom and translated by James H Nichols Jr. New York and London: Basic Books.

Kruks, Sonia. 1998. 'Beauvoir: The Weight of Situation'. In *Simone de Beauvoir: A Critical Reader*, edited by Elizabeth Fallaize, 43–71. London and New York: Routledge.

Lichtenstein, Alex. 2017a. 'Challenging "Umthetho We Femu" (the Law of the Firm): Gender Relations and Shop-Floor Battles for Union Recognition in Natal's Textile Industry, 1973–85'. *Africa* 87 (1): 100–119. https://doi.org/10.1017/S0001972016000711.

Lichtenstein, Alex. 2017b. 'Rick Turner, Participatory Democracy and Workers' Control'. *Theoria* 64 (2) (June): 47–57. https://doi.org/10.3167/th.2017.6415107.

Lloyd, Genevieve. 1984. *The Man of Reason: 'Male' and 'Female' in Western Philosophy*. Minneapolis, MN: University of Minnesota Press.

Lundgren-Gothlin, Eva. 1998. 'The Master-Slave Dialectic in *The Second Sex*'. In *Simone de Beauvoir: A Critical Reader*, edited by Elizabeth Fallaize, 93–109. London and New York: Routledge.

McClintock, Anne. 1991. ' "No Longer in a Future Heaven": Women and Nationalism in South Africa'. *Transition* 51: 104–123. https://www.jstor.org/stable/2935081.

Moi, Toril. 1994. *Simone de Beauvoir: The Making of an Intellectual Woman*. Oxford: Blackwell.

Moi, Toril. 2004. 'While We Wait: Notes on the English Translation of *The Second Sex*'. In *The Legacy of Simone de Beauvoir*, edited by Emily R Grosholz, 37–68. Oxford: Oxford University Press.

Moi, Toril. 2010. 'The Adultress Wife'. Review of *The Second Sex* by Simone de Beauvoir, translated by Constance Bord and Sheila Malovany-Chevalier. *London Review of Books*, 11 February 2010.

NLRC (Natal Labour Research Committee). 1980. 'Control Over a Workforce – the Frame Case'. *South African Labour Bulletin* 6 (5): 17–48.

Pateman, Carole. 1970. *Participation and Democratic Theory*. Cambridge: Cambridge University Press.

SALB (*South African Labour Bulletin*) Editorial Board. 1975. 'The Divided Working Class' (editorial comment). *South African Labour Bulletin* 2 (4): 1–3.

Simons, Margaret A. 2001. *Beauvoir and* The Second Sex: *Feminism, Race, and the Origins of Existentialism.* Oxford: Rowman & Littlefield.

Tarver, Erin C. 2011. 'Rethinking "Intersectionality": Michelle Obama, Presumed Subjects and Constitutive Privilege'. *Philosophia* 1 (2): 150–172.

Turner, Richard. 1972. 'The Eye of the Needle: An essay on Participatory Democracy'. Johannesburg: Special Programme for Christian Acttion in Society (SPROCAS 2).

Turner, Richard. 1980. *The Eye of the Needle: Towards Participatory Democracy in South Africa.* Johannesburg: Ravan Press.

UNCAA (United Nations Centre Against Apartheid). 1971. 'Women under Apartheid'. Unit on Apartheid, Notes and Documents No. 08/71: 1–12. https://www.jstor.org/stable/10.2307/al.sff.document.nuun1971_08.

UNCAA. 1975. 'African Women under Apartheid'. Notes and Documents No. 23/75: 1–12. https://www.jstor.org/stable/10.2307/al.sff.document.nuun1975_23.

UNCAA. 1978. 'The Effects of Apartheid on the Status of Women in South Africa'. *The Black Scholar* 10 (1): 11–20. https://www.jstor.org/stable/41163649.

Unterhalter, Elaine. 1983. 'Women in Struggle: South Africa'. *Third World Quarterly* 5 (4): 886–893. https://www.jstor.org/stable/3990829.

Westmore, Jean and Pat Townsend. 1975. 'The African Women Workers in the Textile Industry in Durban'. *South African Labour Bulletin* 2 (4): 18–32.

5

Poverty and Misplaced Prioritisation: Evaluating 'Human Models' and 'Value Systems'

John S Sanni

Poverty is a major threat to the achievement of social, political and economic goals in South Africa. South Africa is the most unequal society in the world. The nature of poverty in the country has become so normalised, and structures of oppression and economic disparity have systematically disempowered the poor to such an extent, that they are unable to understand and actively engage in socioeconomic justice. Structures of equity and justice, along economic lines, are blurred, and economic justice has increasingly become a distant dream that appears unrealisable. These forms of economic injustice, as I shall argue, owe their existence to various socialisations. In the case of South Africa, economic disparity and injustice emerge out of a history of colonialism and apartheid. These historical socialisations have solidified existing realities of economic marginalisation and inequalities that are prevalent in South Africa today. Socialisations form the foundation of value systems.

Historical socialisations are also racial in nature. South Africa presents a unique space to justify the theory that socialisations are racialised along white and black phenotypical binaries. It is perhaps a lot more complex than this, especially because of the increasing divisions that emerge along ethnic lines. The point here is that the nature of racialised socialisation is the imposition of a particular form of human model. However, when it comes to economic disparity, it is plausible to argue that the socioeconomic divisions in South Africa are mainly along racial lines. This complex case of historical marginalisation engenders and sustains poverty in South Africa. Attempts at resolving this historical marginalisation reveal misplaced prioritisation. As I shall demonstrate, drawing on Rick Turner's work, the focus has often been on goals that are generated from particular value systems – mostly material – that people seek to achieve. I argue that the re-evaluation of socialisations, the value systems and human models they engender calls for a critical engagement with the ethical implications of value systems and human models in South Africa. In this chapter I deal with four issues: first, I look at Rick Turner's 'human models' and 'value systems' and the ethical implications they bring to our attention. Second, I explore the nature of poverty and the structural inequality that remain prevalent in South Africa. Third, I engage instances of misplaced prioritisation as the constituting factor of inequalities in South Africa. Fourth, I argue that there is a need to re-examine conflicting human models and value systems. I debate whether Turner provides a plausible ethical position for addressing inequality in South Africa.

RICK TURNER'S 'HUMAN MODELS' AND 'VALUE SYSTEMS'

At the core of Turner's philosophical position is an attempt to challenge ethical considerations that are conceived to be closed and complete (Turner 2015). This conception of ethics or morality is dangerous to the ethical agenda that Turner advances. The context of his writing was characterised by oppression, injustice, exploitation and racism, among other social and ethical evils. For Turner, the justification for these horrendous acts of injustice emerged from human dispositions toward other humans and the values that have been formulated based on these dispositions, which are often biased, derogatory and exclusionary. 'Human models' and 'value systems' are important concepts that Turner uses to advance his ethical position. By human models, Turner refers to 'the set of values and behaviour patterns that characterise any particular group or individual' (Turner 2015, 10). Value systems therefore emerge from various socialised human models. In other words, human models are informed by socialised value systems. As Turner puts it, value systems emerge from various attempts to respond to the question, '"What am I?",' to which he adds: 'A complete statement of what I am includes a reference to my future, to what I should be' (Turner 2015, 26). There is a tripartite angle to human models and how they inform value systems. Identity is not about the narratives of solely the past, the present or the future. Identity is about the past, the present and human dispositions toward the future.

Turner further elaborates as follows: 'We tend to see the institutions of our society – the type of economic structure, the family, the school system, the existence of nation states, the polity and so on – as natural entities imposing certain rigidities on our behaviour' (Turner 2015, 2). What Turner refers to here pertains to the absolutised or very closed and complete nature of how the individual and collective identities are conceived. He argues for another, different approach to the way human beings see their human models and value systems. As Samuel Scheffler puts it, to value something is to have a favourable disposition towards that thing, or to favour a way of life (see Scheffler 2010). What Scheffler posits is an understanding of particular cultural groups that are bound by a sense of belonging informed by a shared conception of human conducts and values. As he puts it, 'an act is called for by some traditions as giving them reason to perform that act. For convenience, I will say that they see themselves as having "reasons of tradition" or simply "traditional reasons" for acting in certain ways' (Scheffler 2010, 287). The legitimacy of an act is informed by 'traditional reasons' that promote a strong sense of belonging to a group of moral actors. Scheffler uses the term 'traditional reasoning' to refer to actions based on motivations informed by particular values, ideals or principles (Scheffler 2010, 288). The sense of belonging that ties people to particular traditional reasoning is the basis for the rigidities that Turner considers the feature of social behaviours. Social behaviours play out in human models and value systems.

The normative significance of human models and value systems is implied in Turner's critique of social behaviours as constituting rigid tendencies. The point for Turner is not simply the existence of tradition as such, but rather the normative significance of the set of values and behaviour patterns that characterise the traditions of any particular group or individual (Turner 2015, 10; Scheffler 2010). To consider or describe something as a traditional norm is simply to indicate that the norms or values are widely shared, and they make up the normative schema within a certain social group. To be part of a society of norms is to adapt and learn the rules of communicating with other people within that social group (Turner 2015, 12). To exist is to respond to the question 'Who or what am I?' within a social group and all the ways of behaving that align with belonging to that particular group. What this does is simply, as Turner articulates it, 'prepare individuals not just for social living but for living out specific roles in a specific social structure' (Turner 2015, 12). Turner's position bears on the more general themes of the role of social structure in human life and human flourishing, of our attitudes toward the past, present and the future. Scheffler articulates this point succinctly when he writes: 'Traditional practices [social structure] take shape in light of an accumulation of historical experience, judgment, and perspective that outstrips what any single individual can reasonably aspire to achieve in the course of a lifetime, and someone who adheres to the tradition may gain the advantages of that accumulated experience and judgment' (Scheffler 2010, 292).

Human existence and self-identification are informed by a series of historical narratives. These narratives are not immediate, in the sense that they might be outside the temporary period of an individual's own life. They also entail things that happened long before individuals are born and things that might or will happen after they are dead (Scheffler 2010, 289). This is why 'a tradition is a set of beliefs, customs, teachings, values, practices, and procedures that is transmitted from generation to generation' (Scheffler 2010, 290). However, a tradition need not incorporate items or be limited to the qualities just mentioned, because of their complex nature. My focus presents and aligns more directly with most of Turner's argument; I am interested in those traditions or social structures that are seen by people as providing them with reasons for action, and so I will limit myself to traditions that include norms of practice and behaviour.

Turner does not have a problem with socialisations in themselves; what he investigates or interrogates is the standard used in the institutionalisation of oppressive structures. This position finds expression when Turner asserts that 'the process of socialisation can narrow down the individual's range of perceptions and choices to a predefined social reality. One particular human model becomes "human nature"' (Turner 2015, 12). This, to my mind, is the point of Turner's normative interrogation of socialisations. Turner engages the negative moral implications of socialisations that emerge from a narrow range of perceptions and choices. Such negative moral implications include the acceptance of inequality by an oppressed group in an unequal social structure, acceptance of inferiority, and the acceptance of superiority among others (Turner 2015, 12). The point for Turner is that there is a tendency to keep a mechanism going, especially if it constitutes a social structure favourable to one's own group. The moral dimensions of socialisation are very important for Turner. One could argue that Turner was aware of the fact that what constitutes the distinction that is attributed to human beings is the ability to 'evaluate our desires, to regard some as desirable and others are [sic] undesirable' (Taylor 1985, 16). If it is the case that moral actions are judged by an accurate evaluation of our desires in ways that consider moral effects, then it is plausible to argue that our understanding of desires should not be limited to our evaluation of a single group's value system. It has to be based on how we weigh our values with internal and external criteria. In other words, human beings are not to be locked into a single and supposedly complete internal moral framework (Turner 2015, 22).

Charles Taylor presents a similar position when he argues that monologue is a narrow perspective on human relations. Providing practical clarity to the points that Turner presents, Taylor (1994, 32–33) writes:

> The monological ideal seriously underestimates the place of the dialogical in human life. It forgets how our understanding of the good things in life can be transformed by our enjoying them in common with people we love; how some goods become accessible to us only through such common enjoyment. Because of this, it would take a great deal of effort... to prevent our identities being formed by the people we love. Consider what we mean by identity. It is who we are... it is the background against which our tastes and desires and opinions and aspirations make sense.

The point that is of great importance from Taylor's position is the nature of identity. I understand Taylor's conception of identity and its relevance for comprehending other people's horizons or points of departure. Individual points of origin are only important in relation to other points of engagement. Turner seeks to disrupt the social tendency to stagnate within a particular horizon, whereby individuals or groups assume a self-sufficient and absolutised identity. We have already seen that horizons might exist naturally, but they could exist systematically to promote certain kinds of social dominance within society. Conversely, through a normative engagement of potential outcomes such as the imposition of superiority and perceived rights to dominate (Turner 2015, 14), Turner proposes a moment of moral introspection that inspires freedom to love others in their own identity and various attempts to respond to their unique question of identity (Turner 2015, 27).

He expands this point of view with the phrase 'utopian thinking', with which I now proceed to engage.

Utopian thinking is a response that goes contrary to human nature. We have already seen that, for Turner, what we refer to as 'human nature' is not formed by primordial configurations; rather, these configurations come about when human models, informed by value systems of socialisations, become rigid. In fact, Turner 'challenge[s] the natural arrogance whereby individuals believe that their particular way of seeing the world is the only possible way of seeing it' (Turner 2015, 23), a position that necessitates internal morality. It is common that people wish to feel a part of something larger than themselves. Turner explores the normative force of value systems, especially as they influence human models. He proposed a shift from internal morality to 'transcendent morality'. He refers to this transcendent morality as the ethic that challenges the closed, complete and absolutised nature of internal morality by referring to it as only a partial horizon. Turner writes, 'Human beings are always limited to partial perspectives on the world. On the practical level this implies that no particular way of behaving can ever be final. The *transcendent ethic* demands that we question our taken-for-granted ways of behaving, that we must *continually* question them' (Turner 2015, 23). Turner proposes that all closed, internal morality becomes open to internal re-evaluation and continuous reconsideration and thus resolves the challenges of external morality. Morality becomes, for Turner, a continuous internal and relational engagement.

In sum, Turner's conception of social morality breaks free from the standard understanding of society within the framework of logical disjunctions, whereby socialisation is divided into the dual either/or of internal morality and external morality. The freedom that Turner advocates is one that is open to love others by 'escaping from the stereotyped attitudes and behaviour patterns imposed by my background and socialisation' (Turner 2015, 27). The next section seeks to point out Turner's morality within the context of South Africa's complex history of oppression and existential marginalisation.

POVERTY IN SOUTH AFRICA

It is important to note from the outset that for Turner, in South African society, 'whites as well as blacks are victims of social structure. They are of course, victims of a different kind' (Turner 2015, 13). This will play out in the brief account of poverty that this section paints. While Turner recognises the complex nature of South Africa's diverse socialisations, I think that it is a lot more complex than he suggests in his book. This section tackles colonialism and racism and how they are important themes for theorising about poverty in South Africa, as is the capitalist framework that has shaped the economic, social and political reality of South Africa. This capitalist structure on which colonial South Africa was founded, and which was perpetuated during colonial rule, has had a damaging effect on the socioeconomic development of South Africa. The resultant economic and social stratifications of the colonial eras are still reflected in the class and racial demographics of South Africa today, and the contentious issue of land ownership and (re)appropriation is again at the forefront of the South African psyche. As I pointed out earlier, South Africa is currently the most unequal society in the world, and economic stratifications are largely race-based (Sanni 2017; Schotte et al. 2018).

Despite the fact that South Africa is well known around the world for its progressive Constitution and strong public institutions, poverty, unemployment and inequality remain the country's most challenging problems (see Budlender 1999). According to Jayanathan Govender, 'it seems that despite a progressive public policy platform, South Africa's problems appear to be rooted in the legacy of apartheid. The inherited legacy explains why high levels of inequality persist in relation to race, gender and location, which is compounded by inter-generational continuities' (Govender 2016, 248). South Africa's 'double colonialism' (see Woermann and Sanni 2020) is an important starting point for thinking about the economic and social inequality that persists.

Mahmood Mamdani (2012, 49) argues that all colonial powers 'were preoccupied with defining, locating, and anointing the traditional authority – in the singular'. Mamdani (2001, 23) notes that 'direct rule tended to generate race-based political identities: settler and native'. In contrast, 'indirect rule... tended to mitigate the settler-native dialectic by fracturing the race consciousness of natives into multiple and separate ethnic consciousnesses'. He continues: 'A common cultural community signifies a common past, a common historical inheritance. In contrast, a political community testifies to the existence of a common project for the future. The distinction is often blurred because the past flows into the future, as it always does, creating a significant overlap between cultural and political communities' (Mamdani 2001, 23).

Achille Mbembe identifies three major effects of colonialism on African societies. First, 'separation', which 'leads to a loss of familiarity with the self to the point that the subject, estranged, is relegated to an alienated, almost lifeless identity'. Second, 'disappropriation' which, on the one hand, he argues, 'led to material expropriation and dispossession, and, on the other, to a singular experience of subjection characterized by the falsification of oneself by the other'. Third, 'degradation', which 'plunge[d] the Black subject into humiliation, abjection, and nameless suffering' (Mbembe 2017, 78). It also incited a process of 'social death' characterised by the denial of dignity, dispersion and the torment of exile. Richard Leonard (1983, 23) observes that 'the roots of today's problem go back to the first European settlement in South Africa'. Robert Ross (1999, 3), in turn, conjectures that the source of these problems is economic, in that South Africa is 'a capitalist country or at least a country whose economic development has been dominated by capitalist organisations. Colonial South Africa was founded by the premier capitalist corporation of the seventeenth century, the Dutch East India Company, and was taken over by the British at the height of Britain's industrial revolution'.

Colonialism and apartheid established a labour force that was directed to achieving goals that socially and economically alienated the natives, and the resultant economic and social stratifications of coloniser–colonised, well-off whites and worse-off blacks, were further embedded in the apartheid era (Woermann and Sanni, 2020). JE Casely Hayford (1969, 157–158) dramatically captures this partition and the platform it constructs for African–Western relations thus:

> It was like the meeting of the gods, the gathering of the Nations, for they had mastered all knowledge and gotten themselves such power as to make men forget the Power beyond, before whom the Nations are as grasshoppers... 'Come let us partition it among ourselves'.... 'This thing is easily done. We shall go to the Ethiopians, and shall teach them our religion, and that will make them ours, body and soul – lands, goods and all, for all time.'

Hayford's articulation of the effects of colonialism accurately captures the power relations that existed prior to and during colonialism and apartheid. Social and economic powers were very important for the goals that were set to be achieved in Africa. This explains why 'income poverty was strikingly visible and offensive in South Africa because it coexisted alongside great affluence, because this inequality correlated with race and because it was (at least in part) the consequence of the systematic racial discrimination that defined apartheid' (Seekings and Nattrass 2015, 3). Most importantly, apartheid had perpetuated income poverty and exacerbated income inequality in very obvious ways among African people, while the white minority had benefited, and continued to benefit, from discriminatory public policies (Seekings and Nattrass 2015, 4). Most black South Africans were restricted to limited opportunities and they were forced to settle for either unemployment or self-employment, were limited to low-quality public education and health care, and most were physically confined to impoverished parts of the countryside or cities (Seekings and Nattrass 2015, 4).

Inequality and indignity in South Africa were perhaps made starker because racial and class segregation kept the rich and the poor apart. Observers from all parts of the political spectrum unsurprisingly turned to crude dualistic descriptions of this reality, distinguishing, for example, between the 'first-' and 'third-world' parts of the country or analysing the political economy in terms of 'internal colonialism' or 'colonialism of a special type' or identifying two 'nations' (Seekings and Nattrass 2015). Anthony Atkinson (2015) believes that there is a great deal we can learn from the past. The past provides both a yardstick by which we can judge what could be attainable in terms of reducing inequality, and clues as to how it could be achieved. South Africa is among those countries that are grappling with these challenges. Bringing South Africa's structural inequality into clear focus is an urgent task. We find a similar diachronic study in Turner's account of poverty in South Africa, a study that begins with the oppressive socialisation in the past and moves on to an established, systemic exclusion and marginalisation that still exists in contemporary South Africa. Statistics show that inequality in South Africa is structurally embedded, with economic disparity and race taking pre-eminence. Drawing on Statistics South Africa 2014 data, Govender (2016, 239) observes

> the significant differences in poverty levels between the population groups. In terms of poverty share, more than 9 out of 10 (94.2 per cent) poor people in South Africa were black in 2011, a proportion that increased from 2006 (92.9 per cent) to 2009 (93.2 per cent). When framed against the black share of the total population (79 per cent), the deep structural scale of poverty associated with race presents a multi-dimensional quandary for policy makers.

Govender's account shows that South Africa is indeed a divided nation, a nation divided along socioeconomic lines, and the opportunities that open for the future are constituted in the present along lines that are detrimental to black South Africans. Thabo Mbeki's 1998 'two-nation' thesis on Africa captures the fact that the one group is white and prosperous and the other black and poor. 'The contradiction is sharpened by the relative economic growth experienced during the first decade of democracy, yet worsening inequality of incomes persists in current day South Africa'

(Govender 2016, 238). In an absurd twist of logic, poverty, unemployment and homelessness are described to be the fault of poor, black South Africans (Khan 2015).

However, 'inequality has many dimensions, including race, gender, geography and economy which do not work in isolation. It is the concentration of wealth by a few that affect[s] the political, social and cultural processes to the detriment of the most vulnerable' (Govender 2016, 244). Social inequality is a serious feature in the structure and precarious ordering of South African society. Andrew Whiteford and Dirk van Seventer (2000, 28) argue that 'the rise in inequality within population groups and within society as a whole is driven, on the one hand, by rising employment of well-paid, highly-skilled persons and, on the other hand, declining employment of lower-paid, less-skilled persons who are forced into poorly remunerated informal sector employment or into unemployment'.

Whiteford and Van Seventer's analysis of labour market processes, and projections that one of the authors made in another study, has led them to predict that 'the employment of highly-skilled persons will continue to rise while the employment of less-skilled persons will decline, resulting in rising unemployment. Unless there is a fundamental shift in the path along which the economy is moving, there is little hope for a reduction in inequality and income poverty' (Whiteford and Van Seventer 2000, 28). Economic, social and political socialisations have reinforced capitalistic inequality in South Africa. These socialisations carry, sustain, valorise and constantly resuscitate within themselves the traces of historic foundation (Serequeberhan 1994, 34). Pumla Gqola (2007, 115) laments the persistent socialisation of white oppression and black marginalisation when she writes:

> From slave resistance … to the Unity Movement, African National Congress, Pan Africanist Congress, Black Consciousness Movement, the South African Communist Party, … freedom from apartheid was seen as synonymous with freedom from the burden of race … Yet …
> the vast majority of the Black poor … are written out of capital and

most victimised. Although now free from state racism, they feel the effects of a mutating oppressive, capitalist system in their workplaces, for those who have such jobs. For the more affluent, race and class still exert control...

The social imaginaries of oppression have persisted in the South African social and economic mindset. The reality is ingrained in ways that, as Turner articulates it, even 'the process of separation from other people reinforces the socialization process by stopping people from thinking about themselves, and so stopping them from realizing that they could be other than they have been socialized to be' (Turner 2015, 21). For Turner, the centre of focus is often the major problem with socialisations. This is because of how the other becomes excluded in the schema of what a particular group considers as a value system. Different from this outlook, Turner states that 'the refusal to change, the refusal of openness, and the necessity for continuous self-defence wreak the psychological havoc of fear, tension, and half-suppressed insecurity' (Turner 2015, 21). The necessity of change is important for Turner because it challenges stagnant, absolute and closed socialised positions. This chapter suggests that implicit in Turner's work is the reality of misplaced prioritisations. They carry in them supposed ethical considerations that favour a few to the detriment of a vast majority. I argue in the next section that misplaced prioritisation is historical and, as such, complex.

MISPLACED PRIORITISATIONS

Misplaced prioritisation is used here to refer to wrong judgement on what to focus on or do, or not focus on or do. I argue that a closed purview or perception of human models and value systems plays a major role in promoting poverty by reinforcing misplaced prioritisations. As I have already argued above, colonialism and apartheid were characterised by a focus on goals that did not include Africans. Scholars like John Pilger, who proclaimed that 'apartheid did not die', have attributed the lack of significant economic and social change in South Africa post-1994 to the ever-present oppressive structures instituted by the apartheid regime (Pilger cited in Desai 2002). The colonial and apartheid pillaging have continued as an ingrained, systemic aspect of postcolonial society. Turner (2015, 27–28) articulates this accurately when he notes:

> If I concentrate on things, rather than people, I become a slave. I become dependent on things. I behave in the way in which the things need me to behave. In each relationship with the other I am not free to be open to the other as a person. I have to manipulate the other in such a way as to obtain things. And to manipulate the other I have to manipulate myself. This is my essential degradation, for in manipulating myself I finally lose my freedom. I become identified with the role I am playing.

There is an ontological argument at play in Turner's conception of relationship. He argues that freedom is attained when human beings are prioritised, and this means that human beings should not be used as means to an end. When an individual is manipulated by another, the person who manipulates is essentially degraded because the person becomes one with his action(s). Thinking of Turner's position from the context of colonialism will make his point clearer. Colonialists – and supporters of the apartheid regime, one might add – are viewed as oppressors, exploiters, manipulators and such, because they subjected themselves to a state that is beneath their human relational state. To exist in a morally upright way is to expand one's horizon by not being limited to a restrictive socialisation. The expected outcome of an expanded horizon is positive.

Postcolonial South Africa continues to experience various forms of oppression and marginalisation, partly due to the fact that colonialism and apartheid are not to be considered as events, but as structures (Wolfe 2006). The various forms of marginalisation and acts of injustice are not perpetrated through physical force or cruelty as was the case in colonial times; instead, systemic oppression and manipulation are endemic. Amidst signs of change after the transition to democracy, marked by the 1994 democratic election, justice for the poor, and the hope that income poverty would be reduced (Seekings and Nattrass 2015, 4) continue to remain a distant mirage. However, the poor were more sanguine than political leaders (see Charney 1995). The poor were to be enfranchised, the pro-poor and pro-black African National Congress (ANC) would be elected into office, and public policies and private practices would be deracialised (Seekings and Nattrass 2015, 4). It is important to note here that in the last year of apartheid, the formerly disenfranchised African majority had witnessed a rapid upward turn of income and class mobility, but the 1993 income data statistics still showed that the white minority was conspicuously rich: the poverty rate of African people was 57 per cent; it was 20 per cent among coloured people, 7 per cent among Indians and only 2 per cent among white people (Seekings and Nattrass 2015, 3).

Since 1994, the preoccupation of the government and the ANC, it is claimed, has been to alleviate poverty through the socioeconomic rights that were included in Sections 27, 28 and 29 of the 1996 Constitution (Seekings and Nattrass 2015, 55). The rights include:

(1) Everyone has the right to have access to (a) health care services; (b) sufficient food and water; and (c) social security, including, if they are unable to support themselves and their dependents, appropriate social assistance. (2) The state must take reasonable legislative and other measures, within its available resources, to achieve the progressive realization of each of these rights. Section 28 stipulated specific rights for children, and Section 29 establishes rights to education. These … rights were said to be based on the 'democratic values of human dignity, equality and freedom' (section 7, para 2).

The purported goal has been to alleviate the poverty that the majority of South Africans were experiencing. The ANC recognised, however, that 'much more needs to be done' – and it presented itself as a renewed organisation, ready to do so. 'Working together we can do more' was its cautious slogan. According to Jeremy Seekings and Nicoli Nattrass, post-apartheid political senior members and political leaders, 'including Thabo Mbeki (deputy president until 1999, then president until 2008), Trevor Manuel (Minister of Trade and Industry from 1994 to 1995, and then Minister of Finance until 2009), Alec Erwin (Manuel's successor at Trade and Industry)', among others, supposedly 'exploited their positions to ram through business-friendly policies, shifting the ANC from a pro-poor to a pro-business, "neoliberal" position' (Seekings and Nattrass 2015, 7). The starting point of this supposed neoliberal approach was the alleged neglect of the Reconstruction and Development Programme (RDP) and the adoption of the Growth, Employment and Redistribution (GEAR) macroeconomic strategy in 1996 (see Seekings and Nattrass 2015, 7). This shift meant the neglect of the poor who did not have the basic requirements for decent employment. Growth and redistribution were limited to the elite groups, thus promoting structures that prioritised elite groups and trumped justice and redistribution (Govender 2016, 253).

The misplaced prioritisation that is the theme of this section is elitist. A clear indication of this elitism is in the remark made in early 2021 by President Cyril Ramaphosa, that a salary of one million rand per year was not enough for a member of parliament. But the poor citizens of South Africa are to live off a social grant of R350 per month, which amounts to a total of R4 200 per year. Post-apartheid South Africa is complex, not only on socioeconomic grounds but also on ontological grounds. This is why I believe that Turner, in the early parts of his work, seeks to establish an ontological foundation for the moral issues he addresses. Turner (2015, 22) articulates his position clearly when he recommends that we each pose the question, 'What is human life for, what is the meaning of human life?' Turner moves from the particular of socialisations to a general understanding of human models. This, for him, is the meaning of transcendent morality, the foundation of utopian thinking that engages misplaced prioritisations in the search for alternative moral actions.

The nature of misplaced prioritisation lies not only in how the ontological is conceived, it also focuses on the relationships that exist between human beings. Most African leaders are now victims of the same socialisation that they challenged. This is evident in the various policies they prioritise and the commitment that they have toward alleviating suffering, oppression and exploitation. As already noted in the second section, the major flaw of colonialism and apartheid was not only the dehumanisation of Africans, but also its narrow perception of black people. This narrowness reinforced misplaced prioritisations that were material in nature. Most African leaders, assuming their elitist status, have adopted this narrow-mindedness that does not see beyond their material needs. Perhaps the need for utopian thinking has to begin with Africans, who must heed the call of scholars such as Tsenay Serequeberhan, who avers that the African must 'die to himself in order to be reborn to the Other. He is not assimilated; he assimilates himself with the Other. He lives with the Other in symbiosis; he is born again (*con-nait*) to the Other' (Serequeberhan 1994, 37–38). Serequeberhan's philosophical invitation resonates with Turner's critique of socialisations that narrow an individual's or a group's perspective to a predetermined social reality (Turner 2015, 12).

The desire for alternative moral actions can be outweighed by conflicting human models and value systems. The preoccupations of particular human models and value systems are, in most cases, with internal morality even when they do not appear as such. In a multicultural society, conflicts might arise in cases 'when these differences overlap with other significant differences of interest' (Turner 2015, 42). If we are to consider the position of Turner that human models and value systems are socialisations that arise from traditions and beliefs, how do we morally address potential conflicts of interests? In the case of South Africa, where the conflicts are historical and systematically interwoven into the structure of post-apartheid South Africa, what should be the moral compass or the pathway to utopian thinking that would result in the reduction of the poverty rate? To my mind, any attempt to adequately respond to these questions would require a re-examining of human models and value systems from the viewpoint of conflicting interests.

RE-EXAMINING CONFLICTING HUMAN MODELS AND VALUE SYSTEMS

I argue in this section that there is a need to re-examine human models and value systems beyond the conception of utopian thinking that Turner proposes. This is not to undermine or relegate Turner's position to insignificance. On the contrary, I argue that Turner provides us with important theoretical frameworks for thinking beyond his work. From the analysis on the moral implications of Turner's work, it is safe to sum up his work as having a bearing on history, and how history shapes the present and the way the future is imagined. For Turner, therefore, to imagine a more inclusive future entails that we move and think beyond preconceived internal morality to transcendent morality. Turner proposes a utopian reimagination that explores alternative worlds.

Referring to postcolonial African society, Serequeberhan argues that 'As far back as 1952, in *Black Skin, White Masks*, Fanon had convincingly argued that the European "sees" the Negro-African and pastes on him an Image of Otherness that needs to be critically peeled off and rejected' (Serequeberhan 1994, 47). Turner refers to this disposition towards others as human models. The nature of a socialised human model is such that it stratifies society into insiders and outsiders. Neocolonial socialisations have reinforced this toxic stratification by promoting racial exclusion, economic disparity and negative freedom. These realities have been the central pivot on which the need for emancipation turned in Africa during colonial times, and continues, more so, in postcolonial and neocolonial Africa. The pathway to this emancipation entails engaging internal morality. Aimé Césaire forcefully points out that 'I never thought for a moment that our emancipation could come from the right – that's impossible...our liberation placed us on the left, but [we]...refused to see the black [African] question as simply a social [economic] question... after all we are dealing with the only race which is denied even the notion of humanity' (Césaire 1972, 78). This is why the reimagination of the self, as Turner proposes, is an important starting point.

More than Turner has admitted in his work is the reality that socialisations are complex, and historical occurrences have shown that socialisations intersect. There is a need to uncover various socialisations and to engage the reasons behind their existence. It is only on this ground that transcendent morality can be considered as a suitable alternative to internal morality. There is a need to engage with the injunction that 'even in post-colonial Africa, the struggle against neo-colonialism is a struggle aimed and focused on disclosing the historico-political ground on which an African political tradition can be instituted within the context of the present' (Serequeberhan 1994, 37–38). This position is similar to Scheffler's account that 'the normative force of traditional reasons essentially depends on the fact that traditions are collaborative enterprises involving many people over multiple generations' (Scheffler 2010, 310). The nature of the collaborative enterprises of conflicting socialisations in Africa has been an oppressive one.

Amidst the converging socialisations of Africa and the West, the reimagination that I believe is necessary is one that changes the imaginaries of Africans towards fellow Africans. Transcendent morality, as presented by Turner, is susceptible to a new kind of oppression. As Anne McClintock (1993, 93) notes, in the process of engaging with the non-African other, 'the term Africa(n) has received very little interrogation and has been readily adopted on the basis of geography and/or historicity. Such adoption, I argue, is intrinsically linked to and centralises colonialism as the basis of ongoing polarities, Western/African; Aggressor/Victim, such that colonialism keeps "returning" at the very point of its departure'.

Unlike McClintock, who dismisses some kind of return to a unique point of departure, and Turner, who challenges static socialisations,

I argue that Africa's engagement with transcendent morality should be based on critical engagement with historical and current conditions of oppression. We live in a society where 'rather than reversing inequality, it is growing, there is greater unfairness, breakdown of social cohesion, fundamental values are being eroded by the market system, and the political system is under great strain. South Africa is among those countries that is grappling with these challenges' (Govender 2016, 247).

The racialised inequities of apartheid gave way to new 'market' inequities, as the post-apartheid political elite embraced (or was enveloped by) global 'neoliberalism' (Seekings and Nattrass 2015, 7). The point here is that goals give way to new socialisations. South African blacks must begin to engage what their goals and priorities are in their search for the utopia that is uniquely theirs. While it is true that 'one consequence of acknowledging the multiplicity of traditions as a species of normative diversity is to remind us that normative diversity is neither a purely individualistic nor a purely doxastic phenomenon' (Scheffler 2010, 310), South Africans must prioritise their internal moral principles as they search for their own conception of utopia.

While Turner makes a compelling case for addressing socialisation, I think that his position undermines the complex nature of history and how it justifies a closed disposition, as opposed to an open and more receptive disposition, to the way socialisations, over time, have become normalised. The intersection of socialisations has resulted in the oppression that the continent in general and South Africa in particular suffers. Africa was shaped by foreign ideological configurations. Whether Turner resolves this idea of control and domination remains a utopia that we might not live to witness.

CONCLUSION

In summary, I argued in this chapter that Turner's account of human models and value systems provides a significant starting point for theorising morality within the framework of poverty in South Africa.

While I agree that socialisation hinders relationality, especially when certain kinds of socialisation promote oppressive structures, I argue that socialisations in their complex state of contact between Africans and the West compel us to think of the reason why the human models and value systems of a particular society should be reinforced. I further my argument by stating that transcendent morality might become the justification for a new kind of oppression. Therefore, rather than advance an inclusivity, as presented by Turner, I proposed that the reason for upholding internal morality should be reinforced. The effects of colonialism and the apartheid regime have stripped Africans of their dignity. In the various attempts to regain dignity, through economic, social and political enfranchisement and prioritisation, Africans must constantly remember what was lost to colonial invasion and apartheid and remain wary of what might happen to them if they uncritically succumb to the dictates of transcendent morality.

REFERENCES

Atkinson, Anthony B. 2015. *Inequality: What Can be done?* Cambridge, MA: Harvard University Press.

Budlender, Debbie. 1999. 'Patterns of Poverty in South Africa'. *Development Southern Africa* 16 (2): 197–219.

Césaire, Aimé. 1972. *Discourse on Colonialism.* New York: Monthly Review Press.

Charney, Craig. 1995. 'Voices of a New Democracy: African Expectations in the New South Africa'. Research report no. 38, Centre for Policy Studies, Johannesburg.

Desai, Ashwin. 2002. *We Are the Poors: Community Struggles in Post-apartheid South Africa.* New York: Monthly Review Press.

Govender, Jayanathan. 2016. 'Social Justice in South Africa'. *Civitas* 16 (2): 237–258.

Gqola, Pumla Dineo. 2007. 'How the "Cult of Femininity" and Violent Masculinities Support Endemic Gender-based Violence in Contemporary South Africa'. *African Identities* 5 (1): 111–124.

Hayford, JE Casely. 1969. *Ethiopia Unbound: Studies in Race Emancipation.* London: Routledge.

Khan, Firoz. 2015. 'Violence, Grants, Poverty, Inequality, Unemployment and Hope'. *Africa Insight* 44 (4): 14–30.

Leonard, Richard. 1983. *South Africa at War.* Chicago, IL: Lawrence Hill Books.

Mamdani, Mahmood. 2001. *When Victims Become Killers: Colonialism, Nativism, and the Genocide in Rwanda.* Princeton, NJ: Princeton University Press.

Mamdani, Mahmood. 2012. *Define and Rule: Native as Political Identity.* Cambridge, MA: Harvard University Press.

Mbembe, Achille. 2017. *Critique of Black Reason*. London: Duke University Press.

McClintock, Anne. 1993. 'The Angel of Progress'. In *Colonial Discourse and Postcolonial Theory: A Reader*, edited by Patrick Williams and Laura Chrisman, 84–98. New York: Taylor and Francis.

Ross, Robert. 1999. *A Concise History of South Africa*. Cambridge: Cambridge University Press.

Sanni, John. 2017. 'Heidegger's "Potentiality-for-being": Towards Adequate Economic Development in Nigeria'. *Development South Africa* 34 (2): 1–14.

Scheffler, Samuel. 2010. *Equality and Tradition: Questions of Value in Moral and Political Theory*. New York: Oxford University Press.

Schotte, Simone, Rocco Zizzamia and Murray Leibbrandt. 2018. 'A Poverty Dynamic Approach to Social Stratification: The South African Case'. *World Development* 110: 88–103.

Seekings, Jeremy and Nicoli Nattrass. 2015. *Policy, Politics and Poverty in South Africa*. New York: Palgrave Macmillan.

Serequeberhan, Tsenay. 1994. *The Hermeneutics of African Philosophy: Horizon and Discourse*. New York: Routledge.

Taylor, Charles. 1985. 'What is Human Agency?'. In *Human Agency and Language: Philosophical Papers 1*, edited by Charles Taylor, 15–44. Cambridge: Cambridge University Press.

Taylor, Charles. 1994. *Multiculturalism and the Politics of Recognition*. Princeton, NJ: Princeton University Press.

Turner, Richard. 2015. *The Eye of the Needle: Towards Participatory Democracy in South Africa*, revised edition. Kolkata: Seagull Books.

Whiteford, Andrew and Dirk E van Seventer. 2000. 'South Africa's Changing Income Distribution in the 1990s'. *Studies in Economics and Econometrics* 24 (3): 7–30.

Woermann, Minka and John S Sanni. 2020. 'Ethnic and Racial Valorisations in Nigeria and South Africa: How Ubuntu May Harm or Help'. *South African Journal of Philosophy* 39 (3): 296–307.

Wolfe, Patrick. 2006. 'Settler Colonialism and the Elimination of the Native'. *Journal of Genocide Research* 8 (4): 387–409.

6

Should We Take Turner's Democratic Model Seriously?

Daryl Glaser

Taken literally – as a comprehensive model for society – Rick Turner's prescription is implausible, or so I will argue. So how should we view *The Eye of the Needle* now? We could view it as a product of a South African 'moment'.[1] We can also register the attractiveness of Turner's idealism. But the present project invites us to seek – which means to impute – larger meanings that might still resonate in the 2020s. Can we find them?

Some seek the book's ongoing relevance in its model of insistent radical critique, including of materialistic capitalism, Stalinist bureaucracy and narrow race politics. But Turner was not interested, for its own sake, in a politics of criticism and refusal. His prescription for a future participatory democracy was central to his efforts, certainly in *The Eye of the Needle*. He intended to dramatise not just the *possibility* of alternatives, *but a possible* alternative. Yet this means that the weaknesses of Turner's rendition of socialist participatory democracy damage his project. There is also a question about how fully his work resonates with a global moment where, arguably, the 'primary contradiction' is not between liberal and participatory democracy, but between liberalism and forces of illiberalism (some of which forces the mantle of 'truer' democracy).[2] The challenge for a radical democratic theory today is not to find participatory alternatives to liberal democracy but to render liberal democracy more participatory – and participatory democracy more liberal. Some of what Turner says speaks fruitfully to that challenge, but not all of it.

WHAT SORT OF UTOPIAN IS TURNER?

Turner's reflections on utopianism are important, leaving aside his democratic model. It is possible to imagine a version of his book that speaks just of utopian possibility without offering a concrete institutional utopia. This is *The Eye of the Needle* sans chapters four, five and seven. In this abridged version (and especially in chapters one and two) we encounter a searing critique of capitalism's incompatibility with a Christian human model and of its instrumentalisation of human relations. A defence of this Turner does not require defending wild idealism. Turner offers what we might, following Erik Olin Wright, term real utopianism (Wright 2010). He not only invites us to believe that change is possible (and sometimes realistically inescapable); he requires us to distinguish what is changeable, and what is not, in human affairs. Not everything, he acknowledges, is. In this he is right.

Whether utopia is a valuable regulative notion is debatable. Its connotation of human perfection sounds totalitarian in some ears. But can we doubt that higher regulative or inspirational ideals are needed? There is something problematic in the conservative naturalisation of existing orders that Turner rightfully decries, but also in a radical politics that confines itself to challenging manifest injustice. The implication of *The Eye of the Needle* is that Turner would have little truck with compulsive opposition, just as he had no truck with resignation to the status quo.

What both kinds of politics lack is serious engagement with alternative possible social orders.

There are at least two ways to think about the regulative role of ideal futures. In explicit utopianism, utopia serves as inspiration to action, whether revolutionary, prefigurative or both. In the revolutionary version, it inspires a storming of the winter palace; in the prefigurative version, something like Rudolf Bahro's Benedictine commune (Bahro 1978). Revolutionary utopianism paradoxically generates a fearsome realism, because practical violence may be needed now to secure the beautiful future. In the prefigurative case, the beautiful future is built from scratch in the present, and it must express from the outset the humanistic relations envisaged for the future. But in both cases the future is one of transcendence of the world we know, one in which communality replaces division, simplified administration replaces politics and freedom replaces necessity.

An alternative regulative future is Rawlsian 'ideal theory' (Rawls 1999, 7–8, 215–216, 308–309). In enunciating principles of justice, John Rawls distinguished between principles applicable in an ideal world and those applicable in a non-ideal world. But his 'ideal' principles of justice were not designed for a transcendent condition. They were designed to regulate the fair distribution of primary goods in 'circumstances of justice'. These are circumstances in which scarcity persists. Nor is the Rawlsian ideal one in which human nature is remade to tolerate residual scarcities, perhaps through renunciation of materialism. The designers of a future society that go into Rawls' 'original position' may be thoroughly abstracted from history and particularity, but mentally and morally they are still recognisable to us, motivated by both self-interest and a capacity for justice.

Many contemporary social justice champions dislike ideal theory. It seems to them too detached from the particular histories whose injustices shape our present and demand immediate redress, too preoccupied with fair trade-offs as opposed to testing the limits of the possible through struggle. The social justice 'warriors' generally prefer utopia to ideal theory, but action to both.

Where does Turner come down, here? There is clearly in his work some transcendent utopianism. His utopianism is of the prefigurative variety (Turner 2015, 112, 124), proceeding via personal and collective ethical transformation rather than revolution (Turner 2015, 122–148, 197–201). *The Eye of the Needle* invites us to 'live differently' at a personal level, 'in a way that embodies our preference for people over things' (Turner 2015, 123). It also calls on us to transform the organisations we work in (Turner 2015, 124–125). The organisational settings he identifies might surprise: they include the then emerging homelands (Turner 2015, 97, 113–115). But they also include the workplace (Turner 2015, 159–162), foreshadowing Turner's contribution to the 1970s workerism that culminated in the formation of the Federation of South African Trade Unions.[3]

The connection between personal and organisational reform and Turner's vision of radical conciliar democracy is hazy. Turner combines ruminations about small-scale change that could issue from the Institute of Race Relations with a vision of government by soviets. Does he literally think one will yield the other, without passing through revolution? Or had he, as Edward Webster (1993) suggests, discovered a way to combine radical vision with gradualist reforms that could survive apartheid repression? We find here tensions internal to workerism itself, a current that, for better or worse, was at once economistic-reformist and revolutionary-utopian.

For some scientific socialists, Turner's type of reformism is utopian in the negative sense of a pipe dream. If the scientific socialists were utopian, this was not something they admitted. They believed that their future was foretold by hard science. In taking positive ownership of the idea of utopia, Turner seems to be appealing to a 'utopian socialist' tradition that rejects the violence of revolutionary scientific socialism – its physical repressive violence, but the violence also of its coldly instrumental reason. He prefers a utopia of (or built out of) communes and the counterculture.

At the same time, Turner does not seek out Rawls-type impartial principles of justice. Impartial principles of the Rawlsian type are devised by philosophers (even if via contractarian thought experiments) and guaranteed by judges. Turner placed his faith in the people – or rather, in a suitably ethically transformed people. His people would be transformed first personally, and then collectively via 'full workers' control' (Turner 2015, 47). Only workplace-rooted participatory democracy, he believed, would institutionally undergird personal autonomy, the preference for people over things and freely expressed love (Turner 2015, 45–52). By contrast, Rawls saw ideal theory being expressed in constitutional democracy. Turner was a romantic rather than a liberal constitutionalist in this sense. If the danger in Rawls is rule by judges, the danger in Turner is glimpsed in his willingness to entertain versions of the participatory self-management experiments hosted by authoritarian socialist regimes.[4]

But there's another side of Turner, not easily captured by notions either of utopianism or ideal theory. It seeks to figure out what institutions ideals can support in the real world. This is a practical exercise akin (in character if not depth) to Alec Nove's *The Economics of Feasible Socialism* (1983). To see this side one has to look, again, at chapters I initially bracketed. In these, one finds reflections on markets versus planning, representation versus direct democracy, amateurism versus expertise (and Turner allowed a place for markets, representation and experts). These latter chapters are more radically optimistic than Nove was about the possible extent of feasible socialism, yet share his preoccupation with the institutional designs, balances and choices required for real-world socialist governance. In this sense they are, again, realistically utopian, *at least in spirit*.

Taking Turner seriously means taking these democratic-model chapters seriously too, as Turner himself did but his interpreters have mainly not.[5] One can separate the philosophy and the model but, as the discussion has already shown, only up to a point.

TURNER'S MODEL AND ITS LIMITS

To be clear, Turner does not offer a detailed model of participatory democracy. His detailing is deeply uneven; there are vast gaps. His model belongs to the conciliar-democratic family. This family includes guild socialism, anarcho-syndicalism and council communism. It subsequently came to include Yugoslav self-management, Maoist communes and Tanzanian Ujamaa, all three of which Turner scrutinises in *The Eye of the Needle*. The shared aspiration of those advocating these models was to mobilise and empower ordinary people, and in particular poorer and working people. And it was to mobilise them via something that resembled a direct and participatory democracy, one whose base units were located in workplaces, communes and working-class districts. These local units would exercise a high degree of local power, while coordinating their actions at higher levels through instructed delegates subject to recall. In larger political units, this representational structure would involve pyramidal or tiered representation, connecting myriad base units to an apex assembly via intermediate elective bodies. Delegates would represent voters in particular class or functional capacities, rather than as general representatives. The basic idea was that ordinary people would be given real power, in particular real local and economic power, which they lacked under purely political or generalist representation exercised via large territorial constituencies. In other words, council democracy would give producers the real control over their lives that they lacked under 'bourgeois' democracy.

Turner's model belongs to this family, but it is difficult to say exactly where. Clearly, he envisages the organisation of people in workplaces. In it, workers elect representatives who exercise firm-level legislative functions and supervise enterprise directors while retaining their working roles. Turner sees representative bodies as operating at different levels of government, shadowing other (more conventional?) forms of representation at these different levels (Turner 2015, 109). And he sees self-management bodies as having to conform to social plans to ensure a necessary degree of social coordination as well as some degree of freedom for all from the blind forces of market and nature (Turner 2015, 70–78).

Quite a lot is unclear, such as whether there would be a tiered system of elected delegate bodies building up from workplace assemblies to assist with central coordination, as opposed to coordination being carried out by the state. It is also unclear how these delegate bodies relate to conventional parliamentary-type bodies, whether they supersede parliaments or coexist with them and, if the latter, on what basis. A lot rides on both sets of questions. If worker democracy is confined to the enterprise, this looks more like industrial democracy than a 'full' system of worker control. Again, if parliament is sovereign and the workers' elective bodies are subordinate to them, the scheme looks like Western-style corporatism, with functional economic associations participating in economic policymaking but not exercising society-wide legislative authority. However, industrial democracy, if that is what it is, appears to operate in Turner's scheme in a context of cooperative or social ownership rather than private enterprise (Turner 2015, 82–83). And parliament, if it has a role, operates in a fundamentally socialist context. Whether such a parliament would represent also bourgeois and pro-capitalist parties is unclear. In other words, it is uncertain whether the Turner scheme would operate alongside the institutions and rules we associate with liberal democracy, or would break fundamentally with liberal democracy. Part of Turner seems to desire a clear break, as highlighted by his interest in Yugoslavia and cultural-revolutionary China.

But there are some features of the Turner schemes that suggest modesty of ambition. Workers would govern workplaces via elected representatives, rather than directly or continuously. There would be appointed directors and directorial staff, albeit subject to worker supervision and recall. Expertise would continue to play a role, subject, again, to worker oversight (Turner 2015, 48–49). Some inter-enterprise coordination would depend on markets (Turner 2015, 76). Motivation would be bolstered by material incentives. In these details we find the realism in Turner's utopianism. The envisaged system might be non-capitalist, but it does not eliminate reward differentials or the division of labour.

Schemes of this kind were tried by many regimes with lesser or greater good faith, and commonly fell short. Turner himself devoted substantial space to considering what went wrong with them, and to devising countermeasures. At the most general level, the problem was that very often, in practice, power did not lie with ordinary workers but with others: politicians, the ruling party, executive committees, experts or skilled workers. The real interest is in how these problems are diagnosed and in the remedies sought. One diagnostic approach is to focus on betrayal – the idea that proletarian democracy has been actively suppressed by certain leaders or ruling parties (Vladimir Lenin, Joseph Stalin, assorted Stalinists, take your pick). If they do not suppress it, these leaders divest it of real powers. There are numerous examples of leftist leaders who ostensibly supported workers' control but crushed local participatory or workplace democracy, sometimes violently (as did Mengistu's Ethiopia and Angola under the People's Movement for the Liberation of Angola). There is no evidence of Turner pursuing this line.

A second diagnosis is socialist or class-based, and constitutes a second favoured explanation. It basically holds that, in practice, new ruling social strata emerged from or took over popular councils. Their ascent may be the result of choices (like Stalin pursuing 'socialism in one country') or of unfavourable conditions (like economic underdevelopment or neoliberalism). In the more rigidly structuralist version of this diagnosis, there is little that can be done to reassert proletarian democracy unless the structural conditions are themselves altered. In the case of more voluntaristic explanations, various institutional remedies can be sought. It seems to me that this is where Turner is. Turner wants to avoid oligarchic degeneration by ensuring rotation of leaders, requiring that representatives do not become too well off in material terms, and requiring that planning agencies be functionally decentralised (Turner 2015, 60–61, 80). Whether these prescriptions could work is unclear.

These first two explanations typically issue from the radical left, and usually prescribe injections of greater radicalism: more direct democracy or more class struggle. Left critics often see workers' councils less as governing bodies than as revolutionary organs; their historical mission is to intensify class struggle and speed up the building of socialism. A problem for such critics is that the councils commonly disappoint, frustrating the advance of the revolution in some fashion (say, due to penetration by reformists or counterrevolutionaries). The critics are then tempted to think that vanguardist supervision is necessary as remedy, which then precisely reinforces oligarchic tendencies. This libertarian-to-authoritarian oscillation is notable in Lenin.

A third diagnosis is more focused on problems inherent in conciliar institutional design and is advanced by liberal and social-democratic critics more often than by revolutionary Marxist ones. This is not surprising, since, for orthodox Marxists, institutional design is a secondary matter, something to be worked out by collective proletarian agency in the course of the revolution rather than by, say, constitutional lawyers. For them, institutions are manifestations of underlying economic or class power. Liberals, by contrast, are more likely to think that institutional designs make a difference and that certain designs (say, involving free elections or rights-supporting courts) are more conducive than others to the maintenance of democracy. Institutions have an autonomy – and a value – that cannot be reduced to their purported class essence.

This author has joined others, like Tim Wohlforth, Carmen Sirianni and Anthony Polan, in pointing to design limitations of the conciliar family of schemes that might render them less democratic, even with the best will (Wohlforth 1981; Sirianni 1983; Polan 1984). Pyramidal representation is likely to yield highly indirect representation in more centralised polities. Variation and overlap of base units (plus majority voting within them) will yield non-proportional representation. People not rooted in workplaces and other formally recognised base associations will be marginalised. Schemes will co-opt participants into local and practical matters, diverting them from larger political questions. Council schemes premised on the elision of executive and legislative authority threaten, as Polan noted, to politicise bureaucracy while technicising politics. Understood as revolutionary organs, councils limit opportunities for internal ideological debate and pluralism, and invite constant correction by vanguards. Rigidly mandated and rotating delegates are easily manipulated by permanent secretariats. Councils that serve as organs specifically of certain classes are likely to generate unresolvable disputes over class boundaries and eligibility.

It is not clear how many of these criticisms Turner is vulnerable to. Because Turner does not write much about the connecting points between local worker power and central and state power, we cannot say whether he falls foul of criticisms of pyramidalism and non-proportional representation. The absence of clarity on this is, however, a problem in itself. Turner explicitly backs universal franchise for South Africa (Turner 2015, 101), suggesting his scheme will escape disputation about class definitions and boundaries. So does his capacious definition of worker (Turner 2015, 108). There is certainly a workplace bias in Turner's scheme, and this will raise questions about the accommodation of the unemployed and self-employed. Turner does not say whether participants in his scheme will be required to stay within the tracks of an overarching socialist mission, how non-socialists will fit in, and what guidance would be supplied by intellectual and political vanguards. His amateur delegates might be outrun by seasoned bureaucrats. His scheme does seem to be more about local problem-solving than political citizenship writ large, although Turner insists that the former equips workers for the latter (Turner 2015, 81–82). Whether he will allow an autonomy to bureaucracy is not entirely clear, though he respects expertise; nor is it clear how his decentralised planning agencies will be composed, controlled or coordinated.

It is a mixed bag of answers, then, to the question of whether Turner's scheme falls into classic councilist traps. But one point, implicit in some of the above-listed generic criticisms of the council model, is worth amplifying in Turner's case. This is the absence of *politics*. We can register this at three levels. First, in the emphasis on personal and organisational transformation as a road to socialism. Both kinds of transformation are necessary to society-wide political and cultural change. But in Turner's rendering, relatively little adversarial politics seems to accompany them. Second, Turner seems somewhat in the thrall of the sort of *State and Revolution* Leninist libertarianism superbly taken apart by Polan. Essentially, with Lenin, he seems to envisage a participatory 'administration of things' from which politics has disappeared, replaced by ethics, practical problem-solving and accountable expertise. Political parties and movements are nowhere to be seen. Third, there is a bit of end-state utopianism at work in the book, one in which politics has no particular point because its point has been fulfilled. The very society that actors pursue through politics is achieved. In fairness, there's a conundrum here not only for Turner; we can hardly say that there is value in political disputation for its own sake, or that one should deliberately stop short of an ideal for fear of rendering politics redundant. But there is always the temptation, in implementing such schemes, to proclaim the death of politics while politics is still very much alive, even if hidden behind a technicist veneer.

The risk of a post-politics can itself be registered at two levels. First, there is risk associated with naïvity. I refer here partly to the naïvity of thinking apartheid could be dislodged by ethical appeals. It was not, and probably could not have been. That is now academic. More serious was, and remains, the risk of being outmanoeuvred by politicos. One thinks here of Fosatu-style workerism, which in its emphasis on organisational democracy and distrust of parties and political movements found itself, in the end, unable to compete with the African National Congress (ANC) and the South African Communist Party (SACP) on the terrain of national politics. This is not an implicit call for dirtying one's hands in politics, as though politics was a contamination; it is about the importance of acknowledging politics and playing its game, for example by developing parties and programmes.

Second, there is the obvious authoritarian potential of a post-political politics. Because in the real world there will remain irreducible differences of interest and value, these can only be denied political expression by suppression. Society is not the sort of intentional commune that Turner often seems to have at the back of his mind, one governed by love. In that sort of commune, Jane Mansbridge noted, a unitary politics was enabled by shared values and mutual trust. In societies of diverse strangers, equal representation of interests seems the more appropriate maxim (Mansbridge 1980). Shared idealism can neither be assumed nor imposed (which is not to say it should never be advocated or sought).

The issue here is not only whether a society can accommodate diverse personal ends (which are probably accommodated by Turner well enough); it is also about accommodating competing collective ends. In any realistic order, there will be rival visions of society's best overall shape. Turner does not explain how these will appear, find voice, win support, win arguments, or win power (or lose it). It is not clear that the language of utopianism is equipped to provide explanations.

TURNERISM IN POST-1994 SOUTH AFRICA

If the question is Turner's ongoing relevance, a more immediately interesting exercise might be to try to detect traces of Turner's line of democratic thinking in the South Africa that has unfolded post-apartheid. South Africa is no one's idea of utopia, realistic or otherwise. But it does define itself constitutionally as a participatory democracy (as well as a representative one). I am not in a position to track influence back to Turner personally, but he is emblematic of a way of thinking. How much Turnerism did we get, and should we wish we had more?

Two attempts were made to initiate a kind of participatory democracy on the ground prior to the abolition of apartheid. One took the form of workerism, which has been interpreted by Sian Byrne and colleagues as a species of anarcho-syndicalism (Byrne et al. 2017). It was anarchist in its aversion to parties, syndicalist in its faith that a workers' democracy could be built from the shop floor upwards under the rubric of industrial unions. The union structure was pyramidal, and shop stewards constituted its dynamic layer. The ultimate idea was to build a genuinely democratic socialism, avoiding the statist pitfalls of orthodox communism and black nationalism. It is easy to see how this line synched with Turnerism. But workerism lost out in the Congress of South African Trade Unions (Cosatu) to Communism and charterism.

If there is a trace of it today, it is in unions' still remarkably influential role, given South Africa's deindustrialisation. Unions generally preferred to retain an adversarial relationship with employers rather than institute workers' control, perhaps because South Africa retained a capitalist economy. They have also insisted on their independence from the state, even if the Cosatu–ANC alliance attenuates the autonomy of some. Unions have won significantly worker-protective legislation. Unions have been argued to represent a relatively privileged layer, though one into whose earnings a larger unemployed population taps. A hint of functional democracy is to be found in the operation of the National Economic Development and Labour Council. None of this amounts to Turnerian participatory democracy and arguably no such democracy was possible, given the absence of a socialist surround.

The other on-the-ground participatory experiment was the township 'people's power' movement of the 1980s. This was developed in a context of national uprising, and specifically in the power vacuum left in townships by a retreating apartheid state. Many types of organisations filled the vacuum, including alternative educational bodies and courts and sectoral youth and women's organisations. A classically councilist form appeared under the rubric of civic associations. This typically involved, again, a pyramidal set-up, one connecting local street and area committees to a municipality-wide civic. The people's power bodies were understood as, simultaneously, revolutionary organs and prefigurative democracies (Suttner 1986; Morobe 1987). Later, as Inkatha–ANC fighting heated up, armed self-defence units were added to the organisational plethora.

People's power was not Turnerian: it was drawn into a raw, often physical struggle for power; its operation was typically far more hostile, and even violent, than loving. The experience of it was as liable to nurture militarism and 'toxic masculinity' as democratic commitment. Arguably, three traces of it can be detected. One is a formalised state participatory democracy. This manifests in ward committees, participatory planning, community policing forums and school boards. These bodies are generally regarded as either relatively feeble or ruling party dominated. A second is a dense 'civil society' of voluntary associations variously assisting, lobbying or challenging the state, some of which have antecedents in struggle politics (though others have antecedents in a relatively well-established, apartheid-era, 'white' civil society). These associations have often been influential. A final one is ongoing 'insurgent citizenship' (Brown 2015), manifested in service delivery and other local protests (as well as in xenophobic violence).[6]

There is some of Turner in the state's 'invited spaces of participation' (Miraftab 2004), though, to draw on Sherry Arnstein, Turner would likely have complained that they were located too low on the 'ladder of participation' (Arnstein 1969). They are clearly subordinate to legislative and executive branches, and exercise, at best, influence rather than power. It is difficult to imagine quite what Turner would have said about civil society, especially its 'bourgeois' component. If anything, one finds echoes of Turner in early proposals by writers like Mark Swilling and Mzwanele Mayekiso to transform civil society into a kind of progressive associational democracy (Swilling 1992; Mayekiso 1992). The likely result of any such imbrication with state power would have been the technocratic co-option of civil bodies. Democratic civil society is necessarily a plural and open space, rather than a progressive force capable of collective government. For its part, civil insurgency seems un-Turnerian in its determinedly adversarial spirit, though it is open to Turnerians to view such insurgency as the ineluctable product of a failure to transition to socialism. For Turner, fully civil or human relations were impossible under capitalism.

So there is little real Turnerism around. Should there be?

IS THERE A ROLE FOR TURNER'S MODEL?

South Africa's Constitution requires participatory democracy, but in the context of what is basically conventional parliamentary democracy. By conventional here I mean: within the standard range of electoral systems associated with established liberal democracies. For some, like Martin Legassick, South Africa's choice of this model represents a 'counter-revolution in democratic form' (Legassick 2007, 432) compared to the people's power movement of the 1980s; instead of getting proletarian democracy we got 'bourgeois democracy'. The Turner of the early 1970s might have been disappointed too: what South Africa got represents, in his terms, a decidedly un-utopian denouement.

But this sort of discussion can be too easily muddied by the attachment of labels like bourgeois, elitist or even liberal to actually existing parliamentary democracy. What is really at stake is whether or not we want a version of representative democracy centred around five coordinates: direct representation, arithmetic-territorial constituencies, equal weighting of votes, political and ideological choice, and the flexibility/partial autonomy of representatives. A debate about the type of democracy South Africa won is really a debate about these defining features of our current system of representation.

These features can be readily defended on democratic grounds. Direct rather than pyramidal representation increases the chances of successful base to apex communication, especially where power is exercised on larger scales and where intermediate assemblies are ineffective or subject to manipulation. Arithmetic-territorial representation is the best, short of Andrew Rehfeld's scheme for randomly allocating voters to national constituencies (Rehfeld 2005), for underpinning equal-counting votes and direct elections to the centre (by contrast, organic and functional constituencies will be too numerous, overlapping and variable in membership to perform these roles). Equal weighting of votes, made possible by territorial constituencies – though arguably only when accompanied by proportional representation – realises a basic democratic value. So does political and ideological choice, in the absence of which there cannot be truly democratic (truly free or informed) popular will formation. And the freedom of representatives from strict mandates gives them the flexibility to deliberate open-mindedly with fellow representatives, address unforeseen issues, apply expertise to holding executive bodies accountable and champion unpopular causes.

So the real question must be which of these advantages Legassick (he who complained of 'counter-revolution in democratic form') would have been willing to forgo. Why should we favour indirect over direct election, organic constituencies over proportional representation, rigid mandates over public deliberation? The advantages of conventional representative democracy (to which we can add that of simplicity of form) seem, on the contrary, sufficient to establish the case for vesting ultimate legislative power in assemblies that possess them – which is what the South African Constitution does in vesting legislative authority in national, provincial and local assemblies constituted on standard parliamentary models.

Does this mean that Turner has nothing to say to the democratic present, and that the debate around his legacy should concentrate on the other features of his work, *rather* than on his democratic model?

Not necessarily. Investing primary legislative authority in standard representative democracy is not incompatible with vesting certain powers, functions and roles in bodies differently constituted, whether organised interest groups, civil-society associations or organs of industrial democracy. One can enumerate several rationales for doing this. It may be necessary to social peace or system legitimacy. It may give due regard to the special stake that some social groups have in particular areas of decision-making. It may foster political participation. It may counteract atomisation of citizens. It may offer checks and balances to simple majority rule. It may feed useful information into the decision-making process. To be sure, the vesting of formal roles in these groups risks their co-option, or the empowerment of organisational barons, even the undermining of parliament. But so long as parliament's role is defended, and the space for a more fully autonomous civil society is preserved, some amount of formalised associational democracy might well do more democratic good than harm.

Indeed, much hinges on whether such schemes are understood to be *part* of liberal representative democracy or an *alternative* to it. The latter framing is untenable. No attempt to replace liberal democracy with something more democratic has ever succeeded in enlarging democracy. Even amongst council-democracy supporters there is a long subtradition, going back to Karl Kautsky (1964) and the Austro-Marxists (Renner 1978), of favouring some combination of soviets and parliaments. Tripartite-corporatist social democracy took up this mantle; so, in a different way, did left-Eurocommunism. There are hints that Turner places himself within this 'parliament plus councils' subtradition, but it is never clear; there are equally hints that he envisages his model superseding parliamentary democracy. There was certainly little by way of the latter in the 'actual socialist' models that Turner considered sympathetically in *The Eye of the Needle*.

Which raises the next question of how resonantly Turner speaks to this moment in South African and world affairs. The liberal-democratic model triumphant in the early 1990s is everywhere being challenged by populist forces. These invoke the people in their struggle against liberal democracy's established political, economic, professional, legal and cultural elites. They champion the right of silenced majorities to rule, and in the name of the majority they claim decisive authority, pushing aside checks and balances. Some among them praise or employ methods of direct democracy (internet voting and referendums, in particular). As we know, this sort of challenge is primarily issuing from the populist right, not from the 'participatory-democratic' left. But comparable populist challenges from the left may be equally problematic for democracy (think Hugo Chavez, Rafael Correa, Daniel Ortega). Anyone who cares about democracy should defend liberal democracy against *all* these kinds of authoritarian and illiberal challengers.

But having said that, no form of government has an unconditional right to survive. The populist wave is exposing real problems in liberal democracy. These will need to be addressed in some way.

Liberalism's key perceived democratic deficit is its elitism: the role it accords to elected representatives, lawyers, judges, technocrats, corporate executives and even avant garde artists (Mounk 2018). To hear it from the right, the problem is not that these elites are elite, but that they are out of touch. They impose their cosmopolitan preferences on ordinary people, riding roughshod over rooted loyalties and 'common sense'.

From the prospect of these ordinary people exercising the fullest measure of their power, liberal elitists recoil in turn. Who wants Hillary Clinton's 'deplorables' in charge? Even many left elites have come to think of them – the working class – as somewhat deplorable and prefer now the company of educated urbanites.

Turner's work implicitly offered three paths out of the unhappy spectacle of democrats defending democracy from the demos. One was the ethical transformation of the people themselves. Turner, too, did not want 'deplorables' in charge; he wanted to vest power in a population that had imbibed a humanist ethic. A second was institutional: his demos would not gather to hear demagogues at rallies; they would be too hard at work in everyday governing. The second path could join the first: governing could be both practical and morally transformative.[7] But then again, that problem-solving practical people sounds vaguely post-political. You might not want people in thrall to demagogues, but do you want them disengaged from ideological debate?

But if not these paths, then others must be found. Liberal-democratic governments rammed through two epochal projects with little consultation, guided by technocrats and bankers: globalisation and European integration. These forces advanced inexorably, even under left-leaning governments, depriving voters of choice. And they produced a reaction in populism. A democracy that hopes to survive populism is going to have to find ways to sort the legitimate grievances from the parochial prejudices that power populism, and to give greater heed to the former. Liberal and left elites that want to sustain their cultural authority are going to have to re-learn to argue their cases rather than 'cancel' their opponents. Elite condescension will have to be avoided. To that extent, liberal democracy has to make itself more popular, the better to save itself from the populists. Its challenge is to deepen participation while maintaining its liberalism.

It is worth considering that the rise of populism in much of the West was accompanied by a decline in the labour movement. That movement enjoyed a long success in tying working-class assertion to middle-class liberalism. It deepened participation, while remaining faithful to parliamentary democracy. It is not clear what formula might enable the simultaneous democratisation of liberalism and liberalisation of democracy, but it might make sense to consider Turner's economic democracy as a possible third path out of danger, this time as adjunct to liberal democracy. Economic democracy has a possibly unique potential to counteract social atomisation, sustain decent living standards and give people a material stake in democracy more widely.[8] Its prospects are dimmed, in South Africa, by mass non-participation in formal employment. Can an economy be recreated that sustains a labour movement and, beyond it, economic or workplace democracy (or indeed a wider associational democracy) as a component of a larger liberal-democratic order? That is another debate, and one on which the contemporary relevance of Turner as democratic model-builder hinges.

NOTES

1   Turner is considered part of the 'Durban Moment', a period of radical ferment in the early 1970s centred on the University of Natal and emerging worker organisations. The term is attributed to Tony Morphet (1990).

2   Arguably, Turner himself faced 'illiberal democracy' in the form of a whites-only parliamentary government. But he was already looking beyond apartheid to alternative possible post-apartheid futures (Turner 2015, 2, 43, 119). If, in the 1970s, liberals and socialists competed over the future, today liberals and populists compete for it.

3   Or Fosatu (1979–1985). Turner influenced workerism through his central roles in the Institute for Industrial Education and the *South African Labour Bulletin*. Fosatu and its precursor formations emphasised shop-floor worker democracy rather than cross-class political struggle. Fosatu was formed post Turner's murder, and its Turnerian lineage is not uncontested. Whereas Edward Webster sees Fosatu as inheriting Turner's mantle (Webster 1993), Billy Keniston insists that it marked a turn towards centralised forms of organisation that Turner would have rejected (Keniston 2017).

4   Peter Hudson notes Turner's fascination with Maoism's exaltation of revolutionary subjectivity (Hudson 2017, 1–3). Turner was drawn, too, to Yugoslav self-management and Tanzanian Ujamaa (Turner 2015, 53–57).

5   To my knowledge, none of Turner's interpreters has scrutinised his participatory model. Ralph Lawrence briefly considers justifications for participatory democracy (Lawrence 1990, 102–105). Tony Fluxman and Peter Vale offer generic reflections on the strengths and challenges of worker-based participatory democracy (Fluxman and Vale 2004, 180–182). Scott Parker reflects on the history but not plausibility of participatory-democratic thought (Parker 2017). Lawrence is inconclusive

about participatory democracy's virtues; the others mostly admire it and lament the forces – communist authoritarianism and capitalist modernisation for Fluxman and Vale, neoliberalism for Parker – that precluded participatory democracy in post-apartheid South Africa. Webster's reflection on workers' self-management in Yugoslavia (Webster 1990), which briefly references Turner, notes a range of forces that impeded the Yugoslav experiment, including inequality, unemployment and inflation associated with market socialism.

6   For an illuminating recent exploration of how these three types of participation manifest and interact in South Africa's ubiquitous shack settlements, see Trevor Ngwane (2021).

7   And in this sense could combine Crawford B Macpherson's developmental and participatory democracy (Macpherson 2012). See Turner (2015, 52, 81, 111).

8   Turner himself hints at this integrative (and populism-countering) role (Turner 2015, 105–108).

REFERENCES

Arnstein, Sherry. 1969. 'A Ladder of Citizen Participation'. *Journal of the American Institute of Planners* 35 (4): 216–224.

Bahro, Rudolf. 1978. *The Alternative in Eastern Europe*. London: New Left Books.

Brown, Julian. 2015. *South Africa's Insurgent Citizens: On Dissent and the Possibility of Politics*. Johannesburg: Jacana.

Byrne, Sian, Nicole Ulrich and Lucien van der Walt. 2017. 'Red, Black and Gold: Fosatu, South African "Workerism", "Syndicalism" and the Nation'. In *The Unresolved National Question in South Africa*, edited by Edward Webster and Karen Pampallis, 254–273. Johannesburg: Wits University Press.

Fluxman, Tony and Peter Vale. 2004. 'Re-reading Rick Turner in the New South Africa'. *International Relations* 18 (2): 173–189.

Hudson, Peter. 2017. 'Let's Talk about Rick Turner'. *Theoria* 64 (151): 1–9.

Kautsky, Karl. 1964. *The Dictatorship of the Proletariat*. Ann Arbor, MI: University of Michigan Press.

Keniston, Billy. 2017. 'The Weight of Absence: Rick Turner and the End of the Durban Moment'. *Theoria* 64 (151): 20–28.

Lawrence, Ralph. 1990. 'Shaping Democracy in a Future South Africa'. *Theoria* 76: 101–114.

Legassick, Martin. 2007. *Towards Socialist Democracy*. Pietermaritzburg: University of KwaZulu-Natal Press.

Macpherson, Crawford Brough. 2012. *The Life and Times of Liberal Democracy*. Ontario: Oxford University Press.

Mansbridge, Jane. 1980. *Beyond Adversary Democracy*. Chicago, IL: University of Chicago Press.

Mayekiso, Mzwanele. 1992. 'Working Class Civil Society: Why We Need It, and How to Get It'. *African Communist* (second quarter): 33–42.

Miraftab, Faranak. 2004. 'Invited and Invented Spaces of Participation: Neoliberal Citizenship and Feminists' Expanded Notion of Politics'. *Wagadu* 1: 1–7.

Morobe, Murphy. 1987. 'Towards a People's Democracy: The UDF View'. *Review of African Political Economy* 40: 81–87.

Morphet, Tony. 1990. '"Brushing History Against the Grain": Oppositional Discourse in South Africa'. *Theoria* 76 (2): 89–99.

Mounk, Yascha. 2018. *The People vs. Democracy: Why Our Freedom is in Danger and How to Save It*. Cambridge, MA: Harvard University Press.

Ngwane, Trevor. 2021. *Amakomiti: Grassroots Democracy in South African Shack Settlements*. London: Pluto Press.

Nove, Alec. 1983. *The Economics of Feasible Socialism*. London: Routledge.

Parker, Scott David. 2017. 'The Truth is Revolutionary: Mills and Turner as Theoreticians of Participatory Democracy'. *South African Historical Journal* 69 (2): 288–303.

Polan, Anthony J. 1984. *Lenin and the End of Politics*. London: Methuen.

Rawls, John. 1999. *A Theory of Justice*, revised edition. Oxford: Oxford University Press.

Rehfeld, Andrew. 2005. *The Concept of Constituency: Political Representation, Democratic Legitimacy, and Institutional Design*. Cambridge: Cambridge University Press.

Renner, Karl. 1978. 'Democracy and the Council System'. In *Austro-Marxism*, edited by Tom Bottomore and Patrick Goode, 187–201. Oxford: Clarendon Press.

Sirianni, Carmen. 1983. 'Councils and Parliaments: The Problems of Dual Power in Comparative Perspective'. *Politics and Society* 12 (1): 83–123.

Suttner, Raymond. 1986. 'Popular Justice in South Africa Today'. Unpublished paper presented to the Sociology Department, University of the Witwatersrand.

Swilling, Mark. 1992. 'Socialism, Democracy and Civil Society: The Case for Associational Socialism'. *Theoria* 79: 75–82.

Turner, Richard. 2015. *The Eye of the Needle: Towards Participatory Democracy in South Africa*, revised edition. Kolkata: Seagull Books.

Webster, Edward. 1990. 'Self-management in Yugoslavia: A Failed Experiment in Democratic Socialism?'. *South African Labour Bulletin* 15 (1): 60–71.

Webster, Edward. 1993. 'Moral Decay and Social Reconstruction: Richard Turner and Radical Reform'. *Theoria* 81/82: 1–13.

Wohlforth, Tim. 1981. 'Transition to the Transition'. *New Left Review* 130: 67–81.

Wright, Erik Olin. 2010. *Envisioning Real Utopias*. London: Verso Books.

PART III

TURNER AND TEACHING PHILOSOPHY

7

Rick Turner and Teaching Critical Theory

Laurence Piper

The rise of neoliberalism since the 1980s has impacted higher education globally, resulting in its becoming more 'market-friendly' in a variety of ways. These include new forms of university governance, greater requirements to raise money from industry, rankings tables and competitive marketing strategies, and framing students as consumers. In this context, the nature of knowledge researched and taught is increasingly under pressure to be directly relevant to the workplace. As part of this, the traditional academic emphasis on 'episteme', or abstract knowledge, is becoming rivalled by growing forms of 'techne', or applied knowledge (Parry 2014). One manifestation of this shift is the growth of practice-based learning or work-based learning in higher education and the spread of this pedagogic approach to traditional academic disciplines such as Political Studies.

For many scholars of practice-based learning, the epistemological contrast at stake in this pedagogic approach is the divide between abstract or theoretical knowledge and applied knowledge, more specifically the contrast between teaching the general principles of practice on the one hand

and enacting or implementing these capabilities in actual workplace situations on the other (Billett 2013, 104). While these arguments are made with professional or occupational disciplines such as medicine, law or teaching in mind, this conception has now spread to include 'all programs that develop the capacities required for specific occupations' (Billett 2013, 101). In recent times these programmes have spread to academic disciplines that are not directly or obviously practice based, for example, a programme I teach in Sweden, a master's in work-integrated learning (WIL), with a focus on Political Studies.

Now while traditionally academic disciplines like Political Studies and International Relations have a variety of vocational applications in government, party politics, the media, non-governmental and research organisations, they are generally orientated towards developing academic rather than occupational capacities. As reflected in the wide variety of professions that graduates take up, traditional academic disciplines develop forms of knowledge production that are not just abstract, but also normative. That is, in addition to reflecting on the principles of different electoral systems, for example, scholars of comparative politics will also be exposed to criticisms of the mainstream model of democracy as being about representative government through elections. It is the capacity to think, in terms of not only broader principles but also the basic political categories themselves, that is central to the academic undertaking. For lack of a better term, I call this kind of thinking 'normative' although it extends beyond reflection on values to include questions of ontology, epistemology and metaphysics generally.

This critical dimension of academic knowledge in the humanities and social sciences is informed by a recognition of both the contingent and the normative nature of social relations in a particular place and time in human history. It is my view that it is this normativity, central to academic projects in the social sciences and humanities but less central to the vocational disciplines (which are sometimes presented as value-free), that forms a stronger point of contrast between the academic and vocational disciplines than the difference between general principles of occupational knowledge and particular occupational practices. This point takes on even greater significance if one considers the consequences of neoliberalism's depoliticising tendencies for contemporary political subjectivity (Brown 2015), a tendency that instrumentalises education and centres employability in the consciousness of the student body – and helps motivate the move from academic to workplace learning.

In what follows I will show how Turner provides resources both to fill out this conception of critical thinking and to model some ways of how to teach critical thinking, even though his theory leaves little space for teaching. Perhaps appropriately, his model for teaching critical thinking comes more from his practice as a public intellectual of a particular kind, the 'intellectual activist', than from his academic writings. Indeed, in his intellectual-activist work Turner models exactly the relationship between theoretical knowledge, framed as 'the theoretical attitude', and practical knowledge, learnt through doing, that WIL programmes could achieve. The implication is that WIL does not have to be market orientated only; it can also train students to become better democratic citizens, sustainability warriors or even revolutionary subjects.

WHAT IS CRITICAL THINKING? TURNER AND THE 'THEORETICAL ATTITUDE'

The notion that a university education, and in particular a liberal arts education, should teach students to 'think critically' is widely articulated. But what does it mean to think critically? This is an ancient and complex question that stretches back to at least Socrates, who famously argued that critical thinking was important to develop both because people in authority could be wrong in their judgements and because good judgements through reason were crucial to identifying the truth, including the truth about the good life (Wang et al. 2008). Turner's argument about critical thinking, including what he terms developing 'a theoretical attitude', is located in a very different context from that of Socrates, but it shares a scepticism towards authority and the belief that freedom is linked to rational individual choice informed by the truth. I unpack each of these three points in more detail in what follows.

Turner's scepticism towards authority is concerned with the judgements of people in positions of authority but broadens the problem to systems of oppression and exploitation and, especially, the values and ideas that support these systems. Hence Turner famously begins *The Eye of the Needle* with a critique of what he terms 'common-sense' thinking, which he describes as the product of socialisation into the values and ideas of the dominant system. In the context of South Africa in 1972, these common-sense ideas reflected the values, assumptions and judgements of systems of white supremacy, patriarchy and industrial capitalism. Furthermore, these common-sense ideas often obscure reality, are factually inaccurate and, importantly, constrain the imagination of what is possible by falsely naturalising social choices or contingent relationships, or misinterpreting cause and effect. Perhaps most significantly, common-sense thinking often conceals various forms of domination – and Turner gives everyday gender, race and class examples from South Africa in the 1970s to illustrate this claim.

Consequently, to escape domination we must be able to escape the socialisation processes of an oppressive society. In *The Eye of the Needle*, Turner identifies two ways in which this is made possible in a country like 1970s South Africa. The first is by developing the capacity to reflect on what is essential to any society either through nature or the requirements of collective living and to *contrast* this with the contingent way that an actual society works. This is clearly a process of *reasoning* and, as Turner points out, must be learnt. Thus, he says (2015, 7):

> To understand a society…we cannot just describe it. We need also to theorise about it. We need continually to refer back and forth between what we see in society and what is essential to any

society... Theory itself is not difficult. What is often difficult is to shift oneself into a theoretical attitude, that is, to realise what things in one's experience cannot be taken for granted... The present nearly always seems to be at least fairly permanent. In order to theorise about society, perhaps the first step (psychologically) we have to take is to grasp the present as history.

Effectively, Turner is suggesting that the hard part of change is recognising the contingency of our social existence, the inevitability and indeed the necessity of change. Importantly, and this brings us to the third point, the contingency of social relationships means that we can collectively choose a good society – we can choose a society that reflects our values. Hence, he argues, we need to think not in a common-sense way, but in a 'utopian' way that asks two questions: first, why does society work the way it does and second, is there a moral justification for this? (Turner 2015, 6). Thus, the theoretical attitude opens the possibility for rational reflection that includes both causal analysis and moral evaluation (Friedman 2017). This, for Turner, is theory. This, I would add, is also critical thinking.

But how do we learn to theorise or think critically? Furthermore, how do we achieve the first crucial step in this process – 'the theoretical attitude' – when we live relations of domination through which we are socialised into the values and ideas of the powerful? Turner's answer in *The Eye of the Needle* is that socialisation is never complete or perfect, for three reasons. First, socialisation is always partial, as everyone's upbringing is unique 'and in this uniqueness lies the possibility that the socialisation process may fail' (Turner 2015, 111). Turner does not develop this point further, and his subsequent arguments rely more on the following points. Second, the internal contradictions of society create cognitive dissonance that may provoke reflection in individuals. He gives examples of workers whose experiences on the shop floor create resistance to the wishes of the powerful, thus prompting the workers to challenge the ideas and values of the powerful too. Third, he notes the growth of oppositional practices and cultures, such as union organising, that often emerge in response to the contradictions. He states:

> There is an intimate relationship between change in conscious-
> ness and organisation. Consciousness develops along with organ-
> isation. To be effective, organisation must be related to the way
> that people see the world and must help them see the world
> in a new way. There are three essential elements in this new way
> of seeing the world. I must come to see the world as able to be
> changed. I must come to see myself as having the capacity to play
> a part in changing it. I must see that my capacity to do this can be
> realised only in co-operation with other people. (Turner 2015, 6)

Turner then gives examples of 'countercultures' in South Africa that can help people to challenge the common-sense thinking of domination: the enduring culture of tribal society and the emergence of Black Consciousness thought. More famously though, in *The Eye of the Needle*, Turner cites religion as a potential source of the 'theoretical attitude', as it is based on a set of values that run counter to the values of white supremacy and capitalism in South Africa or, for that matter, any system of domination. Hence, he argues that all religions hold the promise of a larger, transcendent morality:

> The essence of religions lies in the concepts of transcendence,
> that is, in the idea of something (whether it be a 'reality' or an 'ideal')
> which goes beyond the present, which goes beyond what people
> are doing in the world at this moment and in the light of which
> the present is only of secondary importance. Religion challenges
> the common-sense tendency to be committed to the present, to
> see the world as we experience it now as the only possible form of
> reality. (Turner 2015, 23)

Religion does this through a transcendent reality (God) and a transcendent ethic that 'demands that we question taken for granted ways of

behaving and continue to question them'. Religion then teaches the theoretical attitude: 'No great religious leader has said: "Change your beliefs, but continue to act in the way in which you have always acted". Each leader has attacked both old social forms and religious forms. They have attacked religious forms that have precisely lost their transcendence and become merely repetitive rituals. They have attacked social forms that have become both unquestioned, hence mechanical and unhuman and unjust, hence de-humanising' (Turner 2015, 23).

In sum then, the theoretical attitude can develop from individuals reflecting on hardship and the contradictions between their lives and the dominant discourses of authority, but tends mostly to develop within organisations and thus, I would suggest, by implication it is usually taught or learnt from the example of others. In essence, socialisation into common-sense thinking by the institutions of the powerful must be challenged by socialisation within organisations formed to resist it. Socialisation, Turner says, is thus both the source and the solution to false knowledge about the world. However, socialisation is but a process of education – of teaching and learning – and thus requires teachers.

HOW TO TEACH CRITICAL THINKING: *THE EYE OF THE NEEDLE*

Turner's account of education in *The Eye of the Needle* involves both a critique of the apartheid-era education system and an account of learning at school and at work in a socialist participatory democracy. While the critique of the actually existing education system is consistent with his general critique of common-sense thinking, his description of future learning does not deal explicitly with how to teach critical thinking in general or the theoretical attitude in particular. Indeed, there is an interesting bipolarity in Turner's account of learning as a child versus his account of learning as an adult in the workplace, which points to his existentialist and his Marxist inspirations respectively. Where the former presents learning as a student-driven process without a fixed curriculum and facilitated rather than taught, the latter presents learning as participation in collective decision-making processes where the public good is primary. Where in the former it is hard to see how the child will necessarily come to the practice of critical reflection, in the latter there seems little space for divergence from the collective norm. Neither learning environment seems particularly amenable to developing critical reflection and neither account has a clearly developed notion of teaching.

The Critique of Traditional Education

Turner's account of traditional school education was heavily influenced by Kurt Danziger, Paulo Freire and Ivan Illich, with whom he shared the view that it was largely oppressive (Lichtenstein 2016). Turner describes the Western education framework as about (i) imparting facts, (ii) in the right sequence, (iii) through special institutions, (iv) with an associated disciplinary structure (Turner 2015, 88). However, for Turner, the whole framework is wrong. There is no body of facts that must be learnt in a particular order. Rather, 'what has to be learned is a particular way of thinking, the ability to analyse, to think critically and to think creatively' (Turner 2015, 88). He goes on to add that if there is a body of facts, children do not need to learn these facts at school, as adults know that they have forgotten most of the facts that they learnt at school. Furthermore, while children do need to learn how to read and write, this is often done badly at school. He adds, 'those who learn to love reading do so at home not at school' (Turner 2015, 89).

Effectively then, traditional schooling is underwritten by the wrong assumptions, including that there is a world of facts ready to be given to one 'rather than discovered'. The world is full of authority figures who are inefficient and can usually be circumvented. Furthermore, it is assumed that children are educated when they leave school, and that studying is not part of life. Turner argues that the real role of traditional schooling is a custodial one: 'to look after the children while their parents are at work' (Turner 2015, 91). In addition, traditional school socialises for 'a hierarchical society of little pleasure and much pain'.

Implicit in much of what Turner is saying is the hidden school curriculum of social conformity and control in order to produce workers for industrial work. In this model, teachers become prison guards as much as they are educators.

Learning as a Child under Socialism

In looking forward to a better form of education for children, Turner follows Danziger's argument that most learning happens through observation and imitation rather than explicit teaching (Turner 2015, 93). He frames this as 'role-playing': students try out many different roles or aspects of roles – 'role as a male, role as a bicycle-rider, role as a symbolic reasoner'. Turner sees this adoption of multiple roles as central to moral development because the self must take over the roles and therefore learn to adopt the perspectives of others. Importantly, he also links this to the adoption of multiple points of view, which enhances the capacity to think hypothetically – and which, I concede, is at least part of the theoretical attitude. Concluding that seeing things from multiple points of view is connected to the development of both self-discipline and intelligence, Turner argues that education needs to be driven by role-taking and internal motivation rather than by external punishment or reward. 'Children naturally wish to expand the number of roles that they can play and are strongly influenced in the roles they want to play by the adults around them, if the right relationship exists between them and those students' (Turner 2015, 95).

Turner argues that a school system informed by these notions of role-playing and moral development would be based on the principles that children must go to 'school' voluntarily and that 'teachers' would become more like advisors or mentors who help in a common search for truth, rather than experts dispensing the truth. Furthermore, learning could happen in many different contexts, including offices and factories. Thus, Turner (2015, 96) writes, 'in a worker-controlled democracy, children could be gradually integrated into the work process in a non-exploitative way at a much earlier age than they are now.' And the combination of work and education could continue long past 'school-leaving age'. In a sense, even schools would disappear. Hence, 'schools' should first become more like community centres where children can play, learn and work. Second, there should be facilities and learning tools such as 'books, telescopes, laboratories and animals' available for use. Third, there should be 'teachers', better described as 'people available for consultation'. Turner argues that there is no need for external disci-pline to force children to learn; they do this by observation and imita-tion and if they set their own learning agenda their interest in the topic and eagerness to learn will help overcome obstacles. He comments: 'And the idea that people shy away from hard work is a myth. People shy away from meaningless work. But hard, directed, motivated work, even if it includes elements that in themselves are dull and uninteresting, is one of the most satisfying and pleasurable of all human activities' (Turner 2015, 97).

My concern with Turner's account of a child-centred approach to education under socialism is that it remains unclear how critical skills will be learnt by the child if it is the child driving the learning agenda and pace. What exactly is the mechanism that will force the child to ques-tion 'common-sense' knowledge, to see the 'present as history' and to ask the questions, 'Why does society work the way it does and is there a moral justification for this'? Furthermore, presuming that a socialist order has fewer contradictions than a capitalist one and less reason for countervailing organisations, what will spur on the child to ask hard questions about the social order? It seems reasonable that some chil-dren supported by some adults will develop critical skills but how can we ensure that enough people or even everyone achieves this? And do we not need this to ensure that participatory democracy works? If socialisa-tion is so important at maintaining the oppressive apartheid social order, should it not also be used to maintain the socialist participatory democ-racy? Ultimately Turner's account of how children learn under social-ism seems naïve on several levels, but for my interests in this chapter, it is very vague about how to ensure that children collectively develop a theoretical attitude and learn how to theorise about social relations. The model also seems highly individualistic with no clear relation to the common good.

Learning as an Adult under Socialism

Turner's discussion of learning as an adult revolves around worker participation in running the factory, farm or enterprise – a notion that Ralph Lawrence (1990) notes was influenced by Carol Pateman's *Participation and Democratic Theory*. Thus, a central tenet of Turner's socialism is that working life proceeds in a participatory democratic way. To address the tension between the basic principle of equality of all workers in making decisions about the enterprise and the fact that some workers will have specialist knowledge, Turner outlines a combination of participatory and representative processes. In this model, key decisions around working conditions and production strategy would be decided by collective meetings of all, whereas the more day-to-day business of implementing the larger strategy would be managed by elected worker councils. To prevent an oligarchy, individuals would occupy these positions for a limited term (Turner 2015, 49). This requirement for the active participation of workers in the enterprise requires a process of education – largely by observation and imitation – but essentially, workers would learn how to run an enterprise by doing it. As Turner states, 'The enterprise is not designed only to produce goods as cheaply as possible. The enterprise is also part of the life of each worker and one of its products is educated and autonomous individuals' (Turner 2015, 62).

Critically, Turner notes that worker control of the enterprise is a necessary but not sufficient condition for freedom, as the activity of the enterprise needs to be coordinated with other enterprises through planning mechanisms. He argues that 'a free society is one in which I cooperate with others in deciding how to maximise our freedoms. Individual freedom means other areas must conform to a plan – a plan is required to protect the rights of individuals from infringement by others' (Turner 2015, 71). How exactly this will happen, Turner does not say, other than to dedicate a significant amount of space to developing some key ideas affirming that 'planning does not require that all decisions be bureaucratically made by a central authority' (Turner 2015, 78). Key here are ideas such as keeping the wage gap low and ensuring that all officials use the same services as the people. Turner concludes by arguing that worker participation 'equips individuals with the psychological confidence to take part in decision-making; and it helps them get good information to make decisions' (Turner 2015, 81). He finishes by citing Julius Nyerere, the former prime minister of Tanzania, as an example of someone who replaced the traditional white model of education with forms of participatory democracy in farm schools (Turner 2015, 99). In this model, teaching is meant to be based on the technical aspects of agriculture but also on the social and financial problems that arise from the communal running of the school. The students should make as many decisions as possible. He concludes that 'it is an education in which "academic skills" are integrated with meaningful work and responsible participation in community self-government' (Turner 2015, 99).

This description of adult learning in the workplace shares the spirit of 'learning through doing' that Turner hopes for in the learning process for children under socialism. However, while it seems clear how workers will learn 'techne', how will they learn 'episteme'? As with childhood learning there seems no clear space or opportunity for workers to learn to question common-sense knowledge or engage in utopian thinking. Yes, workers will be able to debate the goals and operations of the enterprise, but will they be able to question the grand economic plan or the values of the socialist productive system? And if so, where and when would this occur and how would it articulate with a decision-making process orientated towards the collective interests of the enterprise and the economy? Notably, where learning as a child seems orientated towards the pace and choices of the individual child, learning as an adult seems orientated towards the collective goals of the enterprise or the economy. In neither scenario is there an obvious opportunity to learn how to develop the theoretical attitude, or how to conduct theoretical analysis. Most obviously of all, in neither scenario is there a dedicated teacher of theory.

These two learning processes in Turner's socialist utopia function as opposites on a spectrum between child and adult, individual and collective, personal choice and collective imperatives. They also seem to manifest the base values of existentialism and structural Marxism respectively. But perhaps even more interesting is that in Turner's account of participatory democracy there is no account of the university or any post-school institution. His imaginary seems to run from 'school' newly conceived, to the enterprise working towards the grand plan with other enterprises; nothing is said of the state machinery, who gets to work in it and how it will run. In this space, the university is lost, along with the state. This is obviously deeply paradoxical, given that Turner was a much-loved academic who clearly revelled in his profession. It is hard to imagine how a genuine intellectual would give up the world of ideas – and of course the university is far from the only space where ideas matter, but it is an important one. This silence is a little baffling. Perhaps I judge Turner too harshly as he was assassinated before he had time to write more and to think through his ideas and proposals in a more systematic way. Indeed, there is an inkling of how Turner imagined the learning of theory could proceed and that it would involve some kind of teaching and special institutionalisation – but it comes from his practice as a public intellectual rather than his publications as an academic. It is to this that we now turn.

How to Learn Critical Thinking: Turner as Intellectual Activist

In many ways Turner's arguments about critical thinking amount to a version of critical theory like the tradition of the Frankfurt school: the notion that power relations in institutions and ideas dominate us and that ideology critique is central to the process of liberation (Geuss 1981). Crucially for Turner, the process of ideology critique is best coupled with both personal reflection and collective action to bring about social change that is identified through a process of deep personal and collective reflection. This is a journey that is hard for the individual to take alone, and impossible to take apolitically. Hence, in his practice as an intellectual activist, Turner modelled the role of the teacher as a kind of facilitator alongside the student on the collective journey towards political enlightenment and personal liberation. In many ways it is a form of teaching closest to the model of religious learning.

In making this case, one can start by noting that a significant contribution to Turner's stellar reputation was his involvement in politics off-campus as much as his teaching and research on-campus (Lichtenstein 2016, 453):

> By his own count, between 1970 and 1973 he gave at least forty-eight speeches and lectures outside the confines of the university lecture hall and probably many more informally. During those three years, Turner had spoken at dozens of student meetings and addressed numerous local organisations – church groups, women's groups, white liberals – on a wide range of topics, including 'radical thought, socialism, communism and the philosophies of Sartre, Mao Tse Tung and Marcuse,' according to the information collected (probably from the secret police) by the Schlebusch Commission (Republic of South Africa 1974, 93).

Of particular significance for my purposes was the integration of theory and practice represented in this off-campus work. Signs of this were evident from quite early on in his academic career, for example when he initiated a programme of 'action research', where students had to research the working life of African workers in Durban (Macqueen 2014). Much more significant, though, was his involvement with a number of like-minded academics in setting up the Institute for Industrial Education (IIE) and the establishment of the journal, the *South African Labour Bulletin*. As Eddie Webster (1993, 6) and Ian Macqueen (2014, 517) note, 'central figures in the new institute were drawn from beyond the white academy and included: Harriet Bolton, Lawrence Schlemmer, John Copelyn, Alec Erwin, Foszia Fisher, Beksise Nxasana, Omar Badsha, Halton Cheadle and David Hemson, with Chief Buthelezi acting as Chancellor'.

At the heart of these initiatives was the idea of educating the black working class in support of the re-emerging trade union movement. As Webster (1993, 6) notes, in the work of the IIE there was a tension between ideas and action that was repeated in the workerist/charterist debates in the 1980s. Some wanted to focus on training union leadership and others the working rank and file. Webster notes that by the end of 1975, training the leadership had become the major priority. Thus, the general approach was a politics of radical reform in society, although not necessarily radical strategies to achieve this. Turner's politics was more about a battle of ideas linked to organisation, than about organisation linked to violent confrontation. He reflected his belief in the possibility of radical freedom through the development of a theoretical attitude and the practice of theory, but then also through changing behaviour personally and organisationally to prefigure the democratic socialist future in the present (Keniston 2014). As Anthony Egan (2017) notes, this morally informed prefigurative approach anticipates some key positions in liberation theology. Notably, too, this model of social change places teaching at the centre of the process of developing the theoretical attitude necessary for the achievement of individual freedom through conscious choice.

In this way, we can see Turner as a particular kind of public intellectual – a thinker committed to integrating ideas and action to bring about a socialist participatory democracy. In many ways he is modelling what could be termed a 'critical' version of WIL, closer to the tradition of critical theory. It is the centrality of critical reflection imagined in both instrumental and normative terms, along with the integration of theory and practice, that produces self-conscious and free citizens who enact and organise peaceful, revolutionary change. Of course, as noted above, how one integrates theory and practice is not obvious, nor is how one would manage enduring tensions between the two. Nevertheless, the larger point is the value of linking theory to practise in order to generate praxis.

In this way Turner is modelling a left version of the WIL practised at universities today – one that integrated theory and practice so as to create a revolutionary proletariat 'for itself' rather than just 'in itself'.

Notably, central to the learning process and especially developing the theoretical attitude, is a process of dialogue rather than lecturing – what Duncan Greaves (1987, 33) terms 'redemptive discourse': a process of Socratic dialogue that aims to draw out what is already within. Turner was famously brilliant in one-on-one and small-group conversations (Hemson 1996; De Kadt 2017) – but the point is not so much about his style as it is about the idea that learning happens dialogically rather than didactically. Furthermore, this dialogue is one that disrupts through rational reflection on the common-sense values and ideas of systems of domination. It is fact and reason that must ground arguments to understand the world, and the point of understanding the world is to change it to a better, utopian alternative based on shared human values of freedom and love (Piper 2010). For Turner, the meaning of praxis that emerges from the critical reflection on practice requires personal and collective choice to behave differently in the present, and affirming the value of prefigurative practice both individually and organisationally (Hudson 2017). Indeed, organisation was seen as central to producing the consciousness of free individuals (Nash 1982). In the words of Turner's colleague and collaborator, Eddie Webster (cited in Lambert 2010, 33):

> There was a profound feeling of personal liberation being able to explore all these ideas and connect with them in a very action oriented way and I think this is what was so central to Rick's philosophical position. The necessity of utopian thinking applied to all aspects of life. You could actually think about how the world could be different – not just the world, but how personal relationships could be different; how bringing up children could be different; how schools could be different. This utopian thinking was radical at a level of ideas and practice, but not in the way that the Security Police thought of it [that is, not violent insurrection].

To my mind, it is Turner's model of intellectual activism, rather than his academic writings, that is the real locus of his vision for education for liberation. It is through the collective practice of teaching as dialogue to create a theoretical attitude that critical reflection on theory becomes possible, filling out the meaning of 'episteme' and its contrast with the 'techne' practice of daily working life on the shop floor. Through organising this process of reflection, that is, teaching, organisations can facilitate the transformation of the 'instrumental attitude' towards learning as a way of getting ahead in the system, into a theoretical practice that critiques the status quo and imagines a better system. The theoretical attitude enables a particular kind of action-orientated reflection or praxis.

Lastly, if it is in Turner's practice as an intellectual activist that we find the best model for teaching critical thinking in a radical tradition, can this be institutionalised? Clearly, Turner and his colleagues tried to institutionalise it in the IIE programme, but as others have argued, this project was soon overtaken and abandoned by a different political agenda in the trade union movement, much less concerned with changing consciousness and developing worker capacity for individual choice and collective action, and more concerned with a confrontational politics to secure political power (Fluxman and Vale 2004; Keniston 2017; Macqueen 2017). My sense is that it is possible to institutionalise Turner's model of teaching critical thinking in organisations, but that it requires intellectual activists to design and lead processes of learning. In short, it needs a kind of teaching closer to the religious tradition.

CONCLUSION

There is something poetic in the fact that Turner has taught us more about critical thinking through his role as an intellectual activist than in his academic writings. His practice was a brilliant example of a radical form of WIL orientated not so much towards making students employable, but making workers into self-conscious revolutionaries or perhaps democratic citizens of a participatory socialist republic. Notably, this is a practice that requires a particular kind of teacher, to at least design a process of learning that cultivates the critical thinking or 'episteme'. Central to this practice of critical thinking is the development of the theoretical attitude. This means becoming open to the inaccuracy of common-sense thinking and the contingency of existing social relations through conceiving of 'the present as history' in order to do 'theoretical analysis' that rationally separates out the necessary from the contingent and imagines future possibilities based on common human values that transcend the current. This, in Turner's account, is the real meaning of theory, or 'episteme', which is then brought into dialogue with the practical experience of workers, or 'techne', preferably in an organisational context. Out of this engagement on action-orientated problems, new understandings, goals and strategies can be formed. Theory and practice, 'episteme' and 'techne', are combined in these moments into praxis.

From this conclusion, we can make explicit two claims not developed by Turner in *The Eye of the Needle*. First, this practice of critical thinking cannot work in his account of the child-centred learning process, nor can it work in his account of learning through participation in enterprise governance. In neither scenario is there any clear and developed possibility of the child or adult coming to develop the theoretical attitude. In the former scenario, the child drives the learning process and is highly unlikely to develop the theoretical attitude without some kind of intervention. In the latter scenario, learning is orientated towards the strategic ends of the enterprise or the economy, with no obvious opportunity to expand these in more normative ways.

Second, and relatedly, Turner's account of critical thinking implies, but especially models, a teacher – whether an individual or an organisation or both. Someone or some process that is dialogic rather than didactic, disruptive of assumptions but committed to transcend the present for a better future, an egalitarian who tries to live freely in the compromised present and to combine with others organisationally to bring about a utopian future. In many ways this is the archetypal religious leader. After Turner's example, we can conclude that teaching critical thinking in repressive situations is best integrated into worker and other countercultural organisations and arguably into the learning of both children and adults in a participatory socialist democracy. Perhaps, if Marxist-Leninism modelled social change through the development of a small revolutionary party to lead the contestation for political power, Turner's participatory socialism requires a seminary of intellectual activists to drive critical thinking that will transform individual and collective consciousness such that human well-being is achieved.

Finally, these insights from Turner offer resources for academics today to reimagine themselves as intellectual activists who can contest, reclaim or reframe the turn to practice-based learning in ways beyond making students more employable for the market. Instead, one can imagine integrating critical thinking at the university with real-world practice in wider society in ways that produce a revolutionary class, as Turner did, or perhaps sustainability warriors or democratic citizens. Especially through this model of his, Turner opens the door for rethinking and redoing higher education in a neoliberal age.

REFERENCES

Billett, Stephen. 2013. 'Practice-based Learning and Professional Education: Pursuing Quality Outcomes and Sustainability'. In *Practice-based Education: Perspectives and Strategies*, edited by Joy Higgs, Ronald Barnett, Stephen Billett, Maggie Hutchings and Franziska Trede, 101–112. Dordrecht: Springer Science & Business Media.

Brown, Wendy. 2015. *Undoing the Demos: Neoliberalism's Stealth Revolution*. Cambridge, MA: MIT Press.

De Kadt, Raphael. 2017. 'Editorial'. *Theoria* 64 (151): v–vii. http://www.jstor.org/stable/44648072.

Egan, Anthony. 2017. 'Rick Turner as... Theologian?'. *Theoria* 64 (151): 58–71.

Fluxman, Tony and Peter Vale. 2004. 'Re-reading Rick Turner in the New South Africa'. *International Relations* 18 (2): 173–188.

Friedman, Steven. 2017. 'The Nemesis of the Suburbs: Richard Turner and South African Liberalism'. *Theoria* 64 (151): 10–19.

Geuss, Raymond. 1981. *The Idea of a Critical Theory: Habermas and the Frankfurt School*. Cambridge: Cambridge University Press.

Greaves, Duncan. 1987. 'Richard Turner and the Politics of Emancipation'. *Theoria* 70: 31–40.

Hemson, Crispin. 1996. 'Rick Turner and the Politics of Learning'. Rick Turner Memorial Lecture, University of Natal, Durban, 24 October.

Hudson, Peter. 2017. 'Let's Talk about Rick Turner'. *Theoria* 64 (151): 1–9.

Keniston, Billy. 2014. 'Response to Eddie Webster's Review of *Choosing to be Free: The Life Story of Rick Turner*'. *Transformation: Critical Perspectives on Southern Africa* 86 (1): 78–81.

Keniston, Billy. 2017. 'The Weight of Absence: Rick Turner and the End of the Durban Moment'. *Theoria* 64 (151): 20–28.

Lambert, Robert. 2010. 'Eddie Webster, the Durban Moment and New Labour Internationalism'. *Transformation: Critical Perspectives on Southern Africa* 72 (1): 26–47.

Lawrence, Ralph. 1990. 'Shaping Democracy in a Future South Africa.' *Theoria* 76: 101–114.

Lichtenstein, Alex. 2016. 'Rick Turner and South Africa's "Sixties"'. *WorkingUSA* 19 (4): 447–466.

Macqueen, Ian. 2014. 'Black Consciousness in Dialogue in South Africa: Steve Biko, Richard Turner and the "Durban Moment", 1970–1974'. *Journal of Asian and African Studies* 49 (5): 511–525.

Macqueen, Ian. 2017. 'Class versus Nation: A History of Richard Turner's Eclipse and Resurgence'. *Theoria* 64 (151): 29–39.

Nash, Andrew. 1982. 'History and Consciousness in South Africa Today'. Unpublished document.

Parry, Richard. 2014. 'Episteme and Techne'. *The Stanford Encyclopaedia of Philosophy*. https://plato.stanford.edu/archives/fall2014/entries/episteme-techne/. Accessed 14 November 2022.

Pateman, Carol. 1970. *Participation and Democratic Theory*, Cambridge: Cambridge University Press.

Piper, Laurence. 2010. 'From Religious Transcendence to Political Utopia: The Legacy of Richard Turner for Post-apartheid Political Thought'. *Theoria* 57 (123): 77–98.

Turner, Richard. 2015 . *The Eye of the Needle: Towards Participatory Democracy in South Africa*, revised edition. Kolkata: Seagull Books.

Wang, Shin-Yun, Jer-Chia Tsai, Horn-Che Chiang, Chung-Sheng Lai and Hui-Ju Lin. 2008. 'Socrates, Problem-based Learning and Critical Thinking: A Philosophic Point of View'. *The Kaohsiung Journal of Medical Sciences* 24 (3): S6–S13.

Webster, Eddie. 1993. 'Moral Decay and Social Reconstruction: Richard Turner and Radical Reform'. *Theoria* 81/82: 1–13.

8

The Relevance of Rick Turner's 'Utopian Thinking' for a Critical Pedagogy

Crain Soudien

In his postscript to *The Eye of the Needle* Rick Turner closes his analysis of South Africa and its prospects for social transformation with the comment that he is conscious of not having provided a plan or guideline for how change might happen:

> I have shown...that a participatory socialist democracy is not impossible...Nevertheless, I have not considered in any detail the enormous problem of how to bring such a society into existence in South Africa.
>
> In part, this was intentional. I wished to make a moral statement, to offer a yardstick in terms of which the present in South Africa and elsewhere can be judged. I think that such a moral point can validly be made by itself; but of course, it is an invitation to begin the process of trying to change the society in a particular direction. (Turner 1980, 99)

This yardstick he proffers is, importantly, not an ideal in the Weberian sense. It is not a defined thing. It is centred largely on consciousness – 'utopian thinking'. In defending it, he elaborates: 'There are two reasons why it is important to think in long-range "utopian" terms... It constitutes a challenge to all accepted values, an invitation to continuous self-examination, to a continuous attempt at transcendence... [It makes possible] in the light of other possible societies [an understanding of how our society works] and why it works as it does' (Turner 1980, 1–3). Foregrounded here and used orientationally throughout the text are the grounded competencies of consciousness – critical thinking, analysis, theorising and planning.

In this contribution, I work with Turner's insistence on the need to develop the capacity for critical thinking and consider its relevance for contemporary debates that are taking place around education and change. I ask how Turner's (1980, 1) thinking, produced at the apogee of the forty-year period of apartheid, when repression was at its most intense – 'Other things being equal,' he commented, 'it is impossible for a black person to become prime minister of South Africa' – might help us think about how we approach that great task of education and free it of its most limiting inclinations. I take this question to the current South African discussion around decolonisation but seek to hold it, also, against the larger discussion of the place of education in the struggle for human freedom and equality. With this, I work with his general comments on education and its role in the struggle for freedom but concentrate on his thinking on human becoming. Becoming is a central motif in his work. In *The Eye of the Needle* he talks of the importance of 'exploring the absolute limits of possibility' and the challenge of self-examination (Turner 1980, 53). He introduces the idea of transcendence and the immanence of the 'alternative' (Turner 1980, 1). This emphasis on 'self-examination' can, of course, be read psychologically in its relationship to individual consciousness. The approach taken here, however, is to stay with Turner's framing of consciousness as a social phenomenon, especially in its concern with the ethics of human behaviour. My own interest is on the educational implications of Turner's understanding of *becoming human*.

DECOLONISATION AND EDUCATION IN SOUTH AFRICA: THE DEBATE

The decolonisation discussion currently under way in the South African university has brought the question of the process of education to a productive point. While it is by no means new, its resurgence has provoked fresh discussion about the nature of knowledge, the relationship of knowledge to power and, most pertinent for the South African context, the place, function and responsibility of the South African university.

The discussion, as we shall see, has multiple accents, emphases and silences which take it in a range of directions. It proceeds, however, from an agreement that decolonisation and decoloniality – and there are differences (Mignolo 2001) – are about, in the first instance, an awareness of the ideological superstructure of modernity, its logics, metaphysics and ontologies and their accompanying power apparatuses, religion, education, socialisation, propaganda and coercion (Santos 2007). They are in the second instance, also a call to resistance. In the first instance, they draw attention to the totalising impulses of modernity, to its centring of value in the European form – its archive and its telos – and its claims to be civilisation's final signifier. Meaning, anywhere, takes its clearest form and value *only* in relation to it. In this, decolonisation seeks, simultaneously, to decentre and reorient. The decolonial call to arms is a call for the disruption of Eurocentricism and an appeal for the inclusion of the whole treasure store of human knowing. That which is to be disrupted, explains Achille Mbembe (2016b, 3), is whiteness. 'We are…calling,' he said, 'for the demythologisation of whiteness because democracy in South Africa will either be built on the ruins of those versions of whiteness that produced Rhodes or it will fail…For these reasons, the emerging consensus is that our institutions must undergo a process of decolonisation both of knowledge and of the university as an institution' (Mbembe 2016b, 10).

The South African agreement is about re-centring enquiry and the making of knowledge around the full historical and cosmological experience of Africa. To be recuperated are the knowledges of the dispossessed and the disenfranchised and, critically, their ways of being, apprehension and engagement with reality (see, for example, Ndlovu-Gatsheni 2013; Garuba 2015; Essop 2016; Hendricks and Liebowitz 2016; Kamanzi 2016; Mbembe 2016a and 2016b; Nyathi 2016; Pityana 2016; Jansen 2017; Prah 2017; Rudin 2017; Mamdani 2019). Rejected in the discussion are the following: the marginalisation of the African voice; the positioning of Africa as a 'place to learn about and not from' (Hendricks and Liebowitz 2016); and the objectification of Africa as a site for Western scrutiny (Garuba 2015; Kamanzi 2016).

Demanded, on the other hand, is a 'recogni[tion] and [the] according [of] value to the [knowledge of the] previously disadvantaged and... how the object of study itself is constituted' (Garuba 2015). Capturing the implications of the agreement for the university, Ahmed Essop explains that

[decolonisation] is about how knowledge – and the assumptions and values that underpin its conception, construction and transmission – is reflected in the university as a social institution.

It is in essence about institutional culture: the ways of seeing and doing that permeate a university and are reflected in learning and teaching. In this sense it is both about the formal and the informal or 'hidden curriculum'...Decolonisation is first and foremost about inclusion, recognition and affirmation. It seeks to affirm African knowledge and cultural traditions in universities, which remain dominated by western traditions. (Essop 2016)

Not unexpectedly, the questions of inclusion, recognition and affirmation are extremely contentious. It is here that it is important to understand how the decolonisation discussion is unfolding and to what its different interlocutors give emphasis. Giving one a sense of these developments, in his book *As by Fire*, Jonathan Jansen (2017, 158–163) identifies six distinct emergent approaches: (i) decolonisation as the decentring of European knowledge; (ii) decolonisation as the Africanisation of knowledge; (iii) decolonisation as additive-inclusive knowledge; (iv) decolonisation as critical engagement with settled knowledge; (v) decolonisation as encounters with entangled knowledge; and (vi) decolonisation as the repatriation of occupied knowledge.

While Jansen's classification is helpful, the decolonisation angle I seek to explore is the relationship between the epistemological and the ontological. I am interested in how sociological explanation or sociological knowledge, particularly the explanation of subjectivisation – the process through which people come to a sense of themselves as human subjects and their positionalities in relation to each other – influences, inflects and in some cases determines people's self-knowledges, their ontologies. Talking about the knowledge embodied in the hegemonic curriculum, Paulo Freire argued that it played a role in helping human beings to 'relate' to their world in a critical way because '[t]hey apprehend the objective data of their reality…through critical reflection – not by reflex, as do animals. And in the act of critical perception, men [sic] discover their own temporality. Transcending a single dimension, they reach back to yesterday, recognise today and come upon tomorrow' (Freire 1973, 3).

The 'data' of which Freire speaks is, of course, not 'objective'. It has, nonetheless, what Vanessa Andreotti and her colleagues describe as a grammar (Andreotti et al. 2015, 22). With this focus, I identify two basic 'grammars' or classificatory logics, as opposed to Jansen's six. His classification is based on an epistemological grammar – the different perspectives brought to the politics of knowledge, ordered and cohered around particular discursive premises and logics. Mine is on what different ontological representations the knowledge perspectives authorise. I am interested in what the epistemological does for the ontological. Using this, the two basic positions I identify are: *new* Black Consciousness and *new* humanism. I describe the kind of Black Consciousness here as *new* in relation to older forms of Black Consciousness which placed more emphasis on the rejection of the idea of race. In new Black Consciousness (NBC) race is worked with much more ambivalently. The new humanism of Mbembe is unapologetically critical of the anthropocentric order.

Humans share the planet with other life forms. Making that point, it is necessary to acknowledge that blackness is an issue in both NBC and new humanism. In the first a centring of it is sought. In the second, an attempt is made to situate it within a framework of human difference. Giving one a sense of the different ways in which the issues of recognition and inclusion work, Nceku Nyathi suggested that there was what he called a 'glossing over' of the issues in much of the discussion (Nyathi 2016). He asked:

> What is this thing called Africa or African that people wish to infuse into curricula? Unpacking it makes clear that the notion of 'Africa' is largely a social construct that's not borne out by the facts. Somalia is different to Zimbabwe...[a]nd if the continent is just one big happy family as this narrative of an African identity suggests, what is the xenophobia that's played out across South Africa in recent years all about? (Nyathi 2016)

What can be said about NBC as a sociological analysis? It begins with a fundamental rejection of whiteness and its normative framing of space, consciousness and sense-making. It does so drawing on decolonialists, such as Ramon Grosfoguel (2011), and the critical anti-universalist discourse he and the Latin American decolonial scholars developed, but also, significantly, on North American critiques of antiblack racism (Crenshaw 1989; Mbembe 2019a). In the process, it elaborates decolonialism in distinctive ways. It does so through a focus on the 'black body'. The 'black body' is not only recuperated but is reread for the purpose of deliberately constructing an anti-Descartian and an anti-white normativity view of the world. It rejects the discursive and material modalities of whiteness and particularly the ways in which it mediates knowledge and power through the reification of embodiment – white bodies and black bodies. Elemental in this reification is privileging and abjection – the idealisation of the white body against the denigration of the black body. Inscribed into the body in this analysis is an onto-epistemological essence. Significant in the NBC restoration of the unity of the head and the body is the critique of 'worlding', to use Chakrabarty's expression 'worlded' in the present continuous tense; the notion that in embodied white bodies is found the biosocial template for the future of all of humankind, the evolutionary climax of humankind (Dube 2002). This 'worlding' produces the universal standard according to which all history portends. In response, Thuli Gamedze and Asher Gamedze (2015, 1) explain that whiteness is responsible for black people's alienation:

[It seeks to control]…where we live, how we live, how we speak, what we say when we do speak, how we think and perhaps most importantly for us [as intellectuals] what we think, speak and write about…As African intellectuals, as Black people, this process of alienation is one we need to tackle, resist and subvert. To be a radical African intellectual is to challenge, on fundamentally personal, institutional and societal levels, this form of alienation that colonial education encourages.

Elaborating, the #RhodesMustFall Movement commented, soon after the removal of the statue of Cecil John Rhodes from its pedestal on the University of Cape Town's (UCT) campus, that '[o]ur freedom cannot be given to us. We must take it. We want to be clear that our only regret is that we did not take the statue down ourselves. Going forward, we will no longer compromise. Management is our enemy' (Rhodes Must Fall 2015, 12). The movement's mission, the comment declared, was to create new spaces on UCT's campus for black bodies, spaces where 'they could breathe'. Leigh-Ann Naidoo, speaking at the Second National Higher Education Summit in Durban, convened by then Minister of Higher Education Dr Blade Nzimande, on 16 October 2015, said that what students wanted was to alienate their own alienation (notes taken by the author, see Naidoo 2015). The critical task of decolonisation, she said, was to disrupt the norms of the system.

African humanists work with the social in different ways to those advocated by NBC. Although committed to a sense of the African continent and its place in the world, African humanists are critical about the dangers of racial essentialism. Kwesi Kwaa Prah, for example, argued against the tendency, in much decolonisation literature, to reproduce unproblematically racial-biological arguments about African people: 'The Africanisation or localisation [as it is sometimes called] of positions which were previously held by colonial personnel does not in itself necessarily translate as outstanding progress. It must be remembered that Africanisation wherever it has been pursued on this continent is a policy which mainly affects the fortunes of the elite' (Prah 2017, 1). The main point he sought to make was that development was a question of culture and not colour: 'the centring of African culture at the heart of the development endeavour is crucial' (Prah 2017, 2). Sabelo Ndlovu-Gatsheni took a similar position, saying that 'claims to nativity and indigeneity by any single ethnic or racial group ha[d] the potential to render others stateless' (Ndlovu-Gatsheni 2013, 140).

Mbembe, in several contributions, argued similarly (Mbembe 2016b, 1; Mbembe 2019a). He was anxious about the conflation of Africanisation and decolonisation. The object appeared to be, he said, to 'want to finally bring white supremacy to its knees. But the same seems to go missing when it comes to publicly condemning the extra-judicial executions of fellow Africans on the streets of our cities and in our townships' (Mbembe 2016b, 1). The conflation of decolonisation and Africanisation had the effect, he explained, of 'the transfer into native hands of those unfair advantages which were a legacy of the colonial past' (Mbembe 2016b, 11). Mbembe continued: 'Most of these studies (Mavhunga, Hountondji) could be assembled under the rubric of ethno-knowledges, so tight are their connections with the politics of identity and ethnicity' (Mbembe 2019b, 240). In some instances, he argued, 'decolonisation

is easily reduced to a matter of origins and identity, race and location'
(Mbembe 2019a, 241).

Building on these comments, he comes to a different explanation
of the decolonisation project: 'It is the taking back of our humanity.
[It is the]…struggle to repossess, to take back, if necessary by force,
that which is ours unconditionally and, as such, belongs to us' (Mbembe
2016b, 12). Important in this line of argument is his understanding of
how knowledge is mobilised behind the ontological project: 'becoming
human does not happen in time but through time and time, properly
speaking, is creation and self-creation – the creation of new forms of life'
(Mbembe 2016b, 12). European logic, and especially its 'narrativisation'
of history, he explained, was predatory. Its premise was that the future,
what he described as futurity, was the preserve and responsibility of
Europe. Insisting on the necessity of a break with this appropriation of
reason, he argued, in agreement with Latin American decolonial theorists, that decolonisation required a completely different temporal orientation: an engagement with that which was yet-to-come – the 'emergence
of the not-yet' (Mbembe 2016b, 14). Extending the argument, he commented that the dominant Eurocentric explanation of the world, with its
presumptive universalism, had reached its limits: 'knowledge can only
be thought of as universal if it is by definition pluriversal' (Mbembe
2016b, 19).

In taking a 'pluriversal' view he sought to enlarge the social landscape
on which human beings operated. In this way, decolonisation would
obligate human beings 'to see ourselves clearly, always in relationship
to ourselves and to other selves in the universe, non-humans included'
(Mbembe 2016b, 23). Expressed in these terms, it is suggested here, was an
explanation of human possibility that broke with mainstream humanism.
Mbembe made an appeal for a new understanding of being – ontology,
of knowing – epistemology, and of values – axiology. It committed to
a disruptive sense of being in the world. Being in the world, he explained,
involved the recognition and affirmation – and this is the radical challenge he mounts – of a planetary democracy in which the category of

human was no longer sovereign. Humans shared the world with other forms of being:

> Our world is populated by a variety of nonhuman actors. They are unleashed in the world as autonomous actors in their own right… At stake… once again, are the old questions of who is whom, who can make what kinds of claims on whom and on what grounds and who is to own whom and what… It is about humankind ruling in common for a common which includes the non-humans, which is the proper name for democracy.
>
> To reopen the future of our planet to all who inhabit it, we will have to learn how to share it again among the humans, but also between the humans and the non-humans. (Mbembe 2016b, 26–29)

Significant about Mbembe's reading of the decolonisation imperative is the urgency of the development of new ontics that are able to transcend human conceits and, especially, the conceit of human priority over other life forms. This imperative begins with a deconstruction of the logocentric politics which produce African delegitimation. It calls out the racism lodged at the heart of this logocentricism, but refuses the seduction of inversion, of simply turning the world upside down and putting Africa at the apex or the centre of all and every accounting of life.

Having made this move in defining what a decolonial project could be all about, Mbembe powerfully, especially in *Necropolitics*, begins to describe the challenge before the decolonial project (Mbembe 2019b, 113–114). This challenge is the suborning of reason, thought and deliberation in the complex ensemble of power, processes and its products to which modern capitalism has come through technology – electronic reasoning or artificial intelligence. In overwhelming sight, he argues, is the advent of computational media which not only steer and influence but also supplant the capacity for reasoning. Reducing the objective of life to commodifiable outputs, financialisation has produced a new epistemic hegemony. He describes the current state of capitalism as being not so much about the creation of wealth but, rather, driven by processes of devaluation and expendability: 'it increasingly aspires to free itself from any social obligation and to become its own ends and its own means' (Mbembe 2019b, 113). He continues:

> In this context, one of the many functions of computational media and digital technologies is not only to extract surplus value through the annexation and commodification of the human attention span. It is also to accelerate the disappearance of transcendence and its reinstitutionalisation in the guise of the commodity. Formatting as many minds as possible,... colonising their unconscious have become key operations in the dissemination of microfascism in the interstices of the real. (Mbembe 2019b, 113–114)

Important for our analysis here is Mbembe's focus on the phenomenon of 'transcendence' and the disappearance of its possibility. Implicit in this diagnosis, perhaps underdeveloped in its explication of sociality, is an anxiety about the capacity of the decolonisation project to see the scale of the challenge before it. It is not simply domination, but, fundamentally, an order of social 'constitutiveness' in response to which standard and conventional sociology and psychology and their philosophical underpinnings are completely inadequate. The condition, as Mbembe sees it, is 'the accelerat[ion of the] disappearance of transcendence'. What is meant by transcendence here and elsewhere is always conditioned by the context. Broadly, it encompasses the capacity to confront the circumstances of one's formation and to deal with them critically.

TURNER AND 'UTOPIAN THINKING'

What then, in response to this 'acceleration' of the capacity for transcendence, might we take from Turner?

A useful start is to separate out the critical operational elements to Turner's sociology. These are, significantly, his overarching theory of change and within this, sub-theories of self and society. Around the discussion of self lie elements of an explanation, a proto-theory, of consciousness. Objects of analysis in this sociology include 'reality', 'structures', 'behaviour' and almost of prime significance, 'consciousness'. These, to take a view of the whole of *The Eye of the Needle*, take sharp form in the early parts of the book. They do not, in and of themselves, develop into a full theory of consciousness and, critically, into a programme for social change. The latter part of the book, where Turner turns his attention to political options open to South Africa, particularly chapter 7, is not only a shift in semiotic register, but tends to be written with little sense of his earlier analysis of the politics of the self in society. The politics of self on which the extraordinary symbolism of *The Eye of the Needle* is crafted, that 'it is easier for a camel to go through the eye of a needle than for a rich man to enter the kingdom of God', is, in some senses, not developed. He depends, instead, on the standard tropes of conventional sociology – almost, not always, homogenised whites, Africans, coloureds and Indians. It is, effectively, a rainbow sociology. More valuable is his idea of the making of self in society and its politics. We have in this sociology, I would argue, important resources with which to work towards an approach to Mbembe's aporia – the 'accelerated disappearance of transcendence'. However, it has to be reassembled.

In approaching Turner's thinking on change, it is important to begin at the beginning of his understanding of what the problem is that is under examination. *The Eye of the Needle*, almost counterintuitively, does not begin there. The problem is first stated on page 11, where he explains that 'South Africa is a capitalist society and the human model characteristic of the dominant white group in South Africa is the capitalist human model' (Turner 1980, 11). The point to make, this delayed statement notwithstanding, is that the design and presentation of the text are premised on the taken-for-granted fact that we are dealing with the challenge of living in a 'capitalist human model'. The problem is capitalism. His focus, in relation to this problem, is not the economic structure of capitalism but that which authorises it, its value system. At regular points of the text he describes the economics of capitalism. Important for our discussion, he lays out the structure of capitalism and its foundation in its mode of production, the extraction of surplus value. In this is embedded the basic structure of exploitation. This structural system depends on a value or ethical system. It is the content and substance of the value system – its ideological superstructure – that he sets out to explain: 'the values imposed by the socialisation process in capitalist societies are those which that particular form of society needs to survive' (Turner 1980, 11). These values, he explains, consist of two major components: '[t]he justification of exploitation and manipulation as a way of relating to other people' (Turner 1980, 15).

Out of these descriptions emerges what Turner describes as a human model. This human model is given substance to and characterised by socialisation/learning mechanisms 'that tend to keep it going. The dominant group are also being socialised, with the concomitant belief in the naturalness of their dominance…In one sense at least each group is as much a victim of the system as is any other. Each individual's human potential is reduced to a cardboard role, whether it be as male or as female, as oppressed or as oppressor' (Turner 1980, 10). In response to this, he urges that '[w]e need to make explicit the value principles embodied in our actual behaviour and to criticise these principles in the light of other possible values' (Turner 1980, 3).

It is here, 'making explicit' and 'criticising' our dominant values, that Turner's theory of change can be deduced – his 'utopian thinking'. It rests on the ability of human beings to change their values and their behaviour. His approach is to argue that their socialisation into society's dominant values and forms of behaviour is neither inevitable nor desirable. In this is, firstly, his characterisation of who we are as human beings and, secondly, his description of capitalist South Africa and the alternative towards which it could move.

With respect to the question of who we are as human beings, he moves quickly and early to the question of 'race'. He gets to this question in the opening passages of *The Eye of the Needle*:

> Unless we can see our society in the light of other possible societies we cannot...understand how and why it works as it does, let alone judge it. Let us take the example of...race...It is based on white South Africans' experience of the objective 'inferiority' of most blacks...They 'explain' a social fact by direct reference to biology and thereby misunderstand it...If we discover that there is no biological root for this 'inferiority'...then we...ask the illuminating question: What is the social structure that creates the various objective 'inferiorities' of certain groups? (Turner 1980, 4)

A constant motif in this analysis is the problem of the naturalisation of meaning: 'The concept "human nature" plays a very important role in our "common-sense" thinking. We often explain difficult phenomena... as being products of human nature' (Turner 1980, 7). It is evident in relation to the question of gender and, significantly, that of the market (Turner 1980, 4, 53). The point about these social phenomena, he explains, is that they are artefacts of society. White attitudes to other people, he explains, arise out of their culture: 'Race prejudice is a real phenomenon, compounded of ignorance of different cultures, of an unthinking explanation of very real social differences in terms of biological differences' (Turner 1980, 32). In situations of oppression, he argues that 'most people see the social order as being part of the natural order of things' (Turner 1980, 85). In these explanations, he does not quite get to the point of articulating a definition of humanness but he explicitly counterposes being human to being a privileged white South African. In almost Gandhian terms in a few passages where he talks of transcendence, to which we shall come, he says that 'we must realise that love and truth are more important than possessions' (Turner 1980, 92). His objective in this passage is to point to the problems of privilege. Pertinent, however, are his comments at this point about being human:

> We must do this to be human... If we love people we will, when faced by intimidation, fear the loss of our openness towards other people more than we fear anything the intimidators can do to us. We can learn to live differently as individuals and we can also learn to live differently in small groups by experimenting with types of communal living... People can live in human solidarity and learn to work with one another in harmony and love. (Turner 1980, 92–94)

What is this society of 'human solidarity' of which he speaks? It takes expression in his discussion about freedom: 'The principle of our ideal society is freedom' (Turner 1980, 48). He defines 'a free society as one in which: (a) the limits are as wide as possible; (b) all individuals have a say in deciding where it is necessary for those limits to be; and (c) all individuals know how and why they are being limited' (Turner 1980, 53). This free society, he continues, 'is one in which I co-operate with my fellows in deciding how to maximise all our freedoms' (Turner 1980, 54). For the record, it is at this point that he qualifies the kind of socialist ideal towards which he aspires. It is not the centralised economy of Soviet communism, but significantly, nonetheless, depends on cooperative planning. It is hallmarked by individual freedom (Turner 1980, 59) which, however, is never unconditional. Individual freedom is determined, always, by a recognition of the rights of others and their resolution through cooperation. The virtue of cooperation, argues Turner, is that it obliges everyone to consider the issues that are affecting others in the cooperative arrangement: 'On the basis of this, it is possible for the problems of society to begin to make sense to me and so for me to evaluate intelligently what is happening' (Turner 1980, 61–62).

Participation and cooperation are important Turnerian concepts for us to use. In them are examples of alternative socialisation/learning modalities to those available in dominant society. Most useful, here, is his discussion of education and consciousness. As I indicated above, this discussion is distributed in a number of places in the text. I reassemble them here to suggest what the outline of a Turnerian theory could look like and, with this, suggest what value it offers for the decolonisation discussion. The basic line of approach I use is to think of consciousness as the way we experience and adapt to sensory information. In working with this approach, it is important to hold on to Turner's extensive discussion about dominance's socialisation role in the making of consciousness. His contribution is fundamentally about how this *naturalised* learning can be countered.

There are three elements worth singling out in Turner's discussion. The first is about the child's sensory encounter with the world, the second is about the cognitive process itself and the third is about self-consciousness. The first two are relatively familiar to an informed reader. The last, self-consciousness, is not.

Turner's first move is to make the observation, well known, about the value of the formal school and to argue that 'what has to be learned is a particular way of thinking, the ability to analyse, to think critically and to think creatively' (Turner 1980, 67). These qualities, he says, do not need to be acquired in the school. He is insistent, however, about the importance of learning and how important it is for the child to develop the capacity for making moral and intellectual judgements in their lives. This is best facilitated in a learning context which is *not* separate, or cut off, from the rest of society, as was the intention of the dominant school model. Having made this move, he develops his second, which is about resisting dominance and providing children with multiple opportunities to encounter a sensory universe which constantly pushes them to try out new roles for themselves: 'This is the essence of the learning process' (Turner 1980, 71). Referring to Piaget, he says that the significance of 'this for moral development is that "the development of a self involves the taking over of roles and hence the points of view, of others". This process Piaget calls "decentration" – the process whereby the individual moves from a view of the universe as having one centre – oneself – to a view of it as having many centres' (Turner 1980, 71). Seen here, obviously, is a reference to decolonisation.

It is Turner's next move which is most relevant – that about transcendence,

> that is…the idea of something (whether it be a 'reality' or an 'ideal') which goes beyond the present…beyond what people are doing in the world at this moment and in the light of which the present is only of secondary importance. The latent role of the affirmation of a transcendent reality is to challenge the natural arrogance whereby individuals believe that their particular way of seeing the world is the only possible way of seeing it…On the practical level this implies that no particular way of behaving can ever be final. The transcendent ethic demands that we question our taken-for-granted ways of behaving, that we continually question them. (Turner 1980, 17)

Elsewhere he talks of the 'excitement of self-discovery, the excitement of shattered certainties, the thrill of freedom' (Turner 1980, 92). In this is Turner's utopian thinking. It constitutes, he says, 'a challenge to all accepted values, an invitation to continuous self-examination'. The fundamental and driving purpose of this line of thinking is to shift people away from *naturalised* modes of thought to what he describes as a 'theoretical attitude' (Turner 1980, 5). This attitude helps them become aware that they have the basic human freedom, always, to choose: 'Human beings can choose. They are not sucked into the future by stimuli to which they have to respond in specific ways. Rather, human beings are continually making choices. They can stand back and look at alternatives. Theoretically, they can choose about anything. They can choose whether to live or die; they can choose celibacy or promiscuity, voluntary poverty or the pursuit of wealth' (Turner 1980, 7–8).

How they choose is the challenge of transcendence and so, he urges, as part of the 'theoretical attitude', people should be taught to historicise: 'In order to theorise about society perhaps the first step [psychologically] we have to make is *to grasp the present as history*' (Turner 1980, 6, emphasis added).

CONCLUSION

Does this Turnerian approach, reassembled here, pivoting on his conception of transcendence, offer a response to Mbembe's diagnosis of our times – the acceleration of the disappearance of transcendence, our capacity to move beyond the reproductive categories of dominance?

Yes and no.

In Turner's ontological summing up of who we are and what makes us human – our capacity to make choices – is the eternal response to Mbembe's doom-laden diagnosis. The response Turner offered, at a time when possibilities of an alternative to extreme oppression appeared negligible, holds even now in Mbembe's apocalyptic times. It is in his assertion of our ability to choose, even in circumstances of extreme moral ambiguity. And yet that ability – the ability to think critically – is not ever formulaically predeterminable. Turner offers it, to return to his reluctance to lay out a plan, as a *yardstick*. He invites us to reach towards it. Critical to this approach is that it presents a version of decolonialism which is continually vigilant with respect to power of any kind and power's desire to totalise and universalise meaning. This is utopian thinking. Presenting it as a yardstick demonstrates the importance of its necessity. And so, to conclude the argument for why Turner is relevant for our contemporary times, a brief response to make here is that he offers decolonialism the opportunity to reconnect with long-standing critical theory and to see itself as the continuing thread in the maintenance of the education for liberation tradition.

And yet, the Turner ensemble has been overtaken by historical developments. Enduring as his basic positions are, the complexity of the technological turn demands *fresh* politics. It demands an education which is able to anticipate the extraordinary ways in which sociality is being reconfigured by the technological. Particularly challenging is the ease with which technological proximity is able to displace and restructure the ontological – people's sense of self, their sense of self-sufficiency and their sense of solidarity – and the emergence, as a consequence, of new ontics in and through which power is mediated, instituted and policed invisibly, seductively and, most worryingly, in the name of our advancement as a human species.

How Turner himself would have responded to this challenge is, of course, a question that is entirely speculative. *The Eye of the Needle* does not present itself as a pedagogical primer. He would not have wanted it to be read as such. He constantly, however, urged in his work that people should be looking for ways, their own ways, to find an alternative to dominant capitalism. They should exercise their capacity to make choices. He exemplified this stance, powerfully, beyond his ability to say it, in the way he lived. In terms of this, Tony Morphet's tribute remains apposite:

> Turner's whole life-project manifests a profound value statement… In a society of… pervasive oppression all lives are stunted and malformed… The death of the practice of freedom necessarily entails the distortion of the whole range of positive human values… even the bravest individuals are driven towards venal compromise in order to survive. The value of Turner's life lies in its triumphant demonstration of autonomous value-creating thought and action. The demonstration involves a coherent dialectic of action and reflection which has the capacity to transcend all limitations placed upon it by the irrational situation in which the life was lived. (1980, xxxiii)

REFERENCES

Andreotti, Vanessa, Sharon Stein, Cash Ahanakew and Dallas Hunt. 2015. 'Mapping Interpretations of Decolonization in the Context of Higher Education'. *Decolonization: Indigeneity, Education and Society* 4 (1): 21–40.

Crenshaw, Kimberle. 1989. 'Demarginalizing the Intersection of Race and Sex: A Black Feminist Critique of Anti-discrimination Doctrine, Feminist Theory and Antiracist Politics'. *University of Chicago Legal Forum* 1 (8): 139–167.

Dube, Saurabh. 2002. 'Presence of Europe: A Cyber Conversation with Dipesh Chakrabarty'. *South Atlantic Quarterly* 101 (4): 859–868.

Essop, Ahmed. 2016. 'Decolonisation Debate is a Chance to Rethink the Role of Universities'. *The Conversation*, 16 August 2016. http://theconversation.com/decolonisation-debate-is-a-chance-to-rethink-the-role-of-universities-63840. Accessed 12 March 2017.

Freire, Paulo. 1973. *Education for Critical Consciousness*. New York: The Seabury Press.

Gamedze, Thuli and Asher Gamedze. 2015. 'Salon for What?'. *The Johannesburg Salon* 9: 1–2.

Garuba, Harry. 2015. 'What is an African Curriculum?'. *Mail & Guardian*, 17 April 2015. https://mg.co.za/article/2015-04-17-what-is-an-african-curriculum/. Accessed 12 March 2017.

Grosfoguel, Ramon. 2011. 'Decolonizing Post-colonial Studies and Paradigms of Political Economy: Transmodernity, Decolonial Thinking and Global Coloniality'. *Transmodernity: Journal of Peripheral Cultural Production of the Luso-Hispanic World* 1 (1).

Hendricks, Cheryl and Brenda Liebowitz. 2016. 'Decolonising Universities isn't an Easy Process – But It Has to Happen'. *The Conversation*, 23 May 2016. http://theconversation.com/decolonisng-the-universities-isnt-an-easy-process-but-it-has-to-happen-59604. Accessed 12 March 2017.

Jansen, Jonathan. 2017. *As by Fire: The End of the South African University*. Cape Town: Tafelberg Publishers.

Kamanzi, Brian. 2016. 'Decolonising the Curriculum: The Silent War for Tomorrow'. *The Daily Maverick*, 28 April 2016. https://dailymaverick.co.za/opnionista/2016-04-28-decolonising-the-curriculum-the-silent-war-for-tomorrow/. Accessed 12 March 2017.

Mamdani, Mahmood. 2019. 'Decolonising Universities'. In *Decolonisation in Universities: The Politics of Knowledge*, edited by Jonathan D Jansen, 15–28. Johannesburg: Wits University Press.

Mbembe, Achille. 2016a. 'Decolonizing the University: New Directions'. *Arts and Humanities in Higher Education* 15 (1): 29–45. https://doi.org/10.1177/147402221568513. Accessed 12 January 2018.

Mbembe, Achille. 2016b. 'Decolonizing Knowledge and the Question of the Archive'. Unpublished talk given at University of the Witwatersrand and University of Cape Town, 2016. https://wiser.wits.ac.za/system/files/Achille Mbembe – Decolonizing Knowledge and the Question of the Archive.pdf. Accessed October 2017.

Mbembe, Achille. 2019a. 'Future Knowledges and Their Implications for the Decolonial Project'. In *Decolonisation in Universities: The Politics of Knowledge*, edited by Jonathan D Jansen, 239–254. Johannesburg: Wits University Press.

Mbembe, Achille. 2019b. *Necropolitics*. Johannesburg: Wits University Press.

Mignolo, Walter. 2001. 'Coloniality and Subalternity'. In *The Latin American Subaltern Studies Reader*, edited by Ileana Rodriguez, 224–244. Durham, NC: Duke University Press.

Morphet, Tony. 1980. 'Biographical Introduction'. In *The Eye of the Needle: Towards Participatory Democracy in South Africa*, by Rick Turner, vii–xxxiv. Johannesburg: Ravan Press.

Naidoo, Leigh-Ann. 2015. 'Needing to Learn: #RhodesMustFall and the Decolonisation of the University'. Presentation at the Second National Higher Education Summit, International Convention Centre, Durban, 16 October. http://www.dhet.gov.za/SiteAssets/Latest%20News/Independent%20Thinking%20Second%20Edition/dhetpage7.pdf. Accessed 16 March 2017.

Ndlovu-Gatsheni, Sabelo. 2013. *Coloniality of Power in Postcolonial Africa: Myths of Decolonization*. Dakar: CODESRIA Press.

Nyathi, Nceku. 2016. 'Decolonising the Curriculum: The Only Way through the Process is Together'. *The Conversation*, 19 December 2016. https://theconversation.com/decolonising-the-curriculum-the-only-way-through-the-process-is-together-69995. Accessed 9 December 2023.

Pityana, Barney. 2016. 'The 2015 Student Revolts in South Africa: A Call for Dialogue'. Unpublished paper.

Prah, Kwesi Kwaa. 2017. 'Has Rhodes Fallen? Decolonising the Humanities in Africa and Constructing Intellectual Sovereignty'. https://www.assaf.org.za/wp-content/uploads/2015/05/Has-Rhodes-Fallen.docx-ASSAF-Address-15.2.2017.pdf. Accessed 12 March 2017.

Rhodes Must Fall. 2015. 'Rhodes Must Fall Statements'. *The Johannesburg Salon* 9: 6–19.

Rudin, Jeff. 2017. 'Deconstructing Decolonisation: Can Racial Assertiveness Cure Imagined Inferiority?'. https://www.dailymaverick.co.za/opinionista/2017-01-22-deconstructing-decolonisation-can-racial-assertiveness-cure-imagined-inferiority/. Accessed 20 March 2017.

Santos, Boaventura de Sousa, ed. 2007. *Cognitive Justice in a Global World: Prudent Knowledges for a Decent Life*. Plymouth, UK: Lexington Books.

Turner, Richard. 1980. *The Eye of the Needle: Towards Participatory Democracy in South Africa*. Johannesburg: Ravan Press.

PART IV

RICK TURNER AND THE LEFT

9

Rick Turner, an Aboveground Radical

Billy Keniston

When I first began studying the life of Rick Turner (over twelve years ago now), what first intrigued and inspired me was Turner's independence, his unwavering commitment to a utopian vision of socialism, his stubborn refusal to align himself with any of the 'vanguards' of the liberation struggle (such as the African National Congress [ANC] and the South African Communist Party [SACP]). I continue to believe that Turner has yet to be granted full pride of place amongst struggle heroes on account of the fact that he was never a party loyalist, of any kind. Still, there is another layer to the unique contribution of Rick Turner, which both I and other scholars have yet to adequately grapple with. Even though Turner's most active years in the anti-apartheid struggle overlapped precisely with the development of the armed struggle, Turner remained steadfastly separate from the turn to violent resistance.

How should we understand Turner's persistent unwillingness to align himself with the armed struggle? Is it simply that he was a pacifist, morally opposed to violence in all its forms? There are some that knew Turner well who would certainly insist that this was the case. However, I believe that his rejection of the armed struggle reflects a more complex and nuanced stance than 'merely' being a non-violent person. Turner's reticence to participate in the armed underground, I argue, stemmed from a deep critique of the *structures* of clandestine activity that armed movements required and reproduced. Therefore, an investigation into Turner's thinking and choices in response to the armed struggle will not only offer insights into the level of tactics (for example, which forms of resistance are most effective?) but also provide a larger critique of the entire project of seeking revolutionary transformation through violence. In what follows, I summarise the few occasions when Turner reacted directly to the armed struggle, and analyse the broader lessons we might draw from these fragments.

THE AFRICAN RESISTANCE MOVEMENT

Rick Turner's first connection to the armed underground happened largely without his knowledge – and certainly without his consent. Turner's undergraduate years were spent in the predominantly white liberal atmosphere of the University of Cape Town in the early 1960s. During these years, Turner was politically engaged, a curious and dedicated intellectual, steadily outgrowing his liberalism. At the same time, everyone I interviewed who knew Turner during this time insisted that he would have hoped to steer clear of the burgeoning sabotage movement, which began in the aftermath of Sharpeville. For example, Turner's brother-in-law, Michael Hubbard, said that 'Turner was always non-violent, so kept himself out of that'. However, Hubbard also explained that 'he was friends with these people' (Keniston 2013, 27). In other words, several of Turner's close friends in Cape Town were later revealed to be members of the short-lived sabotage organisation, the African Resistance Movement (ARM). While it seems likely that members of the ARM would have been careful to conceal their underground work from Turner, it became impossible to hide once the government began rounding up

ARM members in July of 1964. As Hubbard remembers, this was 'a very tense time. I remember, one Sunday evening, Barbara [Hubbard, Turner's wife] was upset, worrying aloud, "Where is Richard? Where is Richard?" I didn't understand that exactly at the time. But I understood, in retrospect. Suddenly the papers were full of Richard's friends getting arrested' (Keniston 2013, 27).

Amongst those arrested in these raids was Turner's housemate in Vredehoek, Alan Brooks. Brooks had begun as a liberal, but by 1964 was a communist. Brooks was tortured by the police and 'was greatly hardened by the experience' (Keniston 2013, 27). Around the same time, Turner's childhood friend, John Clare, felt compelled to leave the country after it had become clear that his wife Sheila was at risk of being detained for her involvement with the ARM.

Dozens of others were either arrested or went into exile because of the crackdown on the ARM. The collapse of the ARM was remarkably swift. Their last sabotage action was a bomb placed in the whites-only waiting room at Johannesburg's central train station, on 24 July 1964. John Harris, the man responsible for the bomb, called the police and urged them to clear the station, but nothing was done in response to Harris's call. The resulting explosion killed one elderly woman and injured 22 others. Harris was quickly arrested, and soon became the first and only white political prisoner to be hanged for his crime.

The demise of the ARM took place while Turner was completing his doctorate in Paris. Nonetheless, it had a profound impact on Turner's close friends and on the climate of opposition politics that Turner encountered when he returned to South Africa in 1966. This is why Michael Hubbard insists that, 'if you're going to understand Rick's political position, you've got to understand the ARM' (Keniston 2013, 27). Perhaps it is simple to understand Turner's position on the ARM, as he wrote a rather scathing critique of it: 'In fact, the ARM episode, in which disillusioned students tried sabotage, shattered their own and others' lives and did great damage to the cause they were fighting for, made me acutely aware of the danger of students turning to violence' (Turner 1980, xiii).

On the surface, Turner's sentiments here are not particularly notable. The ARM is widely regarded as a failure, including by liberals,
other armed organisations, historians of all stripes and even many
of the participants themselves. However, on a closer reading, one
notes that Turner's driving concern had to do with the ways in which
clandestine armed activity had 'shattered their own and others' lives'.
That is, Turner was not troubled by whether the sabotage attacks succeeded at hitting their chosen targets or weakened the apartheid state
in any tangible sense. Turner was troubled by the impact of this form
of resistance *on the rebels themselves*. Therefore, to understand Turner's
critique of the ARM, perhaps we will need to turn Hubbard's comment on its head and attempt to understand Turner's political position –
particularly in terms of the *forms* of political organisation that he saw
as emancipatory.

PREFIGURE THE FUTURE

Only if the new culture is embodied in the process of moving
toward the new society will that society work when we get to it.
— Rick Turner, *The Eye of the Needle: Towards Participatory
Democracy in South Africa*

As much as it is an outline for a utopian society, Rick Turner's *The Eye of
the Needle* was also intended as at least an initial sketch of the potential
paths towards such a society. In multiple instances throughout the book,
Turner articulated his vision for the kinds of social and political organisation that would embody the new culture of a participatory democratic
utopia. The heart of Turner's vision focused on a radical restructuring
of the economy by placing maximum control in the hands of workers.
Turner's 'participatory democracy' has echoes of anarcho-syndicalism
or council communism in that the consistent refrain stresses the need
to dramatically decentralise decision-making structures, to put the locus
of economic, social and political power on the smallest scale possible.

For Turner, a key reason to insist on direct democracy in the workplace was based on his understanding that 'the enterprise is not only a work place; it is also a socialization process. Once the workers have been through this process, it is scarcely surprising that they do not appear to have the competence to run an enterprise. What the capitalist system has made the workers into is then produced as evidence for the impossibility of any other social system' (Turner 1980, 42).

The notion of 'socialisation' was fundamental to Turner's politics. Throughout his writings, he regularly returned to the question of how human beings are socialised to both accept and reproduce an oppressive system, and how they might unlearn these values and behaviours, to build an ideal society.

While the socialisation process obviously takes place in every domain of society, the core of Turner's proposals in *The Eye of the Needle* referred to the organisation of work:

> On the organizational level we must ensure that all organizations we work in pre-figure the future... Organizations must be participatory rather than authoritarian. They must be areas in which people experience human solidarity and learn to work with one another in harmony and in love. The process of political change through the development of organizational solidarity must itself be a participatory experience if people are to become conscious of the possibilities of freedom. (Turner 1980, 39)

Reading Turner's description of participatory organisations, it becomes clear that his vision of organising for social change was intensely different from – and perhaps openly hostile to – that of traditional trade unions and mainline communism. He supported the emerging trade union movement in numerous important ways, playing a role in, for example, the National Union of South African Students (Nusas) Wages Commission, the establishment of the *South African Labour Bulletin* and the Institute for Industrial Education, and the carefully researched account of the 1973 Durban strikes, *Human Beings with Souls*. Nonetheless, his anti-authoritarian approach to this work led to extensive conflicts with union leaders, and his eventual marginalisation within these circles. As I have written about these conflicts in great depth, in multiple forums, I will not rehash them here (Keniston 2017). Therefore, I would like to interrogate a similar set of tensions, between Turner and the armed struggle.

HOMESPUN MARXISM

In my research on Rick Turner, there was only one occasion when anyone spoke directly regarding Turner's stance on joining the armed struggle. Gerry Maré, who had lived with Turner while doing his undergraduate studies at the University of Natal, decided to go into exile after completing his studies. As an Afrikaner, Maré attempted to establish himself in the Netherlands, but soon decided that there was no viable path for him there. Then 'I came back, and I said to Rick – frustrated beyond belief – "How do I join MK [Umkhonto weSizwe, the armed wing of the ANC]?" I had done military service, so I thought I could be a soldier. But Rick just looked at me and he said, "If you want to talk about this thing, just go away. Speak to someone else; I'm not interested."' (Keniston 2013, 84).

Given Turner's earlier repudiation of 'the ARM episode', this intense refusal to help Maré connect to MK is not surprising. Nonetheless, it is worth thinking deeply about the substance of Turner's refusal to engage with the idea of joining the armed underground. According to Maré, when he followed up by asking Turner what to do *instead* of MK, Turner replied: '"Well, go and stand for the municipality; you've got a right to do that, you are a white person, you've got the vote. Say what you believe in and try to convince people." That,' continued Maré, 'was a challenge. I couldn't do it. But that's what he wanted people to do: to convince people, to find a platform from which you can do it' (Keniston 2013, 84).

On the surface, Turner's suggestion is striking for its liberalism, for the essentially naïve approach to electoral politics in an apartheid society. Perhaps it is possible to read this exchange and determine that Turner was opposed to the armed struggle because he was a liberal, because he was opposed to revolutionary change. Certainly, supporters of the armed struggle would argue – correctly – that the system of apartheid could not possibly be reformed. Therefore, amongst supporters of the armed struggle, there was a firm insistence that the armed struggle was *necessary* precisely because any form of electoral reform or non-violent protest could not possibly succeed against the intensely violent apartheid state. While this is a compelling line of reasoning, it would be an overly simplistic analysis to write Turner off as a 'liberal' merely because he encouraged a young white leftist to run for a local election.

Given the larger context of Turner's writings over a lifetime and his involvement in various political projects, there is no question that he longed for and dedicated his life towards the creation of a socialist South Africa. In fact, Turner's commitment to socialism only deepened over time. There is an important section of *The Eye of the Needle* where Turner analysed various attempts to establish something akin to 'participatory democracy' in different countries. Most of the examples that Turner cites are socialist states, virtually all of which had come to power as the result of an armed revolutionary struggle. For example,

> In Eastern Europe the idea of workers' control is deeply embedded in the Marxist ideology, although obscured by Communist Party practice. However, it tends to emerge in moments of crisis, as in Hungary in 1956, and again at the end of 1970, with the fall of Gomulka as a result of workers' protests. In Czechoslovakia workers' control was one of the most important developments of the later reforms of 1968, and in some industries it even continued to spread for a while after the Soviet invasion. (Turner 1980, 38–39)

187

Once again, Turner's aversion to authoritarian forms of communism is clear here; but what is also clear is that Turner was an avid student of revolutionary socialist struggles throughout the world. As further evidence of this fact, Turner began learning Portuguese in response to the socialist revolution in Portugal, and the corresponding independence of the African colonies of Portugal. He wanted to be able to listen to radio broadcasts from Frelimo in Mozambique. Now, if Turner was simply a liberal, or a morally committed pacifist, why would he have gone to such lengths to follow the progression of an armed revolutionary organisation such as Frelimo?

How then can we make sense of Turner's exchange with Gerry Maré, considering Turner's deep commitment to socialism? First, it is important to understand that the suggestion to run for a municipal election was not merely an offhand comment, fabricated by Turner. In fact, several other white radicals at the time were experimenting with the idea of using their racially exclusive access to the electoral system as a mechanism to make a broader provocation against apartheid. For example, Peter Randall, one of the founding members of Ravan Press and someone that was heavily influenced by Turner through their shared work with the Christian Institute's Spro-Cas project, ran as a social democratic candidate in Johannesburg. In Cape Town, Chris Wood (among the eight Nusas leaders banned at the same time as Turner) created a new political party, called the Alliance for Radical Change (ARC), and ran as a representative of the ARC Party in municipal elections. The idea behind the ARC was to provocatively exploit an intriguing loophole in apartheid law. On the one hand, as a banned person, Wood was expressly forbidden to engage in politics in any form, to publish any kind of political writing, and certainly to engage in political conversations. On the other hand, since the apartheid state sought to present themselves as a functioning democracy, any pamphlets or posters related to an election could not be censored or banned. Therefore, the ARC was able to distribute a pamphlet calling for 'black majority rule now' and stating that 'Vorster is un-South African' (ARC 1974). The ARC directly addressed the issue of running a banned person: 'The person who ARC has invited to stand is a person who is banned and restricted, and whose ideas this government is committed to killing. Although the candidate may not address meetings, campaign or be quoted – he will not be silenced. The ideas of ARC and the platform we represent cannot be banned or stopped' (ARC 1974).

Of course, a political party running on a platform of 'black people know better' in a whites-only election in 1974 Cape Town had no chance of winning. Nonetheless, the ARC represented explicit defiance, and a clear refutation of the power of the state to silence dissent.

Beyond the specific suggestion to stand for municipal elections, it is important to understand Turner's refusal to even discuss the possibility of joining MK within the broader political context that he was operating in. While there is a growing body of historical writing (primarily from ANC members and sympathisers) that insists that the ANC sustained a considerable underground presence inside South Africa throughout the 1960s and into the 1970s, my own research paints an entirely different image.

Nothing in the thousands of pages of archival documents which I have read, nor the dozens of interviews which I have conducted over the past twelve years, has pointed to an extensive presence of the ANC during the late 1960s and early 1970s. Rather, the image I have consistently been presented with is that young white radicals during this period were more or less entirely cut off from previous generations of struggle. As Glenn Moss described it, 'there was very little contact with the past because those who had been involved in the past were either in jail, or banned, or house arrested, or dead, or in exile' (Moss 2019). For Barbara Hogan, this separation from older activists meant that 'we weren't given the givens' (Hogan 2019).

In other words, the process of radicalisation that this group of young people experienced happened largely without the possibility of being mentored, or sculpted into accepting the so-called correct line. Cut adrift from the major African nationalist organisations and the Communist

Party, this group developed their 'own homespun brand of what it means to be a Marxist in South Africa. We didn't call ourselves communists. We called ourselves Marxist and I think that was very much a trend of our generation' (Hogan 2019). According to Moss, this 'homespun' Marxism was 'absolutely and quite consciously' critical of 'what is seen as Soviet communism. There was an explicit attempt to critique and reject a mechanistic or Stalinist Marxism' (Moss 2019). As a result, the politics that developed amongst this group in the early 1970s was 'actually quite utopian'. What Moss describes as utopian is 'a sense that one would actually be helping to create links between students and people off campus, trying to raise the tone of political engagement' (Moss 2019). As post-student radicals, they knew that they needed to develop a politics that was relevant to the broader society, and they tried to make that aspiration tangible, in whatever way they could.

Turner is broadly acknowledged to have been both influenced by, and influential in encouraging and developing, the 'homespun' or 'New Left' or 'Western' Marxism of the early 1970s. To this day, *The Eye of the Needle* remains the most cogent and thorough articulation of the utopian impulse of this political trajectory. One aspect of Turner's influence on young radicals was to encourage people to experiment with radical structures of living and working together, such as communes: 'We must learn that love and truth are more important than possessions. We must do this to be human…We can learn to live differently as individuals, and we can also learn to live differently in small groups by experimenting with types of communal living based on the sharing of property' (Turner 1980, 102).

Amongst the so-called leadership clique of Nusas that were targeted by the state alongside Turner, were a handful who lived together in two different houses – which the government understood to be communes – in the Claremont suburb of Cape Town. For those who lived in these houses, and spent time in them, the idea that these were 'communes' is not quite right; or, at least not in the way that the government intended that word. Clive Keegan, one of the banned eight, did not live in either house, but spent a lot of time socialising in both. From his perspective, 'it's rubbish to call them communes. They weren't dens of iniquity. Obviously, they were intensely political places. But no insurrections were plotted there. If you were a police spy, you frankly would have been very, very bored' (Keegan 2017). Charles Nupen, who was elected the president of Nusas after the 1973 bannings, was also a frequent guest at Mildene Avenue and described the house as 'an intellectually very stimulating environment, because people would constantly talk about affairs of the day, hoping to advance the cause of human freedom' (Nupen 2019). Nicki Westcott, who lived in the same house, is even more emphatic about the intellectually stimulating environment at Mildene Avenue: 'When I think about how my children [now in their 20s] spent their student years, I'm always struck by how little they sit and discuss ideas. We would sit up until the dead of night, every night, discussing. We had people studying history, psychoanalysis, politics, communism, etc. We used to read a lot too, and we would discuss each other's work. So, we had these really fascinating discussions' (Westcott 2019).

Despite their shared enthusiasm for the way of life at Mildene Ave, Westcott insists that calling it a commune 'was intended by the government as a slur' (Westcott 2019), and Nupen will only go so far as to call it 'a rather middle-class type commune' (Nupen 2019). By 'middle-class', Nupen meant that the housemates were busy with their studies (of law, medicine, botany and such) and enjoyed activities like hiking on Table Mountain and rooting out non-indigenous plants.

Despite their strong desire to cast off the slanderous implications of the word 'commune', everyone that spent time in these Claremont houses essentially agrees that they were lively spaces, full of passionate, politically astute conversations. Whatever these houses ought to be called, it nonetheless is clear that they were spaces where young people were actively attempting to 'embody' a different political culture. Spaces such as these were precisely what Turner imagined when he wrote of the need to undo the socialisation of a capitalist society, to prepare for a radically transformed way of life. Throughout his short life, Turner never wavered in his commitment to this style of socialist politics, even as the repression against him and his contemporaries steadily intensified.

Amongst the nearly 1 500 people placed under restrictive 'banning orders' by the apartheid state, many radicalised in response to the restrictions, in one way or another. Presumably, banning orders were intended to confine radical intellectuals to their homes, to separate them from all forms of public discourse. However, a critical irony of this policy, which united the experiences of all banned people, is that the years under a banning order provided ample opportunity for banned people to delve more deeply into their studies. Turner himself maintained a prolific intellectual life during the banning years. He co-authored a book about the Durban strikes, wrote numerous articles for the *South African Labour Bulletin*, wrote speeches for comrades, developed and wrote a series of workbooks for the Institute for Industrial Education, and testified in defence of Biko and other South African Students' Organisation leaders at their trial. He also produced 500 pages of philosophical writing, deepening and expanding on his doctoral thesis. The Special Branch (the security branch of the South African Police) was aware of Turner's continued intellectual and political activities, but they could not understand what Turner was really doing, because it was hidden in plain sight. According to Turner's wife, Foszia Fisher, 'the security police were convinced that we were part of an underground movement' (Keniston 2013, 150). In addition to being constantly surveilled and harassed by the security police, a handful of their neighbours in Bellair (a Durban suburb where Turner and his wife were living at the time) agreed to provide information on them to the police. There were plenty of reasons for Rick Turner to try to hide during his banning years – he simply refused to do so.

Unlike Turner, many banned people went into exile and/or joined the political and military underground structures of the ANC. In fact, of the group of eight people banned at the same time as Turner (27 February 1973), more than half left the country. For many in Turner's generation, the combined pressures of the banning orders, detentions without charge, torture and extended political trials made them feel that aboveground, legal modes of resistance were untenable. Therefore, people who had previously been proud to call themselves 'homespun Marxists', independent from the ANC and the SACP, began to seriously consider clandestine resistance to be the only possible path forward. There was a growing hunger amongst this generation of young leftists to *connect*, to find a way to see their own efforts within the context of a Movement, with a capital 'M'. However, since both the ANC and the SACP were banned organisations, connecting with members of either organisation meant entering a terrain of illegality, of coded communication and subterfuge, a far cry from the robust debates at the Claremont communes. For example, Moss describes his early interactions with Eli Weinberg as being almost entirely devoid of intellectual/ideological engagement:

> If you're working with somebody like Eli Weinberg…the one thing you'd never talk to Eli about was ideology. You certainly did not talk to him about communism or Marxism or something else like that. And that would be true for most of them. I'm not sure they were ideologues…Sydney Bunting once said that the South African Communist Party is the only communist party never to have had a Marxist as a member. That's very crude, but it has a point. (Moss 2019)

Connecting to the underground *did* provide young radicals with an opportunity to move away from the margins of the radical left, aligning themselves with the broader liberation struggle. Furthermore, being in the underground offered a path out of South Africa, a viable life in exile. However, it was not, as many might crudely claim, simply a more 'radical' choice than the internal, non-violent resistance.

Once in exile, the political culture was even more secretive than what Moss had experienced with Weinberg. The ANC's underground structures were, for clear security reasons, divided into distinct cells that had little to no contact with other cells. As Heinz Klug explains, 'There were people in the ANC underground in Botswana that I wouldn't have known. There were people who I recruited and worked with, that other people wouldn't know. You kept within certain circles' (Klug 2018). The idea of using cell structures was not new, and had been practised for decades throughout the world, particularly amongst communist parties. What is perhaps not so obvious about this system is that the division into separate cells cut across close friends, even amongst family. For example, Mike and Carol Kahn 'were placed in separate cells. Somebody gave us our *noms de guerre*. I was Farid, and she was Layla. In some way or other we were referred to as Farid and Layla which suggests a relationship. But I have no idea who was in Layla's cell' (Kahn 2019). The risks involved in underground work – particularly at the military level – required an intense commitment to secrecy; so much so that Mike Kahn can still claim in all seriousness (and despite apartheid having ended 25 years ago) that he has essentially no idea what his wife was doing, or with whom. Similarly, Klug and Kahn lived together for a period in Gaborone, but operated in separate cells, so again, neither has anything to say regarding the other's activities. This kind of political culture would have been absolute anathema to someone like Turner. While the banning order forced Turner to publish his writing surreptitiously (using comrades' names) and to engage in 'illegal' meetings with friends, he otherwise steered clear of any form of clandestine activity. Turner had no desire to engage in the kinds of secretive structures, with limited space for critical conversations, that the underground relied on.

NEW INTERNATIONAL SCHOOL FOR SOCIAL RESEARCH

While Turner was never tempted to join the underground, in 1976 he began working in earnest to find a way to leave South Africa. Turner had been offered a prestigious Humboldt fellowship, which would provide him with funding for a year of study in Germany, and the politics department at the University of Natal approved his request for a sabbatical. However, Turner was still under the banning order, and was furthermore without a passport. Therefore, the final year of Turner's life was spent applying to the Minister of Justice for approval to leave South Africa. As Turner explained in a letter to Frederik van Zyl Slabbert,

> If I go on a South African passport, with the intention of returning to my job here, there is a strong guarantee that I will not engage in any political activity while I am outside the country. However, if I were to leave on an exit permit, or, as seems to be more fashionable, by crossing the border, the state would have no further control over me. Not, I should say, that I have any intention of doing either of those things, inter alia because my children live here. (Keniston 2013, 141)

As these sentiments were expressed in a personal letter, it seems that Turner quite genuinely had no interest in fleeing the country illegally, or of going into exile permanently. 'Because my children live here' is certainly reason enough to stay solidly connected to South Africa. Furthermore, based on Turner's overall stances on these issues it is also reasonable to assume that he objected to the 'more fashionable' idea of 'crossing the border' illegally simply because he was not interested in going underground, for any reason.

Turner was clearly connected to the white exile community in Botswana. Most directly, his brother-in-law, Michael Hubbard, lived in Gaborone for the last years of Turner's life. Furthermore, many young Nusas radicals (whom Turner would have known and in some cases worked closely with) ended up in Gaborone as well. Most strikingly, on the evening that Rick Turner was shot through his bedroom window at 32 Dalton Avenue in Bellair, Durban, Foszia Fisher was in Botswana having dinner at the home of Jenny and Marius Schoon. While the Turners had known

Jenny (née Curtis) during her days as a Nusas student leader, by January of 1978 she was firmly committed to the ANC's political underground. As the Schoons had both fled their banning orders by crossing the border illegally, one might speculate that Foszia's visit to the Schoon household was in the hope of getting assistance to flee the country. Foszia adamantly disputes this claim:

> We were interested in finding a legal means to leave South Africa…[b]ecause this was not good for him. He was doing stuff in South Africa but he needed people to be engaged with. Our plan was, if the worst came to worst – we didn't know there was a worst beyond that – we would leave and go to Germany and work towards having some sort of conference centre in Europe where we would run various kinds of discussion on strategy, on change. It was not just going to be specifically about South Africa. It was going to be about living wherever you are. (Keniston 2013, 147)

Among Rick Turner's papers, there is a handwritten proposal for the 'New International School for Social Research', which appears to be the centre that Foszia described to me, many years later. While Turner's handwritten pages place the location of the school 'at Bellair', I enjoy imagining the project taking hold, as Foszia described it, somewhere in Europe, far away from apartheid South Africa, far away from the assassin's bullet.

The New International School for Social Research was imagined as a postgraduate space where 'our criteria for admissions of students would depend more on personal commitment and intellectual maturity than on formal qualifications', and where the normal 'cleavage' between students and teachers would be dispensed with. All members of the school would be expected to participate fully in the daily operations, in order to 'prevent an alienating "brain-work" vs "dirty work" divide' (Keniston 2013, 138). In other words, as Turner had previously described in *The Eye of the Needle*, the organisational structure of the school was intended to complement and reinforce the social and political aims of the curriculum. In outlining the guiding questions for the school's research priorities, Turner once again returned to the question of socialisation:

> What is the relation between the socialization process necessary to train whites for a position of dominance, the authority structure in education and work, and the dominance of male over female? To what extent are whites oppressed…by their roles in the overall institutional structure? How do Blacks internalize…their oppression? If whites are oppressed, which are the situations in which they can most easily be made aware of their oppression and so motivate themselves to attack the institutions? If Blacks have internalized their oppression…what situations in their daily lives are most likely to make these mechanisms break down? (Keniston 2013, 139)

It is striking that in the last days of his banning order (which were sadly the last days of his life) Turner remained animated by the idea of building an experimental postgraduate school, even as the conditions in both his own life and South Africa grew increasingly dire. Analysed from the vantage point of the armed struggle, such initiatives might appear apolitical, devoid of confrontation or any tangible impact. However, it would be a mistake to characterise this political approach as 'reformist'. Rather, it is important to appreciate Rick Turner's commitment to *pedagogy as politics* as well as to the pedagogical content of political struggle. From Turner's vantage point, clandestine and violent struggle is dangerous because it severs the connection between contemporary politics and a desirable future society. Therefore, Turner clearly and consistently argued that efforts to 'de-alienate' human beings and 'break down' oppressive modes of thinking and organisation are essential components of radical social change.

REFERENCES

ARC (Alliance for Radical Change). 1974. 'Election Brochures'. Palo Alto, CA: Hoover Institute, Stanford University.

Hogan, Barbara. 2019. Interview conducted by the author in Johannesburg, 24 April 2019.

Kahn, Mike. 2019. Interview conducted by the author in Cape Town, 22 January 2019.

Keegan, Clive. 2017. Interview conducted by the author in London, 10 August 2017.

Keniston, Billy. 2013. *Choosing to be Free: The Life Story of Rick Turner*. Johannesburg: Jacana.

Keniston, Billy. 2017. 'The Weight of Absence'. *Theoria* 64 (151): 20–28.

Klug, Heinz. 2018. Interview conducted by the author in Madison, 28 September 2018.

Moss, Glenn. 2019. Interview conducted by the author in Cape Town, 9 March 2019.

Nupen, Charles. 2019. Interview conducted by the author in Johannesburg, 20 March 2019.

Turner, Richard. 1980. *The Eye of the Needle: Towards Participatory Democracy in South Africa*. Johannesburg: Ravan Press.

Westcott, Nicki. 2019. Interview conducted by the author in Cape Town, 9 May 2019.

10

Radical Contingency and Turner's Enduring Message to Relative Privilege

Gideon van Riet

There is a clear religious reference in the title of Rick Turner's *The Eye of the Needle*. There is also a secondary, more obvious, meaning to the title. I believe this secondary meaning goes against much of what is written in the text itself. What is at stake in this apparent contradiction is the definite article in the title, which leads to a paradox between the seemingly idealist or open-ended praxes implied in the book and the idea of a single 'eye' to be threaded through political practice. Much of the current volume is concerned with the tension between philosophical realism and idealism (see the Introduction, chapter 6 and chapter 11). Some have explicitly or implicitly chosen a side, probably revealing an imprecision in *The Eye of the Needle*, which was written in only a few days and consequently can serve as a type of Rorschach blot for those engaging with Turner's work. I will not attempt to escape the implications of this observation. That would be foolish.

Instead, I too will 'project' my own ontology onto this text, by bringing Turner into conversation with the poststructuralism that continued to develop from the time of his banning and after his untimely death. By drawing on Ernesto Laclau and Chantal Mouffe's (2013) theory of poststructural hegemony, this contribution continues the scant attempts to demonstrate how Turner, read from a more idealist vantage point, like Sartre, apparently gained a greater appreciation for the limits to human choice. Poststructuralist views on choice typically still assume that the continuously reiterated social realm is filled with dynamic constraints, while by the same token, creative opportunities for progressive praxes continuously arise. Thus, to highlight the praxes potentiated by Turner and later interpretations of Sartre (Fox 2003; Hudson 2017), which by implication places both Sartre and Turner closer to poststructuralism than they were initially viewed as being, I continue along the path initiated by Peter Hudson (2017), who argued that Turner anticipated this 'new Sartre'. Laclau and Mouffe are used as relevant interlocutors, after the fact, so to speak, based on both theoretical and empirical grounds. Poststructural hegemony as theorised by Laclau and Mouffe – and Turner, it would appear – may help shed light on the contemporary South African problem of crime and the often problematic responses to it, often in the name of the now more diverse category of the privileged.

Although the 'new Sartre', for the most part elaborated by Nik Farrell Fox (2003), is linked to various other poststructural theorists, including Foucault and Derrida, poststructural hegemony is especially suited to demonstrate the richness of potentially progressive praxes amidst continuously morphing constraints to freedom. To be clear, this chapter engages Turner in relation to poststructural hegemony as per Laclau and Mouffe, to suggest a more pragmatic reading of his writing and politics. I embark on this analysis notwithstanding simplistic interpretations that have contrasted Turner with pragmatist thought (see Parker 2017). Instead, my position is that pragmatism is inherent to much of poststructuralism and related orientations, such as that of Turner.

Turner was an idealist and 'restrained' existentialist who engaged in pragmatic politics that, from the vantage point of the contemporary, still potentially inspires a multiplicity of praxes founded in radical open-endedness. This perspective has advantages over the likes of realism in general, including the likes of structural Marxism and the somewhat ironic essentialist slant that decolonial thought has sometimes taken when viewed exclusively as replacing one set of ideas with another, instead of a more radical turn to reflexive thought. Similar insights have been penned for decades. Indeed, notable members of the well-known Frankfurt School (Adorno and Horkheimer 1947; Marcuse 1991) have argued that the fundamental problems facing the world are not socialism or capitalism per se, but rather the institutionalisation of dogma. There is a potential barbarism inherent to any paradigms, especially when they regress into groupthink. Turner had to face this grim reality in the 1970s, when structural Marxism gained ascendency in the left, in opposition to his more pragmatic idealism.

To make the argument that Turner could fruitfully be brought into conversation with poststructural hegemony and offer some guidance towards practice in the wake of multiple contemporary crises, I engage with his critique of white liberals. He famously emphasised that this demographic identified as white first and liberal second. Tony Morphet (1990, 95) substantiates this position. He notes that South African liberals in the 1970s often reverted to false dichotomies between civilisation and barbarism, which meant that they were not particularly reflective and as such not particularly progressive.

Much of this criticism of ignorant privilege remains true for the new expanded and reshuffled South African middle and upper classes. The guiding question throughout this chapter is what kind of use lies in a reading of Turner in conversation with Laclau and Mouffe, when we relate the problematic of the indifferent middle classes to my research into crime and responses to it in the JB Marks Municipality in the North West province?

I maintain that there is an enduring message in the critique of relative privilege – now more broadly defined than was the case in the early 1970s – and its existence amidst the most dire and multifaceted forms of precariousness and insecurity (Van Riet 2022a, 22–38). There is clearly no single eye to be threaded. There are only temporary openings or opportunities, among a range of emergent problems, subject to the reiterations of the everyday. I understand 'iteration' and 'reiteration' as forms of change that exist between the far too simplistic notions of rupture and continuity. They are everyday, secular processes across scales. The remainder of this chapter elaborates the 'new Sartre' in relation to Turner and his critique of relative privilege, and a demonstration of the value such a reading of Turner presents, when applied to societal problems such as that discussed in my case study of crime and the response thereto in the contemporary JB Marks Municipality in South Africa (see Van Riet 2022a).

TURNER AND THE NEW SARTRE

Instead of stating that the elite in South Africa today are 'middle class first and liberal second' we should rather acknowledge that material inequality is an inherent part of contemporary 'liberalism', which is also an increasingly slippery concept. Words have meaning, and create meaning, only in context, and in relation to other words. This chapter only partially takes up the concept of liberalism in dialogue with Turner. Therefore, I will not invoke a specific meaning of the concept, except to note that Turner equated 'liberty' or 'freedom' to a type of emancipation founded in radical social democracy.

By drawing on poststructural hegemony, I acknowledge the unstable nature of concepts, amid the over-determination of the social. At the same time, both Turner and Laclau and Mouffe present visions of pluralist and social democracy. In contrast to the work of Antonio Gramsci (1971), for example, poststructural hegemony is far less of a telos. Instead, it is a continuous process of articulation, re-articulation and praxes considering time- and space-bound opportunities and constraints. Viewing political reality through such an optic allows for more open-ended analyses in comparison to the determinism of many other forms of radical politics. The social is merely a partially *sutured* totality that is always vulnerable to contestation on account of the incompleteness of language.

It always offers recourse to progressives to critique existing concepts and propose and struggle for alternatives. This type of politics reflects how Fox analyses the nuanced subject in relation to Sartre. He states that:

> Thus, although Sartre agrees with [post]-structuralists like Lacan that 'structure produces behaviour' he maintains that we should not pass over 'the reverse side of the dialectic in silence' (1977 (9), 86): 'Man can only "be spoken" to the extent that he speaks' (1971, 1977). In this respect, Sartre's consistent attachment to some form of agency can be seen to contrast with some of the earlier excesses of [post]-structuralist thought and some of the contemporary excesses of postmodernists who dissolve the subject in an acid bath of anti-humanism. (Fox 2003, 44)

Analysing Sartre's *Critique of Dialectical Reason*, Fox (2003, 55) notes that 'this kind of analytical reason which constitutes bonds between individuals only "in the milieu of exteriority" (CDR, 285) forms the basis of capitalist hegemony by reinforcing the "absolute separation between people which is so crucial to the continuing domination of the individualistic bourgeoisie"'. And later, he ascribes the following criticism of historical materialism to Sartre: 'Sartre is also critical of the teleological assumptions of Marxist history which, in his view, effectively deny history its *radical contingency*' (Fox 2003, 96, emphasis added). This observation clearly resonates with the work of Laclau and Mouffe and with that of Turner, as is explained throughout this chapter.

According to Laclau and Mouffe, totalities are relationally constructed through the contradictory logics of equivalence and difference. Logics of equivalence group diverse individuals together. This logic creates an inside and an outside or an 'us' and a 'them'. The contradictory logics of difference potentially undermine logics of equivalence, by highlighting how they are artificially sutured categories. Claims to universal values and identities are always incomplete and open to challenge. Laclau (1990, 8) notes that 'the social never manages to fully constitute itself as an objective order'. It is always dependent on an implied constitutive outside; that which it is not or to which it is contrasted. As a result, equivalences are always vulnerable to being undermined by those emphasising their oppressive consequences. The lack of homogeneity in problematic identities and the fact that no human is a uniform being can be leveraged towards progressive ends (Laclau and Mouffe 2013, 101). Progressives may strategically redeploy logics of equivalence and difference. They may also highlight 'floating signifiers' (time- and space-bound meanings), indicative of the limitations and incompleteness of the abovementioned suturing. Thus, oppressive signifiers may be called out for what they are. This approach to progressive politics resonates strongly with Turner's critique of common-sense politics and political categories.

Laclau and Mouffe define the radical and pluralist democracy for which they advocate as a polity in which a plurality of political praxes, based on the logics of difference and equivalence and the subsequent logics of construction, develop. This form of democracy is very dynamic. Much like Turner's work (1972, 70), these diverse politics extend beyond elections and other formal hierarchical institutions. They include, amongst other strategies, practices deemed contextually useful, such as strategic alliances with religious or other organisations, and political education. Mobilising alternative interpretations of a social order and a new positivity beyond the abovementioned deconstruction is a process Laclau and Mouffe call hegemonic re-articulation. Here the logic of opposition is joined to a logic of construction and there is a type of productive and enduring 'tension in openness' (Laclau and Mouffe 2013, 174). Hegemony cannot be overcome, and progressive change does not inherently require a Jacobian moment of rapid radical change.

Up to this point, I see much similarity with Turner's position – of someone quite in favour of debate above violence (see Keniston in this volume), which has a type of complicating and final quality to it. However, Laclau and Mouffe also argue that decisions and choices, though they exist, are too constrained to make this productive debate likely. It is easy to see that a concept such as 'liberalism' and an associated notion such as 'freedom' may be critiqued and redeployed in such a context if deemed helpful, although we do not have to. As such, in Turner, there is a somewhat more taken-for-granted view on certain political concepts than one would find in the likes of Laclau and Mouffe.

Still, what Turner at least partially shares with poststructural hegemony is a degree of philosophical idealism and an attempt to describe a desired social order that is rooted in, and will stem from, the contingency of the social. Turner, for example, questioned the 'naturalness' of major social institutions (Fluxman and Vale 2004, 177). Duncan Greaves (1987, 32) argues similarly, stating that 'at the heart of these [Turner's] ideas is the conviction that social structures, however complex and tortuous they may appear, are the products of human choices; and for precisely that reason they can be changed'.

Contrary to superficial interpretations of Turner, there is an obvious (hopeful) ambivalence toward the prospects for change. It is a restrained existentialism in the face of very real oppressive structures. The difference between Turner and authors such as Laclau and Mouffe is, at most, one of emphasis in the relationship between choice and constraint. But this is arguably not a major difference. Turner's existential roots perhaps left a greater belief in faster progressive change, for which he offered a worker-centred blueprint in the 1970s, among other interventions such as progressive education. Still, Turner and Laclau and Mouffe share a reserved spirit of hopefulness, in the face of significant odds to the contrary.

A further hint at Turner's recalibrating mindset, like that of the later Sartre, can be found in his critique of 'human nature' – a floating signifier in the vernacular of Laclau and Mouffe – where he emphasises the trappings of common-sense logic in shaping our realities. Very similar to Laclau and Mouffe, his argument that people might always have a choice could be read as acknowledging that such choices might be constrained by material and ideational factors (Turner 1972, 13). Even though Turner might have been in search of a singular solution or 'eye to be threaded' – my main point of criticism in this contribution – an end to this process of constrained choice has never and can never truly be on the cards.

TURNER'S CRITIQUE OF WHITE LIBERALS

To reiterate, central to my exploration of a desired South African polity informed by authors such as Turner and Laclau and Mouffe is a reflection on Turner's critique of white liberals in South Africa in the early 1970s (Turner 1972, 152–153). Given continued racism, a hitherto dominant party that has failed the people in many ways and dysfunctional, invited and often misguided invented spaces (Mattes 2019, 3), additional praxes to electoral politics and participatory processes as they exist now must be considered. The rate of failure of institutions is simply too high for South Africans to place all their hope in them.

We may ask what cause for hope there is when a government is not looking after the people who voted it in. It is here where the only rela-tively unexplored avenue appears to be fluid, pragmatic alliances across historical fault lines, responding to social ills seen as the shared problems that they are. Such a politics is necessarily open-ended and informed by the contingency of the social and the continuously moving definitional targets that are 'liberation', 'equity', 'justice' and, in Johan Galtung's (1969) vernacular, a 'positive peace'. To conceive of such a politics, we could probably benefit from reflexively revisiting Turner's critique of white lib-erals, viewed as an enduring message.

His critique remains relevant and should be viewed as a call to action to relative privilege. Such a call to action will require gradual re-socialisation and conceptual re-articulation towards a new, meaningful, popular sovereignty that holds the elected government and officials at all scales to account (see Mbembe 2015) – thus the very stuff of pragmatic articulation and re-articulation. This politics will entail a set of loosely formed and dynamic institutions that can 'prefigure the future' (Keniston 2014, 79). Dismissal of such a notion by citing a supposed reality of fixed interests would close analysts off, prematurely and unwisely, to important aspects of 'the real'. It would imply a self-contradictory static view of history, which is incompatible with the ontology of reiteration outlined at the start of this chapter.

Merrill Proudfoot and Ronald Christenson (1978) summarise Turner's position regarding the white liberal programme as follows: 'Briefly, the book's thesis is that South Africa's problem is not at its root racial but economic and that correct as they are about the injustice of Apartheid, the liberals' program would never work, even if by some miracle they should succeed in making it the policy of the country, because it would only induct a few blacks into the privileged class while leaving intact the real mechanism of oppression, exploitative capitalism.'

Turner was one of many authors from the 1970s, and later, to consider the relative importance of the relationship between race and class. Though I do not have the space to deal comprehensively with this ubiquitous problematic, I would contest the analysis of Turner and others (Wolpe 1972; Webster 1993) that class trumped race, notwithstanding that Proudfoot and Christenson's summary of Turner's position arguably materialised when democratisation finally happened decades later. Race, too, amongst a myriad of overlapping crises, should not be placed at the heart of exploitation. Rather, the class–race relationship is complex. Turner did, in retrospect mistakenly, see more potential in trade unions than there may have been, given the simultaneous rise of neoliberal dogma with the unravelling of the apartheid state. But praxis closely related to trade unions was his practical recommendation of the time, which Eddie Webster (1993, 8), despite criticism by Billy Keniston (2017), contrasts with values. Indeed, values were important to Turner's politics. To him, liberation also meant changing values and ways of living (Turner 1972, 98; Fluxman and Vale 2004, 176).

Turner advocated for socialism as the only system compatible with Christian values. This too was a pragmatic move. He was not a Christian or religious. *The Eye of the Needle* was published by the Christian Institute because of a collaborative project, based on some aligned ideals.

One could argue that there was something in the notion of 'love your neighbour' that informed his thought. According to Proudfoot and Christenson (1978), 'Turner accepts the Christian view that people find their fulfilment in loving relationships with other people.' Above all else there was an openness to Turner's thought and politics. Greaves (1987, 37) notes that 'at its core it [Turner's thought] was informed, as much as any of his other political engagements, by the attempt to build a critical culture, a coherent and lived set of alternative values and morals'. There is hence much evidence of a radical embrace of conceptual eclecticism and practical flexibility that Turner and Laclau and Mouffe seem to share (also see Keniston 2017, 24; Ryan 2017, 45).

'Love thy neighbour' could perhaps be reframed for our more secular contemporary era as high levels of considerateness or compassion, a valuing of people (and their opposing ideas) above things (see Turner 1972; Keniston 2014, 79) and above a stubborn attachment to one's own preconceived values and concepts. But that does not mean we have to take such a framing as a perfect representation of the dynamic real. Such a framing may be a mere pragmatic tool. The problem then becomes how to convey, in an accessible vernacular, that there is potential for progressive change to those to whom any particular framing of a status quo is imperative. Perhaps more cynically, we may also wonder what they (those more attached to specific ideas and values) would rather sacrifice to save face and maintain a degree of ontological security. Is it capitalism or significant concessions towards socialism, or is it Christianity or major concessions away from the Bible? These are merely a few examples in the far more complex intertwined tapestry that constitutes the contemporary social order.

Any answer would most likely be varied, and as such precisely what one might hope for. As the composition of the middle and upper classes today is more diverse than ever before, a protagonist does not need to win over everyone at once or apply forceful change to leverage the contingency of the social towards progressive ends. Furthermore, as mentioned, Christians are not the only constituency to be engaged. This insight leads us toward various potential praxes or various 'eyes' of 'needles' across space and time, to be 'threaded' as building blocks toward a different, but dynamic and responsive social order, where demands may be somewhat dissimilar across scales. Although Turner might, for example, have been wrong in one time and space by proposing the potential of Christian churches amongst others to influence change in South Africa, this is not really the point of reading and engaging with his work today. He was, fundamentally, against 'dogmatic metaphysics' (Turner 1972, 30). His pragmatic openness led to great discontent as the 'Old Left' gained traction in what Keniston (2017, 26), seemingly drawing on Herbert Marcuse, calls one-dimensionality. Openness and egalitarianism in the resistance was gradually replaced with structural Marxist dogma and hierarchical institutions, with the latter arguably still reigning supreme in contemporary South Africa.

CRIME AS ONE OF MANY OVERLAPPING PROBLEMATICS

In 2013, Karl von Holdt published an important paper in which he framed South Africa as a 'violent democracy'. He references numerous examples of direct violence, including political killings, structural violence and crime of all kinds. This violent democracy may also be seen as embodying the sense of enduring injustice and a lack of hope felt by many (Fluxman and Vale 2004, 173). In this regard, Webster (2014, 146) affirms the fraught nature of the political party system and invited spaces, by emphasising 'disillusionment with current political parties'. Yet, material inequality might be a useful starting point around which to develop ancillary projects. South Africa suffers from staggering levels of unemployment, absolute and relative poverty and high levels of crime (StatsSA 2019, 5; Van Riet 2022a, 10–11). In such a setting we may ask: What does Turner's vehement opposition to violence as a political tool (Greaves 1987, 34) tell us about contemporary South Africa, considering the notion of a 'violent democracy'?

The policing of crime and the management of fear have developed into a set of nodal or networked public and private projects (Shearing and Wood 2003; Du Pont 2004). These projects include diverse security infrastructures (Van Riet 2020, 2022a) such as private security companies, alarm systems and panic buttons, electric fences and live monitored cameras in public spaces, with private security companies often central to looking after the interests of relative privilege. Privilege does what it can to preserve a type of increasingly difficult to define 'purity' that actively excludes marginal residents. Infrastructures such as neighbourhood residents' associations and city improvement districts are cases in point. There are significant asymmetries in security provision (Van Riet 2022b), as not everyone can afford new security infrastructures, such as an armed response contract, and others are excluded from responses to crime on account of being linked to 'the abject' and seen as criminals through racist and classist logics of equivalence (Van Riet 2022a, chapters 8–9). Moreover, based on my fieldwork, it seems clear that not everyone enjoys the same level of respect from the state police, if one takes the asymmetries in resource allocation, distances to police stations and the long queues at many township police stations as evidence (Van Riet 2020, 2022a).

Still, there are many reasons why there remains a semblance of stability in South Africa. These include the social security system, patronage networks, including even small-scale forms of patronage (see Van Riet and Silander 2022) at the local level, and the spectre of a mythical and pending second phase of a supposed two-stage revolution (Mosala et al. 2017). This spectre of a 'red peril' for some and 'meaningful change' for others gives the ruling party power, as the supposed custodians of the revolution. At the same time the official opposition has confirmed perceptions of conservatism, by initiating significant changes when it lost ground to the right in the previous general election. To this we must add senses of historic injustice justified by the fact that poverty remains a largely black phenomenon and, more controversially, that inequality, which is growing, is a legacy as opposed to a *continuous reiteration* of the past. Such a reading of history, to reiterate, is strangely self-contradictory. Of course, racism endures; it has been relatively robust after apartheid. As inhabitants of an

African country, many white residents need to learn how to engage with their black equals, respectfully, around collective causes or even in solidarity with their fellow residents' needs, without allowing asymmetrical power relationships to hijack these causes. Opposing such a set of projects is the reality that the response to crime is driven by fear of an often poorly specified other, based on logics of equivalence (Van Riet 2022a).

It is against this backdrop that I must disagree with the notion of racism as a requirement for capitalist modernisation, argued by Andrew Nash (1999, 67), as an enduring feature of our social reality. This argument is plausible only up to a point. Thereafter, unrestrained marginalisation must be counterproductive for capitalist development, by causing class-based divisions, out-of-control material inequality, under-consumption, and the subsequent threat of conflict. Although deindustrialisation grew post democracy, it did not start with democracy. Racist decision-making was a major factor in this regard. As such, apartheid and post-democracy globalisation have represented two largely distinct forms of biopolitical abandonment of the masses. And these processes of abandonment are what lie behind much of South Africa's scourge of criminality; not all of it, to be sure, but much of it (Van Riet 2022a, 21–38).

There is very little doubt that South Africa does indeed have much crime (BBC News 2019; Conway-Smith 2019). This ranges from white-collar crime to theft, robbery, house-breaking and the scourge of sexual violence. While the latter is perhaps too complex to even begin to explain here, material inequality is a major contributing force to crime in general. Such inequality is exacerbated by the high levels of absolute poverty and senses of injustice. As a country infamous for its Gini coefficient and with often brazen conspicuous consumption by a minority, there is clearly something wrong in the fabric of society. Consequently, strain theory, initially developed by Robert Merton (1938), remains germane. This theory holds that where certain goods (like the luxury or even basic spoils of accumulation) are highly valued by dominant voices in a social order, some will resort to illegal means to obtain these goods if they lack the legitimate means to do so.

The problem of crime and the response to it by and for relatively privileged members of the social order is an instructive example to use in highlighting a politics that arises from a reading of Turner in conversation with Laclau and Mouffe and, thus, from poststructuralism. Compared to rigid existentialism, and in contrast to structural Marxism or decolonial thought based on bounded categories, a poststructural ontology offers greater insight into the dynamic constraints and opportunities for social and political action. It is increasingly obvious that crime reduction is a collective problem. Victims exist across various lines of division. Parties may enter deliberation on this matter for different reasons, but even then, crime presents a set of opportunities for constructive engagement between diverse actors, and as a collective engaging the state. We may use crime as *one* national concern around which residents espousing diverse arguments and values may gather. In relation to the state, they may, following continuous internal deliberation, raise demands and organise through advocacy, demonstration, and thus diverse praxes towards hegemonic re-articulation.

Focusing on examples such as crime does not detract from the fundamental political economic problematic of material inequality, which Laclau and Mouffe (2013) argue against and which is a general poststructuralist point of contention with classical Marxism (Fox 2003, 100). Instead, this fundamental political economic problem is at the heart of much of the crime, be it acts of need, acts of vengeance or more complexly defined. There is no escaping this reality for the privileged minority, no matter how much they spend on security infrastructures. We must thus break, partially, with Turner and Laclau and Mouffe on this point, by temporarily and pragmatically foregrounding material inequality as a fundamental social ill.

WHAT CAN WE TAKE FROM TURNER?

To imagine new possibilities for a new social order, we consider the over-determination and radical contingency of the social and attempt to look past the optical constraints of contemporary realities. This is, of course, a partially impossible exercise. Turner wrote of ideology, manipulation and change. Today, liberal ideology at a global scale has some bearing on our realities, and so, too, in the South African context have political manipulation, manifested in recent looting in KwaZulu-Natal and Gauteng, and the relative success of discourses of radical economic transformation. Both Turner, as a restrained existentialist, and Laclau and Mouffe understand the world in terms of what Morphet (1990, 94) describes as a double hermeneutic. The first is one of hope. It tries to imagine where things can go and then tries to contribute to such progressive change. The second hermeneutic is one of suspicion of the present. The second is arguably a requirement for the first.

Both Turner and Laclau and Mouffe understand that power is diffuse (Turner 1972, 80). Divisions within society are not insurmountable, precisely because there are so many and because there is an increasingly obvious common foe in the form of the government and its tentacles into the economy and big capital and its tentacles into the state, notwithstanding other complex and overlapping tensions. The atomisation of the social order which Turner (1972, 67–71) refers to (in his case the urban workers) remains a perennial problem. This problem can only be overcome through genuine engagement across divisions on a fair footing. Then it becomes a set of opportunities for building productive bridges. Residents of South Africa must realise that the concern of their neighbour is often also their own concern, even where this might not be immediately obvious. Given such a realisation, the notion 'love thy neighbour' or high levels of a considerateness and compassion that values people (and their opposing ideas) above things, does make sense as one potential guideline for praxes.

Following Laclau and Mouffe, there is an important point where I depart from many readings of Turner. This departure, informed by radical contingency and the over-determination of the social, holds that there is not one final formula or solution for the problems of a dynamic whole, which Turner attempted to arrive at despite an overall pragmatic orientation. At best, there can be a general set of values and principles that remain flexible and inform pragmatic tactics. I would also like to challenge the work of Laclau and Mouffe who argue that 'post-Marxism' should, categorically, not start with historical materialism and the economy as the main problem in society. Their point might be well taken, in general, at an ontological level. There are, however, exceptions and spatio-historical specificities and contextualised epistemologies. Currently, we need alternatives to 'neoliberal' capitalism and ways of becoming a socialist democracy (Webster 2014, 152). South Africans need income, as a bare minimum, and indeed inequality was a growing core concern of Turner's (Fluxman and Vale 2004, 179), as it remains for various analysts today. However, reifying the economy is not the solution. Crime and material inequality are not the only challenges facing South Africa.

My argument, in the short term, is simply that reducing inequality may alleviate some of the most pressing displays of frustration, while it should, in theory, reduce crime and the counterproductive elite responses to it. In the long run, however, and even to establish a more sustainably equitable social order that includes greater trust between residents, physical and metaphorical fences need to be reduced. This is more possible than many would like to believe. Turner (1972, 86) challenged the idea that whites (and for that matter the broader privileged group) are a monolithic category and that change will solely come from or is entirely the purview of the black population or, in contemporary South Africa, the relatively marginalised majority. Power is diffuse and notwithstanding constraints to freedom, it can be leveraged towards progressive ends from various entry points. South Africa is a different space now compared to the early 1970s. Many political constraints to relatively free speech, public critique and protest have been removed. There is more scope for praxes. This presents an opportunity for elites to express their distaste and align themselves with some of the underlying causes of these protests.

As regards crime, I have documented how some privileged South Africans are slowly setting new precedents (Van Riet 2022a). This includes challenging established common-sense knowledge in the local newspaper and on social media, and proactively looking for livelihood options for car guards and garbage pickers displaced by a city improvement district (Cilliers 2019; Van Riet 2022a, 185). These interventions are far from enough. Yet, they arguably offer evidence of hope. They are important in that they form the basis for the continuous development of different centres of power in the social order, advocating for the changes in the dynamic challenges faced at different scales and in different spatio-temporal contexts (Turner 1972, 87). Further evidence of Turner's eye for pragmatism is that he, similarly, saw the potential of diversity in white South African society, even when it was possibly far more homogeneous (Turner 1972, 78). The current reality is more intricate than simply dividing privilege into 'verkramp', 'pragmatic' and 'verlig'.[1]

Whether and how Turner was wrong, given how South African politics later played out, is not the goal of reading his work. Instead, reading Turner – as a restrained existentialist, I argue – potentially inspires a type of incessant constructive reflection that is extremely critical of popular categories and prominent common-sense beliefs. Like the theory of poststructural hegemony, Turner allows for a type of reflection that *does not stop at critique*. Both Turner and Laclau and Mouffe advocate for imagining new realities. For academics, this is scary, as such scholarship often 'paints a target on one's back', when we conceive of theories and praxes that can be critiqued. I would, however, argue that such scholarship is more authentic and sincere. Having the courage to speculate about a better future and, better yet, to engage in 'public philosophy' (Nupen 1988, 37; Ryan 2017, 41) and other progressive praxes, demonstrates integrity. Morphet (1990, 95) is quite right that intentions do matter. Critique as the totality of an academic career can be insincere and wastefully unhelpful.

CONCLUSION

By heeding Hudson's (2017) argument that Turner anticipated the 'new Sartre' and by bringing Turner into conversation with the work of Laclau and Mouffe on poststructural hegemony, I have attempted to show commonalities between these perspectives. Recognising, more fully, the dynamic constraints to and opportunities for human freedom points to commonalities between these authors. Reading Turner in this way also highlights his contemporary relevance. One important commonality between Turner, as a restrained existentialist, and poststructuralists such as Laclau and Mouffe, points to a link between idealism and pragmatism. The over-determination of the social implies manifold opportunities for reiteration and, as I have argued, fluid and more meaningful collaboration across historical fault lines. I have drawn on the empirical example of crime and elite responses to reiterate Turner's relevance in our current milieu, albeit with some qualifications. The problem of crime cannot be viewed in isolation. It is merely a case in point, demonstrating how the South African social order has continuously been reiterated and how much constructive change is still needed. Many elite responses, through various security infrastructures, target individuals as reified 'criminals' when they are in fact evidence of societal problems, and in need of greater societal compassion and consequently more inclusive praxes.

Thus, there is a need to reconsider the definite article in the title of Turner's most well-known work. Progressive change is a continuous set of unending projects. There should be open, respectful and unending discussions on how we define 'progress'. For now, I favour meaningful social policy, addressing material inequality as most urgent. Of course, such an interpretation of a complex social order suffering many afflictions is not without danger, most notably the neglect of some important causes.

A key question remains as to how such praxes may be initiated. I do not yet have meaningful suggestions, except for stating that there can be no singular formula. I will, however, raise the following problematic: How do we bring history back into our analysis? What lies ahead, after 'bad governance'? How does this current moment relate to the *longue durée* of South African history? How can we imagine a caring social order without succumbing to teleology? I would add to this: How do we temper discussions on policy and formal institutions where they potentially impinge on productive politics?

This chapter has essentially outlined 'radical reform' as ascribed to Turner by Webster (1993), which has not been without criticism (Keniston 2014). My reading of Turner as a restrained existentialist points to the need for an emergent culture of continuous regeneration and consistent reflection. To this end, the chapter has highlighted the need for South Africans from diverse backgrounds to support each other's causes, as far as they feel comfortable. Only then can the privileged progressives heed Turner's enduring message by not being privileged first and progressive second.

NOTE

1   These are categories used by Turner and by political commentators of the time more generally. *Verlig* refers to more 'enlightened' white South Africans of the time. *Verkramp* refers to more conservative and rigid white South Africans of the time. 'Pragmatic' is a more self-evidentiary category. It was viewed as a type of middle ground.

REFERENCES

Adorno, Theodor and Max Horkheimer. 1947. *The Dialectic of Enlightenment*. London: Verso.

BBC News. 2019. 'South Africa Crime: Police Figures Show Rising Murder and Sexual Offences'. *BBC News*, 12 September 2019. https://www.bbc.com/news/world-africa-49673944. Accessed 27 February 2021.

Cilliers, Juanneé. 2019. 'Potch dis Tyd vir Opruim!'. *Potchefstroom Herald*, 18 April 2019.

Conway-Smith, Erin. 2019. 'Soaring Murder Rate Drives Cape Town up the List of Deadliest Cities'. *The Times*, 1 July 2019. https://www.thetimes.co.uk/article/soaring-murder-rate-drives-cape-town-up-list-of-deadliest-cities-xhqw3k0ld. Accessed 15 January 2024.

Du Pont, Benoît. 2004. 'Security in the Age of Networks'. *Policing and Society* 14: 76–91.

Fluxman, Anthony and Peter Vale. 2004. 'Re-reading Rick Turner in the New South Africa'. *International Relations* 18 (2): 173–189.

Fox, Nik Farrell. 2003. *The New Sartre*. London: Continuum.

Galtung, Johan. 1969. 'Violence, Peace and Security'. *Journal of Peace Research* 27 (3): 167–191.

Gramsci, Antonio. 1971. *Selections from The Prison Notebooks*. New York: International Publishers.

Greaves, Duncan. 1987. 'Richard Turner and the Politics of Emancipation'. *Theoria* 34: 32–40.

Hudson, Peter. 2017. 'Let's Talk about Rick Turner'. *Theoria* 64 (151): 1–9.

Keniston, Billy. 2014. 'Response to Eddie Webster's Review of *Choosing to be Free: The Life Story of Rick Turner*'. *Transformation: Critical Perspectives on Southern Africa* 86 (1): 78–81.

Keniston, Billy. 2017. 'The Weight of Absence: Rick Turner and the End of the Durban Moment'. *Theoria* 64 (151): 20–28.

Laclau, Ernesto. 1990. *New Reflections on the Revolution of Our Time*. London: Verso.

Laclau, Ernesto and Chantal Mouffe. 2013. *Hegemony and Socialist Strategy*. London: Verso.

Marcuse, Herbert. 1991. *One-dimensional Man: Studies in the Ideology of Advanced Industrial Society*. Boston, MA: Beacon Press.

Mattes, Robert. 2019. 'Democracy in Africa: Demand, Supply, and the "Dissatisfied Democrat"'. Afrobarometer Policy Paper No. 54. https://www.afrobarometer.org/publications/pp54-democracy-africa-demand-supply-and-dissatisfied-democrat. Accessed 25 January 2021.

Mbembe, Achille. 2015. 'The State of South African Political Life'. *Africa is a Country*. https://africasacountry.com/2015/09/achille-mbembe-on-the-state-of-south-african-politics/. Accessed 20 August 2020.

Merton, Robert. 1938. 'Social Structure and Anomie'. *American Sociological Review* 3: 672– 682.

Morphet, Tony. 1990. '"Brushing History Against the Grain": Oppositional Discourse in South Africa'. *Theoria* 76: 89–99.

Mosala, Seshupo, Jan Venter and Eddie Bain. 2017. 'South Africa's Economic Transformation since 1994: What Influence Has the National Democratic Revolution (NDR) had?'. *The Review of Black Political Economy* 44 (3–4): 327–340.

Nash, Andrew. 1999. 'The Moment of Western Marxism in South Africa'. *Comparative Studies of South Asia, Africa and the Middle East* 19 (1): 66–81.

Nupen, Michael. 1988. 'Philosophy and the Crisis in South Africa'. *Transformation* 7: 37–46.

Parker, Scott. 2017. 'The Truth is Revolutionary: Mills and Turner as Theoreticians of Participatory Democracy'. *South African Historical Journal* 69 (2): 288–303.

Proudfoot, Merrill and Ronald Christenson. 1978. 'Preface'. *The Eye of the Needle: Towards Participatory Democracy in South Africa*. Maryknoll (NY): Orbis Books. https://www.sahistory.org.za/archive/eye-needle-preface-richard-turner. Accessed 18 February 2021.

Ryan, Mary. 2017. 'Imagining Utopia in an Unfree World: Rick Turner on Morality, Inequality and Existentialism'. *Theoria* 64 (151): 40–46.

Shearing, Clifford and Jennifer Wood. 2003. 'Nodal Governance, Democracy and the New "Denizens"'. *Journal of Law and Society* 30 (3): 400–419.

StatsSA (Statistics South Africa). 2019. 'Inequality Trends in South Africa: A Multidimensional Diagnostic of Inequality'. Report No. 03-10-19. http://www.statssa.gov.za/publications/Report-03-10-19/Report-03-10-192017.pdf. Accessed 22 July 2020.

Turner, Richard. 1972. *The Eye of the Needle: An Essay on Participatory Democracy*. Johannesburg: Spro-Cas Publishers.

Van Riet, Gideon. 2020. 'Intermediating Between Conflict and Security: Private Security Companies as Infrastructures of Security in Post-apartheid South Africa'. *Politikon: The South African Journal of Political Studies* 47 (1): 81–98.

Van Riet, Gideon. 2022a. *Hegemony, Security Infrastructures and the Politics of Crime: Everyday Experiences in South Africa*. London: Routledge.

Van Riet, Gideon. 2022b. 'Topology, Scene and Asymmetries in Security Provision in a Small South African City'. *Critical Studies on Security* 11 (1): 14–23.

Van Riet, Gideon and Daniel Silander. 2022. 'Exploring the Democratic Role of Popular Protests'. In *South Africa's Democracy at a Crossroads*, edited by Daniel Silander, Charlotte Silander, Pieter Heydenrych and Herman van der Elst, 113–125. London: Emerald.

Von Holdt, Karl. 2013. 'South Africa: The Transition to Violent Democracy'. *Review of African Political Economy* 40 (138): 589–604.

Webster, Eddie. 1993. 'Moral Decay and Social Reconstruction: Richard Turner and Radical Reform'. *Theoria* 81/82: 1–13.

Webster, Eddie. 2014. 'Review: Billy Keniston. 2013. *Choosing to be Free: The Life Story of Rick Turner*. Auckland Park: Jacana'. *Transformation* 85: 146–152.

Wolpe, Harold. 1972. 'Capitalism and Cheap Labour-power in South Africa: From Segregation to Apartheid'. *Economy and Society* 1 (4): 425–456.

PART V

ON THE NATURE OF
POLITICAL THEORY

11

Rick Turner and the Vision of Engaged Political Philosophy

Christine Hobden

Our common usage of the term 'utopian' casts the utopian into the realm of the useless; it is unachievable and so not of use to us. In dire political situations, we find ourselves reaching always for the useful, something that can make a difference, that can build or protect. But we should not confuse achievability with usefulness. There is much in our lives that we pursue and never achieve. We are nonetheless often better off for the pursuit. Our destination is shaped by where we were heading, even if it is not in fact the destination for which we originally aimed. While it is accurate that that which is utopian by definition cannot be achieved, we are missing something valuable when we fail to imagine, in great detail, what a better world might look like.

We are also sometimes tempted to believe that the utopian is abstracted entirely away from our world; that the perfect cannot have roots in our deeply unjust reality. But the ideal does not have to be abstract. To be sure, ideal theorising will abstract away from reality in its presentation of what ideally should be the case, but there is nothing inherent to ideal theorising or utopian thought that requires starting from an ideal or imagined world. In fact, Rick Turner's work encourages us to do the opposite: to begin our utopian theorising from a deep understanding of our current realities. For Turner, utopian thinking is useful precisely because it provides tools to better understand, evaluate and change our society as we find it now.

Turner's ideas about, and practice of, political philosophy within the context of his commitment to resisting the injustice of apartheid South Africa can provide valuable guidance to political philosophers and theorists today – for all of us, but perhaps especially for those of us embedded in privilege within the current version of a white supremacist, patriarchal society. Drawing on the insights of Turner's life and work, I will argue for the value of practising what I term 'engaged political philosophy'. Engaged political philosophy as a methodological approach to the discipline of political philosophy is inspired by the work, life and ideas of Turner, but is not a claim to set out his view in its entirety or to imagine his comments on current political philosophy. Rather, it attempts to bring Turner into dialogue with current methodological thinking and use these arguments and theories as tools to explicate my own developing approach to political philosophy.

In what follows, I set out the broad guidelines of what constitutes engaged political philosophy as a method and analyse the source of each step of the method within Turner's life and work, with particular focus on his introductory chapter to *The Eye of the Needle*, 'The Need for Utopian Thinking' (1980), and reference to his earlier 'What is Political Philosophy?' (1968). To end, I offer two main arguments for its value: its potential to transform us, and its potential to transform society.

THE METHOD: ENGAGED POLITICAL PHILOSOPHY

Rick Turner took seriously the injunction that it is the task of the intellectual not merely to understand the world, but also to change it.

— Eddie Webster, cited in Jann Turner, 'Rick Turner: Thirty Years On'

At the heart of Turner's work is the existential idea that ultimately (almost) anything is possible; we are radically free. Our task is to come to accept this, to accept that while we had no choice in the facts of our life and how they have shaped us, we have now a second choice that is not limited by those conditions (Turner cited in Keniston 2013, 25). When we assume, as Turner argued most white liberals do, that the institutions and structures of our society are unchangeable, when we treat them like naturally occurring mountains around which we have to work, we make the mistake of assuming the answer to the most fundamental question in our theorising: What is changeable and what is not? (Turner 1980, 2). Not only do we assume the answer to this question, but, Turner argues, we lean too heavily toward meekly accepting much as unchangeable. We confuse that which is 'other things being equal impossible' with that which is 'absolutely impossible' (Turner 1980, 1). In illustrating this point, Turner compares white liberals at the time to those who do not fight the lion head on, but consider themselves to be doing enough when they offer up their old goats in an attempt to protect their prize lambs (Turner 1980, 1). Turner argues instead that it is only the imperatives of human nature and organisation that are unchangeable – and even those, I would add, are contestable.

Utopian thinking, then, is not purely aspirational for Turner, but an act of freedom itself – and in an oppressive state, the radical act of claiming that freedom. Importantly though, this value of utopian thinking is linked to a belief that society is in fact changeable, that this vision is possible – perhaps not right now, or not without consequence, but possible nonetheless. Turner lived this in his own life: a conscious choice to be free – one that came with severe consequences. His life illustrated that it was possible to make choices, such as speaking freely against the apartheid state and living a marriage that it outlawed, in a way that most white liberals denied, in action if not always explicitly articulated. Dan O'Meara recalls Turner saying as much explicitly when he talked to him about his choice to live openly married to Foszia Fisher: 'I have chosen to be free and I accept the consequences' (Keniston 2013, 76).

Utopian thinking is not, then, abstracted dreaming; it is the serious consideration of an ideal future society and as such is necessarily rooted in an understanding of one's society as it exists now – to identify both what is changeable and what is not, and to build a vision and a path toward it that reflects this distinction. It is both these features held together – radical freedom to choose and deep understanding of the space in which we choose – that present the strength of Turner's approach. As Jann Turner phrased it in considering the intellectual forces that her father might have deployed in our current context, a Turnerian approach brings together 'reason and imagination. Critical and visionary thinking' (Turner 2007).

The Turner-inspired method which I term 'engaged political philosophy' includes four steps: (i) analysis of the societal context; (ii) understanding one's own position within that context; (iii) developing a utopian theory; and (iv) bringing that utopian theory back into dialogue with the societal context. These steps are not strictly consecutive but will often overlap and be repeated in layers as a theory is developed. Importantly, the step of developing utopian theory is always embedded within this process – it cannot happen in isolation, or as our starting point. In this chapter, I illustrate how we can discover the method of engaged political philosophy from within Turner's life and writing, and the value of this method from a Turnerian perspective. The method of engaged political philosophy is not fully developed here in either its theory or practice. I focus instead on a first step of examining its Turnerian roots.

STARTING WHERE WE ARE: SOCIETAL CONTEXT

So the philosophical approach should be the critical one of always checking facts, reading widely to fill in the necessary background, and always looking for the implicit interpretations.
— Rick Turner, 'What is Political Philosophy?'

Turner argues that in order to 'understand a society...where it is going, and where it could go...we need to refer back and forth between what we see in the society and what is essential to any society' (Turner 1980, 5). Theorising, understood as necessarily being directed toward change, always includes an eye on society as it is experienced now. A theoretical attitude requires us to view the present as history – to understand the contingency of where we find ourselves (Turner 1980, 5–6). This contingency does not, however, mean the irrelevance of where we find ourselves: our everyday actions and institutions are representations of the implicit assumptions and beliefs that shape both our behaviour and the lens through which we understand the reality around us (Turner 1968, 1). For Turner, it is identifying these implicit assumptions that is the first step in theorising toward change (the second, as we will discuss later, is building a new ideological lens through which we read our reality).

Although frequently overlooked in the practice of contemporary ideal theorising, it is not a new insight that understanding the institutions, relational power dynamics and general workings of society should be an important first step toward developing normative theories of an ideal society. It is also a central claim in scholarship that critiques contemporary ideal theories, particularly for the ways its conclusions illustrate that it has not begun with an understanding of gender or race dynamics in society (Pateman 1988; Mills 1997, 2005). So, on the one hand, this insight from Turner's approach appears unoriginal, and at least in some circles, uncontroversial, if worth emphasising yet again.

On the other hand, we might think that engaging with the empirical, the 'facts and means', is best left to those with specialised skills: the political scientists, anthropologists, economists or sociologists. Disciplinary divisions do, at least in some respects, track specialised skills. The philosopher, then, might wish to both protect their particular philosophising ground from others and justify their avoidance of engagement with reality as respecting that as the social scientists' turf. Turner offers us some response to such a view: philosophical theorising is essential to understanding a society – our ground is perhaps larger than we thought and the task deeply important. Yet, in engaging with the realities around us, a political philosopher does so with a philosophical lens. There is no call to shift the fundamental method and contribution of philosophical thought; the aim of the engaged political philosopher is not to gather observations or provide descriptions of the facts but to interrogate such observations and descriptions in order to understand the hidden assumptions that shape the societal presentation of these observations and descriptions. For Turner, it is only once we have identified this deeper layer of societal workings that we can understand what is changeable, and what might need to be changed.

CONSIDERING WHERE I AM: PERSONAL CONTEXT

> For two people with identical moral codes will behave very differently if they understand the situation differently.
> — Rick Turner, 'What is Political Philosophy?'

Alongside this analysis of the society in which one is theorising, Turner's work encourages us to interrogate our own position within this society – and the extent to which this will shape our understanding of the society we analyse, and so our theorising and our enacting of our theory. Contemporary ideas of positionality were not in Turner's vocabulary but, I argue, the beginnings of these kinds of ideas are implicit in his arguments on the nature of ideal political philosophy and its methods. I think, as I argue below, that there is evidence that Turner's work can accommodate the role of positionality argued for in contemporary decolonial and feminist philosophy (consider, as an example of this work, arguments on the role of race, gender and language in knowledge creation [Collins 1986; Dotson 2011; Kumalo 2020; Mellor 2022]). We should note, however, that here we begin to build *from* Turner rather than interpret solely what is explicitly present and articulated in his written work and his life. This consciousness was not always explicit in Turner's life or the utopias he envisioned. As Billy Keniston writes, his first wife, Barbara Hubbard, in her words, 'would say to Richard and his male friends, "I don't know how you can talk about liberating people when you guys still behave like white South African men, expecting women to make you tea, drop your clothes on the way to the bathroom and expect someone to pick it up"' (Keniston 2013, 54). While Hubbard adds that 'he did change, and began to lose the "I am here to be waited on" attitude' (Keniston 2013, 54), there is much to interrogate around blind spots in Turner's texts on gender, and the intersection of race and gender, as Paula Ensor so aptly illustrates in chapter 4 of this book in her analysis of African women workers as the 'unrecognised other'. Despite this, which can be interpreted as a critique of Turner's self-reflection on his own position within his life and work, there are two features of Turner's presentation of ideal political philosophy that, I argue, offer resources to include reflection on one's positionality as a feature of practising engaged political philosophy of a Turnerian kind. First, I examine his emphasis on the need to show a universalistic idea in action, and second, his emphasis on distinguishing the changeable from the unchangeable.

Argument from the Need to Show a Universalistic Idea in Action

This first point links directly to the need to analyse society as a first step. Turner offers a further reason for this in 'What is Political Philosophy?': 'moral principles are useless without an understanding of the situation' because theory cannot have use unless we understand how the theory will be enacted (Turner 1968, 2). Drawing on a Christian example, Turner makes the fairly self-evident case that people's actions often diverge even when they claim to be following the same moral principle, such as 'love thy neighbour as yourself' (Turner 1968, 2). We could consider a familiar South African example as illustrative here: though many may agree on the principle that extreme social and economic inequality is morally wrong and ought to be rectified, there is widespread difference in how

South Africans live out that belief. While some of this may be ascribed to apathy, fear and other forms of resistance to the change required to rectify it, difference is also created by different understandings of our context. As Turner points out, one can 'love thy neighbour' through alleviating their pain with some soup or warm socks or you can 'love your neighbour' by challenging the political, economic and societal structures that subject them to their oppression and poverty (Turner 1968, 1–2).

Theory cannot predict all the many ways individual agents may interpret or act upon its ideas; I do not think that is what Turner had in mind. It does, however, illustrate that moral principle alone is not enough to change a society – our theory needs to reflect the nature of society, why it is the way it is, and how these principles speak to change. To develop good theory we need to bring these two things into dialogue – a critical understanding of the context and our moral imperatives.

Linking this to positionality – our personal context in relationship to the societal context – my claim is that the mandate to critically understand societal context inherently includes a critical understanding of one's own position within that context. Turner's claim is that this need to understand a universalist principle *in action* is not a next, 'application' step to the intellectual project but a central part of theorising. It is a claim that the theoretical idea or argument is, or should be, shaped by (or constrained by) considerations of what that principle looks like in action, in the specific context in which we theorise. Such a view, I suggest, implies, or at the very least would be sympathetic to, the related claim that the relationship between the theorist's position within the context and the ideas they develop plays a significant role, not as an add-on consideration, but within the core of what constitutes theorising and theory.

Argument from the Attention to What is Changeable vs What is Unchangeable

In the introductory chapter to *The Eye of the Needle*, 'The Need for Utopian Thinking', Turner speaks frequently of the conditions needed to reflect on our values as a society (Turner 1980). As mentioned earlier, he argues for the value of utopian thinking because of the ways in which it helps us to identify what in our society is a necessary imperative of human nature or organisation and what is, in fact, changeable (Turner 1980, 3). We often, he argues, assume our social institutions are unchangeable, like mountains, when in fact, with collective behaviour change, our institutions could be changed fundamentally (Turner 1980, 2).

This argument against the kind of conservatism that assumes the fixity of our social and political institutions can also be read as a mandate to interrogate our own assumptions about what is changeable. Utopian thinking, in Turner's view, seeks to break open the range of what is possible in social and political life. As practitioners of utopian theory, then, I argue there is an implicit mandate to constantly interrogate the extent to which one's own positionality limits one's view of the possible. It is not just that our own position within society might normalise institutions and privileges that must be addressed if we wish to imagine a different way of organising society, or the need for it. It is also that privilege blinds us to the obstacles that others might face – the gatekeeping and structural challenges – that not only do not impact upon the privileged but, at times, are also invisible in the uninterrogated privileged position. Positionality can thus limit us in how much change we see the need to envisage, how big we imagine and, at the same time, how realistically we imagine. Our position in society can influence the extent to which our theory reflects a recognition of the deep-seated realities of power and history that cannot be ignored or 'unseen' if we wish to meaningfully change society.

We can think here, for example, of Charles W Mills' critique of John Rawls that the difference principle cannot protect us against racial inequality (Mills 1997). Rawls' difference principle aims for impartiality and fairness but fails to account for the possibility that the 'worst off' in society (the group to whom inequality is justified on the basis of it making them better off) may all belong to one racial group. Similar to Ensor's critique of Turner, Mills argues against an ideal vision of society that assumes rather than actively ensures the inclusion of currently marginalised groups. This is because this assumption (or neglect) fails to recognise the deeply complex, unique and historical factors that characterise each marginalised group's oppression and so fails to speak to the institutional arrangements required to prevent its perpetuation. Turner's writing on utopian thinking carefully distinguishes engaged but utopian philosophy from the kind of ideal theory that Mills identifies and critiques in contemporary political philosophy and theory: ideal theory understood as 'reliance on idealization to the exclusion, or at least marginalization, of the actual', theory that views 'the actual as a simple deviation from the ideal, not worth theorizing in its own right', or theory that claims that 'starting from the ideal is at least the best way of realizing it' (Mills 2005, 168). These Turnerian resources include a deep engagement with the context in which we theorise and an honest interrogation of what within this context is changeable and what is not, and as I have argued here, self-reflection on how one's own position shapes this analysis.

What Work Does Positionality Do in 'Engaged Philosophy'?

The arguments above have illustrated that positionality plays a role both in inevitably shaping our theory, and in the mandate to interrogate, and to some extent mitigate, this influence. It does not make a claim against universalistic principles or push for a purely phenomenological approach to philosophy. The argument is, instead, that good theory has to begin from both a recognition and an interrogation of our own relationship to the society in which we live. We can see this as another way of expressing Turner's view that philosophy's mandate is to interrogate the assumptions behind the patterns of behaviour and beliefs of society (Turner 1968, 1). Our first role as philosophers, then, is to interrogate the implicit assumptions in our own worldviews.

We can also see here two closely related ideas: that the scholar's positionality will shape the theory they produce and, secondly, it will shape how those ideas are presented, leveraged and used within a political context. The latter gives us reason to also see considerations of audience as an important element of engaged philosophy. A clear grasp of the context and our position within it should be at the forefront of an engaged philosopher's mind in choosing the audience for which their theory is written, and where and how such theory is funded and published. The engaged philosopher believes that theory has a role to play in changing society and, as such, how the theory can lead to change is a central consideration: Who is it attempting to influence? How might it shape ideas and actions? It is an outward-looking position that sees producing theory as a way to participate, at some level, in the project of working toward justice.

This is a different perspective from that of the professional academic theorist producing theory as a personal project toward personal career objectives. In reality, many hold some mix of these understandings of the goal of theorising, and they do not necessarily always have to work against each other. The practitioner of engaged philosophy, however, aims to prioritise choices that serve the goal of participating in the project of change in the direction of justice. They recognise that both our personal and societal contexts shape when, and to whom, and in what manner it is appropriate to address our theory. These are complex considerations in today's academic space. Some examples might be attention to issues of open access, how we engage with journals within the global South versus the global North, and who we are published alongside (the publishing equivalent of all-white or all-male conference panels, for example).

WHERE IDEALLY WE SHOULD GO: UTOPIAN THEORY

Utopian thought is an 'invitation to begin the process of trying to change the society in a particular direction'.
— Rick Turner, *The Eye of the Needle: Towards Participatory Democracy in South Africa*

In one sense, Turner can inspire us to be radically bold in our imaginings of a different future. *The Eye of the Needle* is, in his own words, 'pejoratively utopian', illustrating merely, but importantly, that a 'participatory, socialist democracy is not impossible' (Turner 1980, 99). We are also invited to work toward universal moral principles – a bold act in our context where such universalistic claims have frequently been shown to be, in fact, distinctly un-universal in scope. The arguments presented above suggest, however, a better foundation for this kind of bold, utopian and universalist theorising. It does not claim to be neutral or from a place of 'nowhere'; it acknowledges its roots in where and who we are. These roots are both the key to boldness (because deep understanding of society identifies much more as changeable than we often make room for in our theory), and the key to acknowledging how these roots may limit us, whether in our ability to fully capture all required for a just future or, perhaps more positively, in providing clear boundaries for how our theories can contribute to a small, defined part of the required change.

We should note here perhaps that this exploration of engaged political philosophy contains two normative claims: first, it presents the case for how analytic, ideal political philosophy can and should play a role in transforming society. This is a broader claim, directed to both philosophers and others involved in working toward a more just society: utopian thinking should not be dismissed but leveraged to play a particular and valuable role. Second, directed toward philosophers, the method of engaged political philosophy contains the normative claim that it is a more just way to practise ideal political philosophy in contrast to some versions of ideal, universalised thinking present in the field today (as critiqued by Mills above). It does not argue that ideal theorising should be our only or central tool in resisting injustice nor that it is more valuable than non-ideal theory. It responds instead to the way that, on the one hand, we sometimes lose sight of the value of utopian thinking and, on the other, we frequently do damage with our ideal theorising. This exploration of Turner's writing and life offers us both an argument for valuing the role of utopian thought, justly done, and the tools to guide us in this engaged approach.

We can also consider, I propose, that this view of utopian thinking provides motivation for forms of hybrid ideal/non-ideal thinking. Consider, for example, the cantilever strategy – introduced by Joseph Carens (2013) and David Miller (2016) and developed as a method in my own work (Hobden 2021). In this approach, one starts from identifying an existing societal commitment – either implicit or explicit – and exploring what that commitment, properly justified (if it is plausible to do so), requires of those who hold it. Using Turner's example, we might present a theory based on the principle of 'love thy neighbour as thyself' to Christians, pushing them to see the more radical implications of such a commitment through a deeper understanding of the justificatory roots of such a principle. Politically speaking, we might consider examples such as the ostensible commitment to the equal sovereignty of states as a fairly widely held commitment, even if only performatively. One approach to theorising with a goal to change is to address those who claim to hold such a view, and argue for the full, ideal implications of what such a commitment requires. We begin within the non-ideal, analysing and identifying the hidden assumptions, those commitments that are doing the work – or failing to do the promised work – and we direct our ideal theorising into those specific places, acting 'as a goad – inducing people to reconsider beliefs previously taken for granted, to notice the fuller implications of their value-commitments, or perhaps to recognise the incompatibility between different goals that they espouse' (Miller and Siedentop 1985, 1).

BRINGING US BACK TO OUR CONTEXT

Unless we can see our society in the light of other possible societies we cannot even understand how and why it works as it does, let alone judge it.
— Rick Turner, *The Eye of the Needle: Towards Participatory Democracy in South Africa*

The final element of this approach to political philosophy is to bring the utopian thought back into dialogue with reality – both as a tool to work toward change, and as a way to deepen and enrich the theory. Turner argues that one of the reasons utopian thinking is valuable is that it provides us with tools to understand and evaluate our society. He argues that 'until we realise what other values, and what other social forms, are possible, we cannot judge the morality or otherwise of the existing society' (Turner 1980, 3). We need the 'yardstick' of the utopian in order to truly evaluate (Turner 1980, 99). Relatedly, seeing our society in the light of other possible societies provides us with the tools to better grasp why our society is the way it is (Turner 1980, 3). Note that for Turner, 'possible' is all that is not impossible by virtue of the imperatives of human nature and organisation. It is not a comparison to that which we can currently see the steps to achieve, but a much bolder vision of the possible against which we should evaluate our current society (and our choices that continue to create this society).

A further aspect of this engagement with reality is evident in Turner's postscript to *The Eye of the Needle*. Here, Turner explicitly analyses the society from which one might act toward a socialist Christian society, laying the groundwork for potential strategies of action (Turner 1980, 99–152). We return then to the analysis of society but, importantly, with a more reliable lens through which to do so. Turner believed, as laid out in the discussion on positionality, that there is no non-ideological lens through which we view society; the goal of the philosopher is not only to identify and challenge societal assumptions, but to build new assumptions – with the aspiration that they form a more accurate lens through which to interpret, analyse and understand society (with the goal, ultimately, of changing it) (Turner 1968, 1).

We should recall here, then, that the steps of the method are not consecutive – and neither, for the engaged political philosopher, are our philosophical projects entirely discrete. The use of our philosophical tools of analysis and our utopian theories in engaging with society are both the start and the end of political philosophy with an eye to changing society. This creates a kind of dialogical, almost circular process that moves us deeper and closer to something like the truth of our moral and political commitments to one another. It creates, then, theory that is bold in its vision, but not absolute. The engaged political philosopher never sees the task of theorising as complete – whether it be continued by themselves or others. This gives us reason to participate in theorising collaboratively, not defensively. We can see ourselves as sharing the aim of a more just society – an aim that should leave us open to the dialogue of ideas and visions, even for those commitments we hold most fundamentally. It is not a call to remain uncommitted, but a call to epistemic humility that drives a desire to bring our theory into dialogue with others' theory, analysis and experience, and the ever-changing societal context in which, and for which, it is created.

THE VALUE OF THIS APPROACH

> Choosing to be free.
> — Billy Keniston, *Choosing to be Free: The Life Story of Rick Turner*

Transforming Ourselves and Society

For Turner, rooted in Sartrean existentialism, the act of reflecting deeply on what is possible is itself a step toward freedom. Ultimately, for Turner, while we do not have a say on the society into which we are born, or how it shapes us and our beliefs, we are radically free to choose our beliefs and actions going forward. Critically engaging with our society and building resources to make those choices wisely is thus at the heart of what it can mean to live with freedom. We can understand, then, engaged political philosophy to be an act of freedom, especially within an oppressive context. It is a transformative act, enabling us to notice and better live out this freedom.

Not all (or even many) analytic ideal philosophers are Sartrean existentialists, so we cannot assume a shared commitment to radical freedom of choice. We should note the central role of this commitment in Turner's method and life, but it is not a commitment essential to practising the method of engaged philosophy presented here. Even without this existentialist commitment, we can see the potentially transformative power of the method: the power in developing critical understanding of the oppressive nature of society and finding the freedom to develop a vision for another way. We might think here of the appeal and power of Black Consciousness way beyond those who delved into its existentialist roots.

An implication of this personally transformative power is that it provides a strong argument against philosophy, and especially political philosophy, being only an elite academic endeavour. If it contains the power to transform us (and so, we will see soon, the power to transform society), it is a good that we should seek to make accessible to others. While I think it is a virtue of this approach that it enables us to see the radical power of political philosophy *as philosophy*, this makes philosophical tools particular and valuable for their distinctive offering, but not exclusive. Turner's life illustrates this inclusivity with his strong emphasis on education – both in his theory and in his role as an academic – and in his openness to hosting and engaging in critical discussions with a large social and political circle (Keniston 2013). Just as the engaged political philosopher might think carefully about providing access to their ideas and bringing their ideas into dialogue with others, so too might they be mindful of how to share their philosophical tools – and importantly, how to bring those two goals together in the classroom and in civic space.

In the face of white patriarchal supremacy, there is great power in choosing to reimagine society and reimagine our own place within it. While the actual ideas may never be fully realised, society is changed through the transformation of those who are empowered by the understanding of the contingency of their own oppression, and the potential for another way. Since much of the structures of oppression is psychological (while, of course, enforced through physical violence), Turner recognised the power of the simple yet deeply difficult task of thinking outside the system, of radically imagining an ideal society. Practising engaged philosophy is then not only a personally transformative experience, but also one that, collectively, can provide the soil to grow the desire and vision for societal change.

Turner argues that utopian thinking provides the tools to understand why society is the way it is, to evaluate our societal institutions, to identify what is changeable and to provide the invitation for change in a given direction. Understanding the present as history is a gift because it provides a source of hope. It facilitates the understanding that change is hard to envisage because 'the present nearly always seems to be at least fairly permanent' (Turner 1980, 6). But in reality, 'societies, including our own society, have been changing in many ways, great and small, throughout time, and there is no reason to believe that they have stopped now' (Turner 1980, 6). This standpoint enables us to see, with hope, that 'it is probable that many of our social institutions and personal ways of behaving will change' just as they have throughout time (Turner 1980, 6). Participating in guiding and creating that change is thus not just a possibility, but an imperative.

CONCLUSION

Let us draw together then what it is to practise engaged political philosophy. Most centrally, it is the practice of political philosophy grounded in the belief that change is possible, and that philosophical analysis and utopian thinking have a role to play in this change. It centres the use of philosophical tools, such as identifying assumptions and making connections and distinctions, not only as valuable to understanding society but as an ongoing process central to building a new vision for society. It sees both the act of developing theory, and the theory itself, as potentially transformative. In both, then, we pay attention to the goal of changing society, considering audience and tone, accessibility and wide engagement, the limits of the imperatives of human nature and organisation, and the vast expanse of the possible.

REFERENCES

Carens, Joseph. 2013. *The Ethics of Immigration*. New York: Oxford University Press.

Collins, Patricia Hill. 1986. 'Learning from the Outsider Within: The Sociological Significance of Black Feminist Thought'. *Social Problems* 33 (6): s14–32.

Dotson, Kristie. 2011. 'Concrete Flowers: Contemplating the Profession of Philosophy'. *Hypatia* 26 (2): 403–409.

Hobden, Christine. 2021. *Citizenship in a Globalised World*. London: Routledge.

Keniston, Billy. 2013. *Choosing to be Free: The Life Story of Rick Turner*. Johannesburg: Jacana.

Kumalo, Siseko H. 2020. 'Resurrecting the Black Archive through the Decolonisation of Philosophy in South Africa'. *Third World Thematics: A TWQ Journal* 5 (1–2): 19–36.

Mellor, Kate. 2022. 'Developing a Decolonial Gaze: Articulating Research/er Positionality and Relationship to Colonial Power'. *Access: Critical Explorations of Equity in Higher Education* 10 (1): 26–41.

Miller, David. 2016. 'Is There a Human Right to Immigrate?'. In *Migration in Political Theory: The Ethics of Movement and Membership*, edited by Sarah Fine and Lea Ypi, 11–31. Oxford: Oxford University Press.

Miller, David and Larry Siedentop. 1985. 'Introduction'. In *The Nature of Political Theory*, 1–16. Oxford: Oxford University Press.

Mills, Charles W. 1997. *The Racial Contract*. Ithaca, NY: Cornell University Press.

Mills, Charles W. 2005. '"Ideal Theory" as Ideology'. *Hypatia* 20 (3): 165–184.

Pateman, Carole. 1988. *The Sexual Contract*. Cambridge: Polity Press.

Turner, Jann. 2007. 'Rick Turner: Thirty Years On'. South African History Online. https://www.sahistory.org.za/r-turner/node/33. Accessed 15 January 2024.

Turner, Richard. 1968. 'What is Political Philosophy?'. *Radical Philosophy*. South African History Online. https://www.sahistory.org.za/sites/default/files/What%20is%20political%20philosophy.pdf. Accessed 14 December 2023.

Turner, Richard. 1980. *The Eye of the Needle: Towards Participatory Democracy in South Africa*. Johannesburg: Ravan Press.

12

What is the Point of Political Theory?

Lawrence Hamilton

> Common-sense thinking obscures reality.
> — Rick Turner, *The Eye of the Needle: Towards*
> *Participatory Democracy in South Africa*

> Politics is the art of the impossible, made possible.
> — Oby Ezekwesili, 'Politics is the Art of the
> Impossible, Made Possible'

Contemporary political theory of a wide variety of stripes has become obsessed with the difference between normative and descriptive political theory, non-ideal versus ideal political philosophy, realism in political theory as against idealism in political theory and so on. In short, despite a lot of spilt ink (or 'screen time') on the subject, the troubled distinction between description and prescription in political theory has, if anything, become even more entrenched. This has led some otherwise sensible political theory realists to undermine the role and function of utopian thinking as central to critical and engaged political theory (Galston 2010; Markell 2010; Valentini 2012; cf. Estlund 2020).

As is apparent in all of the chapters in this volume, despite an otherwise wide variety of interpretations, applications or concerns, Rick Turner does quite the opposite. Admittedly in a different context, he is firmly focused on the role of utopian thinking, living, pedagogy and associated practices. Though, for at least two reasons, this should not surprise. First, the stubborn legacies of apartheid, exemplified *in extremis* during the July 2021 civil unrest in South Africa, as well as the many crises and protests across the globe, suggest we are a lot closer to his own conditions than we might hope. Second, there is a core of ideas, whose imaginative powers speak to many oppressive contexts, including our own, exemplified in the fact that all of the authors collected here, even the most critical (for example chapters 3, 4 and 6), find instructive guidance or at least stimulus for fresh leaps of the imagination as regards how better to live collectively. In *The Eye of the Needle*, Turner emphasises the role of utopian thinking with great force and application. He argues that this thinking is necessary for social and political change as it counters the tendency to think of existing institutions, needs and values as natural and fixed. It enables us to understand our society better and thus judge well how to improve it.

Various components of this are brought out in different ways by the majority of contributors to this volume. Eze and Omar (chapters 1 and 2) focus on the overlaps and creative differences brought out by comparison with other thinkers on the nature of freedom, resistance, decolonisation and political change, as does Sithole (chapter 3), if from a more critical perspective. This is true also of Ensor's, Sanni's and Glaser's contributions in the second part of the volume (chapters 4, 5 and 6), picking up Turner's glaring gender blindness via a reading of Turner through both Simone de Beauvoir and the standpoint of black women workers in Durban at the time; showing how some of his philosophical insights regarding apartheid's horrors still obtain today due to misplaced priorities around how to alleviate poverty; and questioning whether his participatory democratic model is viable or even desirable today. Turner's fascinating works and ways of living provide the inspiration for Piper and Soudien, in the third part of the volume (chapters 7 and 8), to engage his critical pedagogy in light of the instrumentalisation of education today and our important contemporary process of decolonising education.

Then, in chapters 9 and 10, Keniston and Van Riet focus more directly on violence and its legacy in South Africa. They provide accounts of how Turner kept himself out of violent struggle in apartheid South Africa, choosing rather to 'live free', the tragic irony of which made him more of a target for the South African state; how the violence of that state still bedevils contemporary South Africa, and how we could learn from Turner's firm messages to white privilege. In chapter 11, Hobden takes lessons from Turner as regards how to live the life of the engaged philosopher, with particular focus on ideas in action, changeability, positionality, direction and context, while reiterating why any utopian proposal cannot get anywhere without a proposal for how to overcome gender oppression. In their various ways, all of these contributions highlight the significance of Turner's life and ideas for both theory and practice today, particularly around the idea of how part of the job of the engaged, radical political thinker is to uncover what may be possible by adopting a politics for seeing beyond the givens of their time, elucidating how the impossible may be possible, and thus convincing others of the need to escape the confines of the present.

My argument in this chapter is that we can learn from resuscitating this lost part of the African archive, though we also need to move beyond Turner's slightly simplistic views on the central role of utopian thinking in political theory, particularly by showing how realism in political thinking is vital for a utopian theoretical attitude. This seemingly contradictory focus on realism flies in the face not only of the usual distinction between idealism and realism as well as Turner's own critique of 'realism', but also many of the views contributors to this volume have expressed thus far, taking Turner at his word, or at least assuming, that in being a utopian thinker, he is an idealist. I shall explain why I dispute this and how this could help us get beyond the distinction, or at least why it is unhelpful in understanding the power of utopian thinking. In doing so, it becomes possible properly to identify the point of political theory, or so I shall argue.

Turner develops two closely linked arguments as to why utopian thinking is vital for political theory and thus politics, which I argue are brought out best by homing in on what he means by the need for the theoretical attitude that grasps the 'present as history'. Although undeveloped, I suggest three ways in which this is understood and how it enables us to see two important (and often overlooked) things: (i) that this utopian attitude rests on a form of realism quite unlike the one Turner himself discusses and refutes; and (ii) it enables us to focus in on the key point of political theory: answering or being guided by the question, 'How should we live together?' Political theory that focuses on history in the way that Turner suggests and I elaborate, enables us to see that what we now view as impossible may be both possible and desirable. I then bring this out by means of an account of the value of radical representative democracy in the global South, which would enable a collective process of (sometimes antagonistic and often utopian) learning to assess 'how we should live together'.

Of course, there are other reasons for doing political theory – intellectual curiosity about ideas, the need to figure out my own political orientations and so on (Floyd 2019) – but here my interest is not the intentions of any particular political theorist but the broader historical point (or you might say political consequences) of analysing, critiquing and ordering our ideas, values and principles in order to determine how we *should* live together. The kernel of how best to go about this is to be found in Turner's ideas, but a full explanation thereof requires us to get to the point of political theory and unearth the bidirectional function of realism and utopianism in political theory.

TURNER ON THE ROLE OF THEORY

Turner argues that utopian thinking is vital for two reasons. First, even the basic outline of an ideally just society enables us to *see beyond* the supposedly natural givens of our society and explore possibilities that its current assumptions regarding 'common sense' deem impossible or unfeasible. Second, unless we see our society in the light of actual other societies and (even seemingly unattainable) possible societies, we are unable to *understand* how and why our society works as it does and thus judge it.

In making these arguments, Turner employs a distinction between 'absolute impossibility' and 'other things being equal impossibility'. For example, he says it is 'absolutely impossible to teach a lion to become a vegetarian'; while 'other things being equal it is impossible for a black person to become prime minister of South Africa'. Recall when he is writing and the beliefs, institutions, behaviours and values of early 1970s South Africa. Liberals, he claims, tend to take these societal conditions as given, even natural, and then search for a more just arrangement within them – they think along these lines: 'let us try to see what changes they [whites] can be persuaded to accept within that context [of whites in power and continuing to want that]. Can we perhaps persuade them to eat old goats instead of our prized lambs?' He mocks this attitude and its use of 'reality'. We should not ask what whites can be 'persuaded' to do, what concessions they might make, other things being equal. We should rather 'explore the absolute limits of possibility by sketching an ideally just society' (Turner 2015, 1).

This is the first way in which utopian thinking is valuable, he argues. By positing or sketching an ideally just society, it invites us to think beyond the supposedly 'natural' givens of our particular society and 'explore' – even 'attack' – all of the 'implicit assumptions about how to behave towards other people that underlie our daily actions in all spheres'. This enables us to *free ourselves from the common sense* that our society – its institutions and associated ways of behaving – is fixed, rigid or somehow natural. Using examples such as private property, gendered social relations and the (often biologically explained) superiority of whites and inferiority of blacks, he argues that these social institutions are simply made up of how people behave towards one another in the here and now of apartheid South Africa. And, unlike a mountain or an ocean, these social institutions can be changed, but only if we adopt a different *attitude* to them: that yes, they exist, but they are our creation and we can change them (Turner 2015, 2–3).[1] This emphasis on what might be called a human's 'radical freedom to choose' is a common theme in most of the chapters in this volume.

Turner then makes a distinction between the 'imperatives of nature' and the 'imperatives of organisation'. Examples of the former abound; the classic example of the latter is that collective action may require some sort of decision-making hierarchy. He continues:

> In order to reflect on our values, then, we have to see which aspects of our society are the necessary result of the imperatives of human nature and of organisation and which aspects of it are changeable. We then need to make explicit the value principles embodied in our actual behaviour and to criticise these principles in the light of other possible values. Until we realise what other values and what other social forms are possible, we cannot judge the morality or otherwise of the existing society. (Turner 2015, 4)

The 'other possible values' and 'other social forms' are perhaps left intentionally unspecified here as this kind of imaginative process, driven by utopian thinking, is by its very nature relative to a particular context and thus difficult to specify theoretically antecedent to the practical process. However, very clear hints as to what he has in mind here are given throughout the rest of *The Eye of the Needle*, particularly at the start of chapter 4 on participatory democracy. In the language of the pared-down Christian ethics he adopts in the book, he begins with individuals and their needs for freedom and for love. He then extends these to include being 'free from hidden conditioning processes' and 'external social coercion' and the need for 'meaningful and creative work, work that is an expression of my own autonomous being'. He suggests that this leads directly to two ideas that are combined in the idea of participatory democracy. The social system must: (i) enable individuals to have maximum control over the social and material environment; and (ii) encourage them to interact creatively with other people. He argues that the institutions required to bring about the fulfilment of these needs and the associated means to their satisfaction require us to 'theorise', as these institutions do not yet exist (Turner 2015, chapter 4; Turner n.d.).

There is remarkable overlap between Turner's view of these general needs and my own account of agency needs, which I developed well before ever coming across Turner (Hamilton 2003). Yet, unlike Turner, I make clear that not that much follows from these universal needs for, at least at the level of everyday politics, most of the needs that are felt, judged and prioritised are what I call social needs, that is, needs with much more particular expression than the very general need for love and freedom and so on. Yet, they can and do constitute the basis of genealogical and other forms of judgement and critique of existing needs, values, principles, priorities and institutions. I return to this at the end of the next section of the chapter.

This then brings Turner to the second important function of utopian thinking. As he puts it, 'unless we can see our society in the light of other possible societies we cannot even understand how and why it works as it does, let alone judge it' (Turner 2015, 4). The example of racism is a case in point. For whites then (and for many still today) it was 'common sense', that is, accepted as given, that blacks were inferior and (it was supposed) this was also explained via biology. Turner argues that this is revealing, for to explain a social fact by direct reference to biology – nature – is to misunderstand it and thus obscure the avenues through which to explain and understand the social causes of the actual 'inferiority', that is, the actually existing forms of domination and exploitation. This is why Turner is insistent on the idea that 'common-sense thinking obscures reality' (Turner 2015, 5). It tends to take the world (the society) as it is 'now' and then reify it as given, natural. He also uses the example of gendered relations and ends off as follows:

> Similarly, unless we think in utopian terms about South African society we will not really come to understand how it works today. We will take for granted inequalities, power relationships and behaviour patterns that need to be explained. Nor will we be able to evaluate the society adequately. We will not understand on how many different levels there are alternatives and so the possibility of choice and so the possibility of moral judgement. (Turner 2015, 6–7)

He is making two critical arguments here. Many would prefer to keep them separate. I suggest, as I think Turner does, that they are firmly connected. He is arguing that utopian thinking is necessary both for *understanding* how a society works and *evaluating* it, that is, assessing it in the light of other possibilities and the associated moral and political judgements in this process of critique, assessment and choice. As Hobden also notes in chapter 11 of this volume, many have criticised utopian thinking using an argument that moves in exactly the opposite direction. That is, that utopianism tends to disconnect us from the reality of our collective existence in the here and now, and thus fails to provide much insight into how best to get from this distorted reality to a prized future reality. How (and why) is Turner able to reverse this received opinion?

The clue comes immediately after the passage I have just quoted, when Turner argues that, in order 'to understand a society, to understand what it is, where it is going and where it could go, we cannot just describe it. We need also to theorise about it. We need continually to refer back and forth between what we see in society and what is essential to any society' (2015, 7). He puts this very succinctly in an earlier, shorter piece:

> The point that I want to stress is that, while it is important to have as complete a description as possible of the society, of its

institutions, of the way in which it produces and distributes wealth, of how it is ruled and so on, it is perhaps even more interesting to know why it is as it is. And if we want to *change* the society, it is absolutely necessary to know why it is as it is. (Turner 1968, 3)

When discussing this in *The Eye of the Needle*, Turner focuses on what he calls the 'theoretical attitude'. Central to this is the role of history or at least the ability to grasp the 'present as history' (Turner 2015, 7). If we do, we will avoid a series of pitfalls: seeing history as a linear process of unfolding into perfection in our current 'civilisation' and believing that our social institutions and forms of behaviour have and will remain the same when in fact, these have changed and will continue to change. They are mutable. Or, in other words, as he puts it, '[t]he fact that something exists is no guarantee that it will continue to exist or that it should exist' (Turner 2015, 8).

In sum, utopian thinking is vital, as it enables both a critical attitude to the supposed natural conditions of our own societies and it enables a certain form of understanding them, that is, which parts of them we can draw out and emphasise in order for us to see that what may have seemed impossible can become both possible and desirable.

UTOPIA AND THE POINT OF POLITICAL THEORY

Yet, we need to parse this somewhat opaque or underdeveloped account to identify the different component parts of political theory that enable this capacity, art or attitude.

First, the point of political theory is quite easy to state in a broad questioning outline: 'How should we live?' (Floyd 2019, 7). However, we may want to add something to this to delineate it from purely moral or ethical concerns and questions: 'How should we live together?', which, given some basic Turner-style 'imperatives of organisation', quickly becomes, 'Who does what to whom for whose benefit?' (Lenin 1972; Geuss 2008, 25). Even if we agree with Karl Marx's famous formulation that the point is not simply to interpret the world but to change it (Marx 1977), we still need to know a little bit more about what this really means, how we go about it and why theory is thus so important. In doing so, we can add further nuance to Turner's insistence on grasping the present as history. Beyond the obvious, the present is history in at least three important ways: it is necessary and helpful in our *analysis* and *critique* of our extant political world and in how we *order* our values, principles and priorities.

To see this, it may be helpful to first expand upon an assumption that most would agree with. Politics involves judgements by rulers and ruled within a particular concrete context regarding our agency, needs, interests and values as well as how best to improve the social, political and economic conditions in this context (Hamilton 2009, 2014b). This is undertaken with the greatest prudence when it draws from theoretical analysis that builds on historically informed critique of the conceptual, normative and ideological frameworks that inform these everyday political judgements. The existing theoretical frameworks for our judgements heavily affect how we collectively conceive of our most pressing power relations, priorities and penalties. The practical, historical context of concept formation is therefore of utmost importance in politics.

This is the first way in which we must constantly grasp the present as history, that is, in our *analysis* of our extant political world. When we analyse our social and political world we do so by means of the conceptual tools to hand and these, like the very ideas, values, needs, principles, priorities and institutions we are thereby analysing, do not come out of thin air. They all have particular histories that can be traced and understood. The present is a consequence of a set of histories that have produced our ideas, institutions and ideologies. Thus, in attempting to understand the present via its analysis, even when we do not set out intentionally to do so, we cannot avoid either analysing particular histories or at least making assumptions about these histories. This is the case even when that assumption is based on ahistorical analytical methods that lead to the rather strange idea that ahistorical conceptual analysis alone is *the* only real goal of political theory, as is still so prevalent in analytical political philosophy today.

Political theory is the means through which we marshal or invent concepts, norms and ideas to comprehend and thus contest our politics. Like most other things that involve language, politics cannot proceed without concepts and ideas to overcome pressing practical problems: how to hold to account our political leaders; which collective goods require public provision; how best to engage with global political power relations; and so on. While conceptual innovation is a central part of this, to argue from this that the main (or only) role of political theory is conceptual or normative clarification is to cripple political theory.

The second, crucial (related) way in which the present is history is when we *critique* our existing, contextual political order, hierarchies, structures, values and principles. As with our everyday needs, interests and values, these broader institutional and normative structures are not given by nature but are the result of individual and collective choices in the past. Their presence today as formative of the way we think and judge is, often, not because of 'natural' or 'organisational' imperatives, but due to the extant power relations, priorities and privileges of the past. And this past can be traced, unearthing avenues not taken and possibilities now deemed impossible. Jonathan Floyd breaks this process of critique down further into three key varieties: (i) 'dangerous implications', (ii) 'inconsistency' and (iii) 'suspicious roots' (Floyd 2019, 59).

This is a neat categorisation and one that can be brought out well by providing examples such as Isaiah Berlin's account of the 'dangerous implications' of positive freedom or Charles Taylor's view of the inconsistencies in Berlin's very distinction between positive and negative freedom and Marx's, Nietzsche's and Foucault's use of history and genealogy to expose the troubling histories behind some of our most cherished beliefs and seemingly legitimate institutions. However, Floyd brings out the deeply historical nature of only the third of these forms of critique.

In line with Turner, I suggest that all of these varieties of critique will involve grasping the present as history. In fact, the very examples chosen by Floyd bear this out well. Berlin's argument is a deeply historical and contextually determined account of how we have come to the position of holding two conceptions of freedom and why we should favour one over the other (negative over positive freedom). The distinction and the preference are determined to a significant degree by cold war proclivities. For this and other reasons, many dispute Berlin's two conceptions of liberty, and as they do, they draw on history again to highlight his missteps and resuscitate 'republican or neo-Roman' (Pettit 1997; Skinner 2002) views or develop other accounts such as 'freedom as power' (Sen 2009; Hamilton 2014b), often using genealogical and intellectual historical tools to identify when and how these alternatives may have been ignored or actively quashed. As John Dunn puts it well, riffing off another famous Marx quote: 'not only do men make their own history; but some men make far more of their fair share of the history of others' (Dunn 2002, 94). In other words, our histories are replete with examples of choices imposed on others, paths not taken, chances missed.[2] Political theory that focuses on history can bring these out best and thus, sometimes, enable us to see that what we now see as impossible may be both possible and desirable. It may also help us see that, although we have the power to choose, especially to choose to live freely, à la Turner, the substance of the choices as well as how we conceive and respond to them are heavily affected by our and our societies' pasts – how we are socialised, as Turner also emphasised. How to move beyond this aporia in Turner's writings is resolved via greater focus on his actual life and choices, as some contributors here have argued (chapters 7, 8 and 9), though I would suggest it is only partially resolved.

The third way in which we need to grasp the present as history is with regard to how we *order* our values, principles and priorities. In short, because of the inherently practical nature of politics, we cannot simply identify an array of values, needs, interests and so on and assume that these can all be met with the same urgency, in the way Turner seems to suggest when discussing our needs for freedom and love – freedom and love may even, after all, sometimes be in direct conflict with each other. Liberty must sometimes trump equality and vice versa. Though, having said that, various clear political *evils* – from more obvious ones, such as slavery, to more complex ones, such as domination – can be ruled out of court (or, at the very least, kept at bay). The very process of working out our existing priorities and then determining whether or not we have the ordering right is the main concern when answering the central question: 'How we should live together?' This process is inherently historical. We need history to find out our own orderings and history to assess and critique the priority we give to certain values and principles over others.

One way of bringing these insights together comes from the origins and development of the term 'utopia'. The word 'utopia' is a coinage of Sir Thomas More, the title of his book published in Latin in 1516. As Raymond Geuss notes, this is an erudite pun with its roots either in Greek or Latin. In short, it means 'no place' *and* 'good place', that is, a place that is very good or a place that is nowhere, that does not exist in reality, but since it is being discussed at all, must exist at least in the imagination. These were often subsequently conflated to the point that 'utopia' came to mean a place that is too good to be anywhere, too good to exist, thus often the basis of easy critique of the very idea of utopian thinking.

This, obviously, takes us far away from realism. But it is not the last word on utopia. In 1907, Gustav Landauer published a book entitled *Revolution*, in which he distinguishes two factors in human history: topia and utopia. 'Topia' is the total state of a society at any given time, the existing world as it now really is, say. 'Utopia', on the other hand, 'designates all those individual impulses which under certain circumstances can come together and move the world in the direction of a perfectly functioning social formation that "contains no harmful or unjust elements"' (Geuss 2020, 111). That is, at any given time, a given population will have (various) conceptions of what is harmful or unjust and these changing conceptions provide the kernel of their utopian aspirations. Landauer maintains, therefore, that at any given point in time our utopian impulses derive from two sources: dissatisfaction with the given topia and remembrance of all previous utopias, that is, memory of practically attempted or merely theorised alternative possible worlds or ways of living together.

As in Turner, the role of history here is vital: it spurs us to revitalise past utopian impulses and ways of thinking. In doing so, Landauer appeals to the twofold sense of the English word 'realise', that is, both 'come to an understanding of' and 'bring into existence'. History is supposed to realise previously embodied utopian impulses in both senses of the word. History, he thought, much like Turner again, was at least as much about creating new forms of cooperative human action and thus about the future, as it was about the past (Geuss 2020, 110–112). In other words, contrary to Turner's rather short reduction of realism to mere empirical description of the social and political world 'out there' (Turner 2015, chapter 8), it is more helpful to see the theoretical attitude espoused by Turner in terms akin to Landauer's: to be realist as regards understanding and prescription requires both utopian thinking (in general) and a view of the present as history (in at least the three ways noted here); and to be utopian, at the very least, one needs to be realist in the sense of having enough knowledge about one's society and its history to understand and explain why it is as it is. In other words, utopian thinking is necessary for us to realise – understand and bring into existence – better ways of living together.

In sum, utopian thinking is necessary for realism in political theory and realism is necessary for utopian impulses. This is the case because, when properly understood and not reduced to mere empirical description of the social and political world 'out there', realism in political theory involves both a description of reality plus a historically informed judgement of how best to proceed to a more prized reality, something unattainable without utopian thinking and the historical and imaginative elements that constitute utopian impulses. In other words, utopian forays are required both as springboards for imaginative leaps out of the confines of the present, enabled by an attitude of grasping the present as history, and as the very means of realising these imaginative leaps, of making the impossible possible. This is no easy feat, but the art of good judgement in politics is, in part, the process of determining which of the seemingly impossible alternatives brought out by utopian thinking may in fact now be possible and desirable, that is, which of them to choose and how to make them achievable.

DEMOCRACY IN THE GLOBAL SOUTH

It follows, therefore, that all citizens need these imaginative and historical capabilities and the educational, experiential and institutional means to acquire them (and this idea chimes very well with Turner's insistence on the role of the public intellectual in the lifelong education of his or her fellow citizens, as discussed in a few of this book's chapters). Elsewhere, I have discussed at length, in general and in the context of democratic South Africa, the kinds of institutional reform (or transformation) that would enable this: a set of radical local and national representative institutions that would enhance political judgement regarding realist, democratic and utopian possibilities (Hamilton 2014a, 2014b). I will not rehash these arguments here, but rather elaborate a little on how the kind of realist, utopian attitude we find in embryonic form in Turner can best be created, not in the advanced democracies of the global North, but in the more fragile, fraught and often frightening democracies of the global South. The point of political theory thus becomes more obvious and pressing here than in the stable and supposedly sound democracies with longer histories and firmer institutional grounding.

If politics is about who rules whom and how, and good judgement depends on a realism infused with utopianism (and vice versa), theorising about politics seems like a luxury, especially in the global South, where many live precariously in the daily struggle to survive. Democratic political rule can seem secondary to more pressing needs, such as securing enough water, food, shelter and security. But this is wrong. Politics determines the extent to which 'basic' needs can be met, and under democratic conditions it is where ordinary citizens collectively select their representatives who determine both these supposedly 'basic' needs and the more complex needs that constitute their lives and livelihoods. And, of course, the very point of political theory – determining in context how we *should* live together – becomes all the more pressing exactly because existing conditions are so parlous.

The nature and role of democracy in the global South brings this out well.

If we ignore or remain passive vis-à-vis politics, we vacate the space within which it is decided who does what to whom for whose benefit. This is perilous, for citizen passivity allows the more wealthy, voracious and venal quickly to fill the space and dictate our politics. Our politics then becomes not about our collective, if often plural and competing, needs, interests, powers, values and ideas, but about the lives of those who thus capture the state. This is no mere theoretical threat, as Zuma's South Africa, Chavez's Venezuela and Bolsonaro's Brazil have made graphically clear. Populism is a dangerous by-product of our passivity as citizens. By contrast, if our focus is on the quality of our lives and the powers to secure and improve them, democracy remains the only real contender. It is impossible to see this and improve it without political theory.

'What is the point of political theory?' is therefore a practical question. It is about working out how best to proceed at a particular moment in local, national and global contexts. This is about comprehension, orientation and judgement with regard to our lives' central questions, facts and values. For this we require knowledge of where we are and where we would like to end up, and judgement as to how best to get there. We also need to understand why we are where we are.

This is not easy. It requires capacities that constitute the *art* of good judgement in politics: a view of the world that acknowledges how our individual security, well-being and freedom is linked to our collective security, well-being and freedom (Hamilton 2014a, 2019); a willingness to deliberate over and critique everyday facts and deeply held values and beliefs; the timing and courage to find ways of judging collectively under conditions of likely disagreement; the capacity to persuade others of the collective worth of a proposal; and so on (Hamilton 2009). In sum, what is needed is the skill, individually and collectively, to decide when and how to act and what to prioritise. This is not easy, as I have said, but nor is it parochial, something exemplified by the existential threats posed by the global Covid-19 and climate crises.

Political theory is the framework through which we acquire these skills and practices. As I have argued, contrary to received theoretical opinion, this is not just a matter of conceptual or normative clarification. It is about learning to acquire and pass on the craft of political judgement: a theoretical attitude, impossible without a view of the present as history and the central role of realist and utopian thinking. One of the reasons that democracy stands out in the modern world is because it is the one political arrangement that enables this collective process of (sometimes antagonistic but always imaginative) learning. A lot of political theorists have supposed the panacea lies in innovative institutional blueprints (constitutional or otherwise), on the assumption that there may exist an institutional fix for democracy's deficiencies. But we need more, always and everywhere. Democracy must be constantly worked on, by leaders and ordinary citizens, to ensure it prioritises and enables this collective process of learning for good political judgement (Cabral 1974; Hountondji 2002; Dunn 2014). In other words, the health and vitality of everyone's democracy is, ultimately, each individual person's responsibility.

This, then, is the main point of political theory, especially in precarious democratic contexts: continually to remind fellow citizens of this responsibility and how best to meet it; and to arm them with the conceptual and factual tools to carry it out, the tools to see the present as history while they analyse, critique and order their needs, interests, values and principles in order to determine how we should best live together. If democracy is necessary for the free, collective determination of individual needs and interests, good political judgement at all levels is a requirement for the health of democracy. Political theorists must guide this political judgement. If they shirk this responsibility, the very existence of the globe is imperilled.

Most political theory that emanates from the global North does just this as it retreats into the life of the 'ivory tower' or actively turns away from the messy business of real politics, often in the dry pursuit of ever sharper and clearer conceptual tools. Political theorists from the global South are well placed to resist this 'flight from reality' (Shapiro 2005) due to the visceral nature of their politics. They are forced to face the actual politics of their time rather than build philosophical castles in the sky. Critical realist political theory from the global South is a practical, post-colonial imperative. It aims to empower everyone to judge well in politics: to be historians focused on utopian futures.

CONCLUSION

In sum, although relatively undeveloped as an argument, I have suggested here that we can learn from Turner's emphasis on the role of utopianism, history and what he calls the theoretical attitude, arriving at a clearer account of the *relationship* between description and prescription and thus realism and utopianism in political theory. Inspired by the rich variety of arguments collected together in this volume, I have shown that we thereby arrive at an answer to the question posed by this chapter: the point of political theory is to change the way we live together for the better and, in order to enlighten us in this regard, our theory must be both realist and utopian, directed at the constant revitalisation of our democracies. Our skills and responsibilities as political theorists and as active, creative citizens are not as distant as many assume (or would like). We all have the capacities to see the 'present as history', identify our interdependent needs and interests and assume the responsibility to ensure our democracies enable utopian forays that, while rooted in a realist account of where we are and how we got here, instantiate the art of making the impossible possible.

NOTES

1 We can dispute Turner's relatively simplistic nature/society dichotomy and we can critique his proposal for how better to organise society, that is, live together, as others do in this volume. However, my concern here is about an attitude, or approach or art of how best to do political theory.
2 This example regarding the nature of freedom also, obviously, problematises Turner's unqualified use of the term 'freedom' to describe a seemingly universal need alongside 'love'. Which conception of freedom is at play in his account? I leave the answer to one side here as it is not material to my main argument.

REFERENCES

Cabral, Amilcar. 1974. 'Análise de Alguns Tipos de Resistência'. In *Colecção de Leste a Oeste*. Lisbon: Seara Nova.

Dunn, John. 2002. 'Practising History and Social Science on "Realist" Assumptions'. In *Political Obligation in its Historical Context: Essays in Political Theory*, 81–111. Cambridge: Cambridge University Press.

Dunn, John. 2014. *Breaking Democracy's Spell*. New Haven, CT: Yale University Press.

Estlund, David. 2020. *Utopophobia*. Princeton, NJ: Princeton University Press.

Ezekwesili, Oby. 2018. 'Politics is the Art of the Impossible, Made Possible'. *The Guardian*, 27 October 2018. https://guardian.ng/guardian-woman/politics-is-the-art-of-the-impossible-made-possible/. Accessed 15 January 2024.

Floyd, Jonathan. 2019. *What is the Point of Political Philosophy?* Cambridge: Polity.

Galston, William. 2010. 'Realism in Political Theory'. *European Journal of Political Theory* 9 (4): 385–411.

Geuss, Raymond. 2008. *Philosophy and Real Politics*. Princeton, NJ: Princeton University Press.

Geuss, Raymond. 2020. 'The Metaphysical Need and the Utopian Impulse'. In *Who Needs a World View?*, 92–115. Cambridge, MA: Harvard University Press.

Hamilton, Lawrence. 2003. *The Political Philosophy of Needs*. Cambridge: Cambridge University Press.

Hamilton, Lawrence. 2009. 'Human Needs and Political Judgement'. In *New Waves in Political Philosophy*, edited by Christopher Zurn and Boudewijn de Bruin, 40–63. London: Palgrave.

Hamilton, Lawrence. 2014a. *Are South Africans Free?* London: Bloomsbury.

Hamilton, Lawrence. 2014b. *Freedom is Power: Liberty through Political Representation*. Cambridge: Cambridge University Press.

Hamilton, Lawrence. 2019. *Amartya Sen*. Cambridge: Polity.

Hountondji, Paulin. 2002. *The Struggle for Meaning: Reflections on Philosophy, Culture, and Democracy in Africa*. Athens, GA: Ohio University Press.

Lenin, Vladimir. 1972. *Materialism and Empirico-criticism*. Beijing: Foreign Language Press.

Markell, Pratchen. 2010. 'Review of Raymond Geuss, *Philosophy and Real Politics*'. *Political Theory* 38 (1): 172–177.

Marx, Karl. 1977. 'Theses on Feuerbach'. In *Karl Marx: Selected Writings*, edited by David McLellan, 171–174. Oxford: Oxford University Press.

Pettit, Philip. 1997. *Republicanism: A Theory of Freedom and Government*. Oxford: Oxford University Press.

Sen, Amartya. 2009. *The Idea of Justice*. London: Allen Lane.

Shapiro, Ian. 2005. *The Flight from Reality in the Human Sciences*. Princeton, NJ: Princeton University Press.

Skinner, Quentin. 2002. 'The Idea of Negative Liberty: Machiavellian and Modern Perspectives'. In *Visions of Politics, Vol. II: Renaissance Virtues*, 186–212. Cambridge: Cambridge University Press.

Turner, Richard. n.d. 'Rousseau and the Problem of Reason'. Unpublished manuscript.

Turner, Richard. 1968. 'What is Political Philosophy?'. *Radical Philosophy*. South African History Online. https://www.sahistory.org.za/sites/default/files/What%20is%20political%20philosophy.pdf. Accessed 14 December 2023.

Turner, Richard. 2015. *The Eye of the Needle: Towards Participatory Democracy in South Africa*. Kolkata: Seagull Books.

Valentini, Laura. 2012. 'Ideal vs Non-ideal Theory: A Conceptual Map'. *Philosophy Compass* 7 (9): 654–664.

CONTRIBUTORS

Paula Ensor is Professor Emeritus in the School of Education, University of Cape Town.

Michael Onyebuchi Eze teaches Africana Studies at California State University, Fresno, and is a research associate of the SA-UK Bilateral Research Chair in Political Theory, University of the Witwatersrand and Cambridge.

Daryl Glaser is Professor of Political Studies at the University of the Witwatersrand, Johannesburg.

Lawrence Hamilton is Professor of Political Studies at the University of the Witwatersrand, Johannesburg, and holds the SA-UK Bilateral Research Chair in Political Theory, University of the Witwatersrand and Cambridge.

Christine Hobden is a senior lecturer in Ethics and Public Governance at the Wits School of Governance, University of the Witwatersrand, Johannesburg.

Billy Keniston is Visiting Assistant Professor of History and African Studies at St. Lawrence University, Canton, NY.

Ayesha Omar is a British Academy International Fellow at the Department of Politics and International Studies, SOAS, and a senior lecturer in Political Theory in the Department of Political Studies at the University of the Witwatersrand, Johannesburg.

Laurence Piper is a political scientist at University West, Sweden, and the University of the Western Cape, South Africa.

John S Sanni is a lecturer in the Department of Philosophy at the University of Pretoria, South Africa.

Tendayi Sithole is Professor in the Department of Political Sciences, University of South Africa. He is also a senior research fellow at the Institute for Pan-African Thought and Conversation, University of Johannesburg.

Crain Soudien is a sociologist and Professor Emeritus in Education and African Studies at the University of Cape Town, an Honorary Professor at Nelson Mandela University and the President of the Cornerstone Institute.

Gideon van Riet is an Associate Professor of Political Studies and International Relations in the School of Government Studies at North-West University, South Africa.

INDEX

A

Achebe, Chinua 9

activism xv–xvi, 18, 41, 189
  of Rick Turner ix, xii, xviii, 30
  see also Turner's intellectual activist
    model

African National Congress (ANC) xi, 11,
    21–22, 37, 105–106, 123, 181
  alliance with Cosatu 125
  shift from pro-poor to pro-business
    approach 106, 110
  see also ANC underground structures

African political elite 164
  responses to poverty and inequality
    106–107, 110, 214, 216
  see also structural inequality:
    misplaced priorities as factor in

African Resistance Movement (ARM)
    182–184, 186

African women textile workers, Durban
    Frame Group factories' brutal labour
    regime 82, 84–86
  impact of Natal Code on 83
  see also gendered oppression: of
    African women

Africanisation 161, 164

Alliance for Radical Change (ARC)
    188–189

ANC underground structures 182, 189,
    192–196
  Umkhonto weSizwe (MK) 186, 189
  see also armed struggle

antiblackness *see* antiblack racism

antiblack racism 47, 52–53, 162
  lived experience of 57–59, 66
  ontological scandal of 54, 59–60, 62
  see also racism

apartheid
  colonial legitimation of 8
  institutionalised segregation under
    7, 21, 30, 100
  racial domination as driving
    force of 33–34, 46–47,
    49–50, 110
  as simulation of capital accumulation
    12, 19, 35–36, 99
  see oppression: apartheid as epistemic
    foundation of; resistance to
    apartheid; Suppression of
    Communism Act

armed struggle 37–38, 125, 197
  non-violent versus xxi–xxii, 182,
    187, 193
  Turner's position on 181–184,
    186–188, 194, 209

B

Bantu Education 10–11

bantustans 82, 84

Beauvoir, Simone de
  freedom as fundamental aspiration of
    xx, 72, 78, 80–81, 86
  positioning within existential
    tradition 77

Beauvoir, Simone de (*continued*)
    take on Hegel's Master-Slave dialectic
      78, 88n3
    on similarities between sexism and
      racism 80
    see also gender: Beauvoir on;
      The Second Sex (Beauvoir)
Berlin, Isaiah 251–252
Biko, Steve x, xii, xviii, 7, 66
    activism of 38
    banning of 47–48
    Black Viewpoint 10
    death in police custody of 30, 53
    see also Turner's relationship
      with Biko
Biko's BC philosophy xviii–xx, 8,
    64–66, 102
    and creation of envisioned self 56–57,
      62–64
    decolonial turn of xx, 54, 63–65
    on education/knowledge
      production 12
    and perception of apartheid as evil
      49–50, 53, 60–61
    phenomenological significance of 53,
      56
    'separatist' stance of 45, 55
    understanding of resistance in 4,
      18–19, 23–24
    see also decolonial turn (of Biko);
      decolonising resistance; white
      liberalism: Biko's critique of
Black Consciousness x, xiv–xv, xix, 142
    as epistemic resistance 12–15, 17–19
    existentialist roots of 46–47, 57,
      65–66, 238
    see also new Black Consciousness
Black Consciousness Movement (BCM)
    apartheid strategies of curtailment of 29
    Turner's responsive engagement with
      xix, 15, 30, 38–42, 45, 52,
      59–61, 65
    as vehicle for radical change xix, 28,
      37–38
    see also Biko's BC philosophy;
      Nolutshungu's theory of political
      change

black inferiority (myth of) 7, 12, 17, 36,
    41, 63–64, 245, 247
    acceptance of 95
    white ignorance as problem behind
      51–52
Black Skin, White Masks (Fanon)
    72, 108
black subjectivity
    apartheid/colonial dehumanisation of
      7–9, 49–50, 53, 58, 107
    see also Fanon, Frantz
blackness 7, 162
    BCM on 13–14, 59
    resistance as resignification of 10, 19
Botswana 29, 194–195
Burgos, Adam
    on resistance 6–7

C
Cambridge School xii–xiii
capitalism xiii, xv–xvi, xix, 37
    Turner's critique of xxi, 4, 20, 35–36,
      38–39
    see also racialist capitalism
Césaire, Aimé 9, 108–109
*Changing South Africa: Political
    Considerations* (Nolutshungu)
    27, 29, 31
Christianity
    and Biko's concept of 'black
      theology' 23
    as ideological platform for liberation
      21–22
    as subterfuge for oppression
      20–23
    see also The Eye of the Needle:
      elaboration of Christian human
      model in
climate crisis xiv
colonialism xiv, 104
    indirect rule under 99
    model of subservience under 7, 9
    white settler 35–36, 50, 52,
      59, 66
coloniality 17
    Biko and Turner's rejection of
      acceptance of 4–5, 17–18

common-sense thinking xi, xvi, 74, 146,
  154, 204, 205, 241, 247
  and assumptions about human nature
    73, 95, 97, 167, 170, 205
  countercultures that challenge
    142–143
  elite challenges to 214–216
  as product of socialisation 140–141, 143
  utopian thinking as alternative to 141,
    148, 152, 245
consciousness 152
  class xii, xx, 73, 77
  Turner's framing of xxi, 17, 42, 142,
    155, 158, 168
contemporary political theory xiv, xviii,
  xxiii, 26
  bidirectional function of realism
    and utopianism in 241, 243–244,
    248–249, 254–255, 257–259
  distinction between description and
    prescription in 241–242, 254, 258
  grasping the present as history in 244,
    249–252, 254–255, 257–258
Cosatu 124–125
crime in South Africa
  JB Marks Municipality study 201–202
  material inequality as factor in 209,
    211
  policing of 209–210
critical thinking, Turner's teaching of xxi,
  143, 149, 155, 249
  and criticism of his child-centred
    approach 144, 146, 154
  as process of dialogue 152, 154
  see also developing 'theoretical
    attitude; Turner's intellectual
    activist model; Turner's views on
    education

D
Danziger, Kurt 144–145
decolonial thought/theorists xiv, xxii,
  162, 165, 201, 212, 228
decoloniality 159
decolonisation debate xxi, 4
  as call to resistance 159–160
  emergent approaches to 161

new humanism approach in 161–162,
  164–167
#RhodesMustFall Movement 163–164
value of Turnerian theory for 158,
  172–173, 243
see also Mbembe, Achille: explanation
  of decolonisation project; new
  Black Consciousness: elaboration
  of decolonialism
decolonising resistance xix, 3–4, 7,
  15–18, 23, 242
  as tripartite process 16
  see also Maldonado-Torres, Nelson
developing 'theoretical attitude' 139, 147,
  149, 152, 243
  as first step in critical thinking
    practice 140–141, 154
  that grasps the present as history 12,
    141, 154, 174, 227, 239, 244, 249,
    254, 257
  possibility of radical freedom through
    151, 173
  realism as vital for 243, 258
  relationship between practical
    knowledge and 139, 153
  religion as potential source of 142–143
  see also critical thinking, Turner's
    teaching of
disenfranchisement 20, 105, 160
dispossession 20, 36, 55, 59, 99
'Durban Moment' see Durban strikes of
  1973
Durban strikes of 1973 ix–x, 75–76
  dockworkers' strike as key event of
    x–xi
  female textile workers
    as unrecognised Other in xx, 75,
      77, 81–82, 86–87, 129, 242
  New Left ideas as central to xi–xii
  Turner's role in x, 46, 131n2, 186, 192

E
engaged political philosophy 224
  and ongoing task of theorising 237
  role of positionality in 228–233, 243
  role of utopian thinking in 226, 231,
    234–236, 239, 242

engaged political philosophy (*continued*)
use of cantilever method in 235
see also Turner's utopian thinking:
transformational potential of
Engels, Frederick 75–76

F

Fanon, Frantz 9, 16–19, 47, 72, 78,
88n3, 108
Federation of South African Trade
Unions (Fosatu) 116, 123, 131n3
Floyd, Jonathan 244, 251–252
Foucault, Michel 200, 251
Fourier, Charles 75–76
Fox, Nik Farrell 200, 203, 212
Freire, Paulo 144, 161
Friedman, Steven 27, 35, 43, 141

G

gender
Beauvoir on overcoming burdens/
limits of 86, 242
Turner's treatment of xiv, 74–77, 86,
229, 242, 247
gendered oppression of African women
xx, 78, 82–83, 85, 87, 88n5 *see also*
African women textile workers,
Durban
see also Durban strikes of
1973: female textile workers
as unrecognised Other in
Geuss, Raymond 149, 253–254
global capitalism xiii, 110
global North 233, 255, 258
divide between global South and
xv, 233
global South 258
nature and role of democracy in 244,
255–256
Gordon, Lewis 53, 56–57, 64
Govender, Jayanathan 98, 101–102,
106, 110

H

Hegel, 8, 78, 88
higher education
contrast between academic and
vocational disciplines in 138–139

growth of practice-based learning in
137–138, 155
see also critical thinking, Turner's
teaching of; neoliberalism: impact
on higher education of
Hubbard, Barbara ix, 183, 229
Hubbard, Michael 182–184
Hudson, Peter xxii, 131n4, 152, 215
human becoming
place of education in struggle for xxi,
158–159, 165

I

identity
black 14, 162
impact of colonialism on 99
politics 162, 164–165, 203–204
see also socialised human models and
value systems: identity aspect of
inequality
class 34, 100
economic/income xvi, 37, 100–102,
105, 214
link between crime and xvi
material xvi, 31–32, 209, 211
racial 17, 31, 100
see also structural inequality
Institute for Industrial Education (IIE),
xi, 76–77, 185, 192
programme of action research
150–151, 153

K

Keegan, Clive 190–191
knowledge production 11–12, 16, 138
Kruks, Sonia 79–80, 88n3

L

Laclau, Ernesto xxii, 200–206, 208,
212–216
Landauer, Gustav 253–254
Legassick, Martin 126–127
Lessing, Doris 8–9
liberal
democracy xvi, 114, 119, 121,
126–130
paternalism 17, 23, 41, 47, 54–55,
59, 63

liberalism
  elitism as democratic deficit of
    129–130
  illiberal foundations of 35, 114, 129,
    131n2
  Turner's critique of xix, 34–37, 42
  see also Nolutshungu: views on
    liberalism; white liberalism
liberation xi, xxi
  BC views on 10, 13, 17–19, 24, 41,
    53–54
  decolonisation as pathway to 63
  education for 149, 153, 174
  New Left ideals for xii, xvii, xxii
  and reimagination of the self 108–109
  theology 20–22, 151
Lichtenstein, Alex
  critique of The Eye of the Needle 76,
    84–85
Locke, John xix, 34–35

M
Macqueen, Ian 38, 43, 56, 61, 150
  'progressive space' of 53–54
Maldonado-Torres, Nelson 63–65
Mamdani, Mahmood 98–99
marginalisation 160, 214
  as counterproductive for
    capitalism 211
  escalation of poverty by xx
  historic 28, 91–92, 97, 232
  systemic 101–102, 104
Maré, Gerry 186, 188
Marxism 33, 121, 129, 143, 187, 193
  homespun xxii, 190, 193
  structural xi, 149, 201, 209, 212
  see also New Left Marxism;
    poststructural hegemony
Mbeki, Govan 11
Mbeki, Thabo 101, 106
Mbembe, Achille 206
  explanation of decolonisation project
    159, 162, 164–168, 174
  on three major effects of colonialism 99
migrant labour system 82, 84–85
Modisane, Bloke 7
More, Mabogo 47
Morphet, Tony 30, 32, 175, 201, 213, 215

Moss, Glenn 189–190, 193
Mouffe, Chantal xxii, 200–206, 208,
  212–216

N
Natal Labour Research Committee
  (NLRC) 82, 84–85
National Union of South African
  Students (Nusas) 45, 185, 188,
  190–191, 195–196
Nattrass, Nicoli 100–101, 105–106, 110
neoliberalism 106, 110, 120, 207, 214
  impact on higher education of 137,
    139, 155
new Black Consciousness (NBC)
  161–162
  elaboration of decolonialism 162–164
  fundamental rejection of whiteness
    162–163
New International School for Social
  Research 196–197
New Left Marxism
  criticism of structural Marxism by
    xi, 33
  prioritisation of consciousness-
    building within xii
  Turner's blend of existentialism and
    x, xii, xxii, 143, 149, 205, 212–213,
    215, 217
'new Sartre'
  and Turner's critique of relative privilege
    xxii, 200–202, 212, 215, 243
Nolutshungu, Sam C 30–31
  criticism of Marxism 33
  views on liberalism xix, 34–37
  see also white liberalism:
    Nolutshungu's views on
Nolutshungu's theory of political change
  27–28, 43
  and emancipatory potential of BCM
    xix, 29, 37–42
  through radical engagement with
    race/class issues 31–34, 36–38,
    40, 42
  see also Changing South Africa:
    Political Considerations
Nupen, Charles 191
Nyathi, Nceku 162

O

oppression
  apartheid as epistemic foundation of
    xiii, 5, 8–9, 12, 17, 39, 47, 49, 82,
    100, 104
  denunciation and subversion of
    ontology of 4, 17
  institutionalisation of structures of
    30, 95
  normalisation of 5, 7, 11, 17, 30, 91
  ongoing systemic 104–105
  persistent socialisation of 102–103
  white liberal accommodation of
    12, 15
  see also Christianity: as subterfuge for
    oppression; gendered oppression
    of African women

P

Pan African Congress (PAC) xi, 37
participatory democracy model 26,
    37–38, 60, 65, 71, 74, 119
  absence of politics in 75, 122–123
  contrast between Rawlsian 'ideal
    theory' and 115–117
  influence of workers' control models
    on 76, 117–120, 134n4, 187
  limitations/criticisms of 51, 113–114,
    116–118, 120–122
  marginalisation of African women in
    xx, 72–73, 75–76, 81, 87
  pyramidal representation within 118,
    121–122
  radical restructuring of economy in
    184–185
  relevance in post-apartheid South
    Africa 124, 126–127, 242
  see also gender: Turner's treatment of;
    The Eye of the Needle: elaboration
    of Christian human model in;
    people's power movement
Pateman, Carole 76, 147, 227
patriarchal society xiii, 80, 83, 85, 87,
    140, 224
  obstacles inscribed on women's
    bodies by 72
people's power movement 125–127

Pilger, John 103–104
Polan, Anthony 121–122
political philosophy of Turner xv, xviii, 7
  ethical agenda of xx, xxii, 92–93, 103,
    116–117, 123, 169
  fusion of theology and 22–23,
    142–143
  as tool to address societal injustice
    xxii, 226–229, 232
  see also engaged political philosophy;
    radical freedom
political power 4
  relationship between moral resistance
    and 5–6
  resistance as challenge to 4–6, 23–24,
    143, 153, 155
  see also people's power movement;
    power
political theology 19–23
political theory 31, 40, 138
  comparative xix, 28–29, 42–44, 138
  see also contemporary political
    theory; resistance: politics/
    political theory of
populism xvii–xviii, 129–132, 256
poststructural hegemony
  Turner in conversation with xxii,
    199–202, 205, 212, 215–216
  and views on choice 200, 204–206
  see also 'new Sartre'; radical
    contingency
poverty in South Africa xx
  associated with race 101–102, 210
  as legacy of colonialism and apartheid
    98–100
  normalised nature of 91
  Turner's account of 101
  see also structural inequality
power
  decolonialism's vigilance concerning
    174
  diffuse nature of 213–214
  imbalances/inequalities 32, 35–37,
    39, 60
  relationship of knowledge to 159,
    162–163
  tied to race 8, 14, 18

power relations 20, 149
    asymmetrical 8, 35, 120, 211, 213
    colonial 4, 7, 100
    gender 85, 87

R
racial hierarchy 8–10
racialist capitalism 7, 33–34
    Turner's understanding of 8, 12, 22
racism xiii, 12, 14, 18, 56, 62–63, 98, 247
    implication of colonial Christianity
        in 21
    infrastructure of 51, 53–54, 60
    internalisation of discourses of 11, 197
    as requirement for capitalist
        modernisation 83, 211
    as source of subjective legitimation 7
    see also antiblack racism; apartheid
radical conciliar democracy 73, 76,
        116–118, 120–121, 128 see also
        people's power movement
radical contingency 212–213
    contradictions between Marxist
        reification and xxii, 203
    and over-determination of the social
        202, 212–213, 216
radical freedom
    Turner's affirmation of x, xiv, xvi, 104,
        147, 151, 225, 238, 246
    utopian thinking as act of 225–226, 246
radical reform, Turner's vision of 27–28,
        30, 38, 116, 197, 217
radical utopian traditions
    emancipation of women as central to
        75–76
    see also utopianism
Rawls, John 115–117
    Charles Mills' critique of ideal theory
        of 231–232
resistance x–xi, xxii, 4
    broad definition of 4, 6–7
    politics/political theory of 4–5, 13, 15,
        18–20, 37–38
    reclamation/restoration of subjectivity
        through 8–10, 13, 16–17
    Turner's understanding of xix, 3–4,
        7–8, 19, 23–24

    utopian vision of 10
    see also Biko's BC philosophy:
        understanding of resistance;
        Black Consciousness: as epistemic
        resistance; decolonising resistance;
        political power: relationship
        between moral resistance and

S
Sartre, Jean Paul xxii, 200, 238
    criticism of historical materialism 203
    influence on Beauvoir of 77
    influence on Turner of 15, 30, 38, 150,
        200, 205, 237
    thesis of anti-racist racism 15
    see also new Sartre
Scheffler, Samuel 93–95, 109–110
Schoon, Jenny and Marius 195–196
Seekings, Jeremy 100–101, 105–106, 110
self-consciousness 78, 172
Serequeberhan, Tsenay 102, 107–109
Sharpville massacre 30, 182
socialisation 38–39, 75, 98, 101–104, 197
    as critical aspect of social
        change 71–72, 140, 185,
        191, 206
    see also common-sense thinking:
        as product of socialisation;
        socialised human models and
        value systems; Taylor, Charles: on
        monological ideal
socialised human models and value
        systems 14, 39, 91–92, 97, 103,
        105, 140
    capitalist 168–169
    identity aspect of xiv, 93, 96
    moral dimensions of 95–97, 104,
        106–111, 246
    re-examining conflicting xx, 92,
        107–109
    'traditional reasoning' informing
        93–95
    tripartite angle to 93
socialism
    Turner's commitment to 187–188,
        191–192, 207
Sorbonne, University of Paris x, 30, 183

South African Communist Party (SACP) 123, 181, 193

South African Constitution 98, 105, 124, 126, 128

South African Labour Bulletin xi, 81–82, 131n3, 150, 185, 192

South African Students' Organisation (SASO) manifesto
    on racial integration 15–16

Stalinism xxi, 113, 190

1976 Soweto uprisings 30
    and rise of BCM 41–42

structural inequality 37
    drivers of 102
    as legacy of settler colonialism 16, 35–36, 91
    misplaced priorities as factor in xx, 92, 103, 106–107, 242
    racialised 31, 102–103
    Turner's views on 32, 35, 50, 74, 95, 101
    see also socialised human models and value systems

Suppression of Communism Act
    bannings under xi, 10, 47–48, 87n1, 188–193, 196

T

Taylor, Charles
    on monological ideal 95–96

The Eye of the Needle (Turner) 20, 35, 38
    elaboration of Christian human model in 21–22, 24, 32, 73, 114, 207–209, 229, 235–236, 246
    ongoing relevance of xiv, xxi, 26–27, 43, 113, 124, 130–131, 129
    as product of the moment xii–xiii, xii, xxi, 26–27, 113
    see also developing 'theoretical attitude'; participatory democracy model; Turner's utopian thinking

The Second Sex (Beauvoir) 77–78, 88n2
    female body as impediment to transcendence in xx, 72, 78–79, 81, 86
    criticism of 80–81

trade union movement xi–xii, 84, 116, 124–125, 151, 153, 185–186

transcendence
    Mbembe on disappearance of 167–168, 174
    Turner's conception of xvi, 23, 71, 74, 97, 116, 158, 167, 170, 173–174

transcendent morality 142–143
    shift from internal to 97, 106, 108–111

Turner, Foszia (née Fisher) ix, 73, 77, 87n1, 151, 192, 195–6, 225

Turner, Jann ix, 226

Turner, Rick
    assassination/murder of ix, 29–30, 41, 53, 131, 149, 195, 200
    banning of 47–48, 188, 191, 194–195, 200

Turner's existentialism 27, 72, 225
    link between idealism and pragmatism in 200–201, 207, 216, 243
    see also New Left Marxism: Turner's blend of existentialism and, Sartre, Jean Paul: influence on Turner of; Turner's relationship with Biko: and shared existential philosophy

Turner's intellectual activist model 139, 149, 153
    integration of theory and practice in 150–152, 155
    see also Institute for Industrial Education: programme of action research

Turner's relationship with Biko xiv, 192
    commonalities and differences in xix–xx, 3–5, 15, 19, 50, 53
    impact of differences in lived experience on 47, 56–59, 62–63, 65–66
    as dual targets of apartheid lethality 48–49
    and shared existential philosophy 46–47, 53, 55–57

and shared vision of radical change x,
    xviii–ix, 30, 38, 45, 66
    see also: Black Consciousness
        Movement: Turner's responsive
        engagement with
Turner's utopian thinking xiii, xv, xix,
    xxiii, 32–33, 54, 56, 59, 86, 97,
    107–108, 114
    and concept of human solidarity 171,
        175, 185
    as invitation to self-examination 23,
        71–72, 158, 173
    on need to theorise society 224,
        227–228, 230, 232, 243–245,
        247–249
    relevance to contemporary education
        xxi, 157–158, 169, 173–174,
        241–243, 248–249
    transformational potential of xxi,
        224–226, 231, 233–234, 237–239
    see also critical thinking; Turner's
        teaching of; participatory
        democracy model; radical
        freedom; transcendence: Turner's
        conception of
Turner's views on education
    on adult learning under socialism
        147–148
    critique of existing system 143–145
    and child-centred socialist model
        145–148, 172
    in relation to contemporary critical
        theory xxi, 45
    see also critical thinking, Turner's
        conception of

U
Ujamaa villages, Tanzania 76, 118, 148
unemployment 98, 100, 102, 122, 125,
    209
University of Cape Town (UCT) 163, 182
University of Natal x, 30, 33, 186 *see also*
    Institute for Industrial Education
utopianism 115–117, 223 *see also*
    Turner's utopian thinking

V
Verwoerd, HF 10–11

W
Webster, Edward 116, 131n3, 131n5,
    150–152, 209, 214, 217
Weinberg, Eli 193
white liberalism
    Biko's critique of xx, 3, 12–15, 18–19,
        23, 47, 54–56, 60–62, 66
    Nolutshungu's views on 40–42
    Turner's position on xix, 12, 17, 20,
        23, 34–35, 37–42, 54–55, 206–207,
        224
    see also oppression: white liberal
        accommodation of
white subjectivity
    black people as antithesis to 8–9
white superiority 5, 8, 13, 20, 36, 95–96,
    245
white supremacy 40–41, 49, 140, 142,
    164, 224, 238
    Turner's rebellion against ix, xiii–xiv
whiteness 7, 11, 163
    calls for demythologisation of 159
    dethroning of 23, 27, 162
    as paradigm of rightness 17
    of Turner 54, 58–59
Williams, Patrick 28
work-integrated learning (WIL)
        138–139, 151–153 *see also* Turner's
        intellectual activist model
workers' control 125
    betrayal of idea of 120
    as condition for freedom 147
    in participatory democracy 73–74, 76,
        87, 117–119
workerism xxi, 116, 123–124, 131n3, 151

X
xenophobia 126, 162
Xuma, AB 11, 21

Y
Yugoslavia 76, 118–119, 132n5

Printed and bound by CPI Group (UK) Ltd, Croydon, CR0 4YY

09/06/2025

14685821-0003